Daniel Miner Gordon

Mountain and Prairie

A Journey from Victoria to Winnipeg, viâ Peace River Pass

Daniel Miner Gordon

Mountain and Prairie
A Journey from Victoria to Winnipeg, viâ Peace River Pass

ISBN/EAN: 9783337128029

Printed in Europe, USA, Canada, Australia, Japan

Cover: Foto ©Andreas Hilbeck / pixelio.de

More available books at **www.hansebooks.com**

From a Photo. by Dr. G. M. Dawson.

MOUNTAIN AND PRAIRIE;

A JOURNEY

FROM VICTORIA TO WINNIPEG,

VIA PEACE RIVER PASS.

BY THE
REV. DANIEL M. GORDON, B.D.,
OTTAWA.

WITH MAPS AND ILLUSTRATIONS.

MONTREAL:
DAWSON BROTHERS, PUBLISHERS.
1880.

Entered according to Act of Parliament of Canada, in the year 1880, by DAWSON BROTHERS, in the Office of the Minister of Agriculture.

GAZETTE PRINTING COMPANY, MONTREAL.

PREFACE.

IN May, 1879, the Canadian Parliament, having decided that additional information should be obtained regarding certain proposed routes for the Canadian Pacific Railway, resolved that a party be sent to examine the country from Port Simpson, on the Pacific, across northern British Columbia and through the Rocky Mountains by way of Peace River and Pine River Passes to the prairies. Copious information had already been procured regarding several other routes connecting the Prairie Region with the Pacific, but the final selection of a Pacific terminus was reserved until this northern route to Port Simpson had been examined and fuller information had been obtained regarding the general character, the resources, and the engineering features of the country.

The party appointed to make this examination consisted of Messrs. H. J. Cambie and H. A. F. Macleod, of the Canadian Pacific Railway engineering staff, and Dr. G. M. Dawson, of the Geological Survey of Canada. The writer accompanied them. They travelled together from Victoria, V. I., to the mouth of the Skeena thence across the northern part of the Province to Fort McLeod, where the party was divided,—Dr. Dawson proceeding by Pine River Pass, the others by Peace River Pass, to meet at Dunvegan. From Dunvegan the writer came eastward in advance of the others.

The following chapters, consisting chiefly of notes taken by the way, record his impressions of the country traversed from the Pacific to Winnipeg, across the "sea of mountains" and the more inviting sea of prairies. The illustrations are from photographs by Dr. G. M. Dawson, Mr. Selwyn, and Mr. Horetzky—the frontispiece being taken, by permission, from the Geological Survey Report for 1878-79. The maps are from the most recent and most authentic in the Departments of the Canadian Pacific Railway and of the Interior.

Carlyle says that "some books are suited for immediate use and immediate oblivion." It is the writer's hope that ere the accompanying record of his journey across mountain and prairie passes into oblivion it may be of use in acquainting some of his fellow-countrymen, in a slight degree, with the character and the resources of that half of the Dominion that lies between Winnipeg and the Western Sea.

        DANIEL M. GORDON.

CONTENTS.

CHAPTER I.

VANCOUVER ISLAND AND THE LOWER FRASER.

    PAGE

Ottawa to San Francisco.—Victoria.—Indian and Chinese Labourers.—Resources of British Columbia.—San Juan.—The Lower Fraser.—New Westminster.—Burrard Inlet.—Yale to Boston Bar 1

CHAPTER II.

VICTORIA TO THE SKEENA.

Along the Coast.—The Chain of Channels.—Nanaimo.—Bute Inlet and the Route of the Canadian Pacific Railway.—Port Essington and the Mouth of the Skeena.—Metlahkatlah.—Mission to the Indians.—Port Simpson.—Work Inlet 32

CHAPTER III.

UP THE SKEENA.

Leave Port Essington.—Canoes, Crews, and Stores.—No Trout.—Tracking and Poling.—Indian Watch-tower.—Catching and Curing Salmon.—Carved Posts.—Burial Customs.—The Sweating-booth.—Height of Steam Navigation.—Division of Coast and Cascade Range.—Indian Villages.—Gold-washing.—Medicine Man.—The Forks of Skeena.—Lip-ornaments and Nose-rings.—Mosquitoes 56

CHAPTER IV.

FORKS OF SKEENA TO LAKE BABINE.

Our Packers.—The Trail.—Up the Susqua.—Coal.—Women Packing and Nursing.—Skilokiss Suspension Bridge.—The Ooatzanli.—The Nataltsul.—Cascade Range compared with Swiss Alps.—Indian Legends.—Taim-Shin.—Scene on the Summit.—Approach Lake Babine.—Engage Crews.—Offended Chief.—Babine Indians.—Neighbourhood of Lake 87

CHAPTER V.

BABINE TO FORT M'LEOD.

Up Lake Babine.—Fort Babine.—Indian Farming.—Indian Reserves in British Columbia.—Reluctance in telling names.—Lake Stewart.—R. C. Missions.—Fort St. James.—Home-sick Indian.—Mule Train.—Following Trail.—Fort McLeod.—Attractions of the H. B. Service.... 113

CHAPTER VI.

THROUGH THE MOUNTAINS BY BOAT.

Explorers of Peace River.—Division of Party.—Leave Fort McLeod.—The Parsnip.—Fur Traders and Gold Hunters.—Mining.—The Nation River.—Pete Toy and Nigger Dan.—Finlay River and Rapids.—The Unchagah.—Peace River Pass.—Parle-pas Rapid.—Moose Hunting.—Buffalo Tracks.—Terraces.—The Canon Coal.—Navigable Extent of River.—Indian Hunters.—Charlie's Yarns........................... 139

CHAPTER VII.

HUDSON'S HOPE TO DUNVEGAN.

The Prairie Region.—H. B. Company and the North-West Company.—Hudson's Hope.—Moose.—The Climate.—Fertile Flats.—The Plateau.—On the Raft.—Appearance of Country.—Fort St. John.—Massacre at the Old Fort.—Bear Hunting.—Dunvegan.—Highlanders Abroad. Moostoos and his Fight with a Grizzly.—Missions to the Indians..... 168

CHAPTER VIII.

PEACE RIVER COUNTRY.

Province of Unchagah.—Outfits of Exploring Parties.—Old Journals at Dunvegan.—Records of Climate.—Beaver Indians.—Cree Music.—Expedition to Battle River.—Character of Country.—Bear Hunting.—Size and Character of Peace River Country.—The Climate.—Danger of Summer Frosts.—Increased Sunlight.—Temperature.—Coal-beds.—Facilities of Communication.................................. 196

CHAPTER IX.

DUNVEGAN TO EDMONTON.

Leave Dunvegan.—Farewell View of Peace River.—Cooking.—Lesser Slave Lake.—Another Stage.—Postal Arrangements.—Indian Hospitality.—Athabasca River and Landing.—Gambling.—Road to Fort Edmonton.—Telegraph Office.—Cree Camp.—Our Indian Policy.—Farm Instructors.—Treaties.—Sioux.—Edmonton District.—Canadian Pacific Railway 224

CHAPTER X.

EDMONTON TO BATTLEFORD.

Steamers on Saskatchewan.—Prepare to cross the Prairie.—Trails.—Prairie Travel.—Pemmican.—Victoria.—Half-breed Farmers.—Christian Missions in North-West.—Victoria to Fort Pitt.—Royal Mail.—Dog-driving.—Fort Pitt.—The Trail again.—Treeless Prairies.—Tree Culture.—Battleford.—Government of North-West.—Climate.—Character of Country.—Great Plain.—Homestead and Pre-emption Law.—Prospect of Settlement 253

CHAPTER XI.

BATTLEFORD TO WINNIPEG.

Battleford to Carlton.—Duck Lake.—A Blizzard.—Fellow-travellers.—Cross South Saskatchewan.—Delayed by Snow.—Humboldt.—Alkaline Lakes.—Touchwood Hills.—Indian Farming.—Break-downs.—Prairie fires.—Qu'Appelle.—Fort Ellice.—Township Surveys.—Colonisation Companies.—Prohibitory Liquor Law.—Shoal Lake.—Salt Lake.—Little Saskatchewan.—Enter Manitoba.—Joe's Temptations.—Heavy Roads.—Portage La Prairie.—Winnipeg.—Prospects of Immigrants.—Loyalty to the Empire.. 281

MAPS.

Map shewing part of the North-West Territories and British Columbia...................................	To face page	1
Map shewing the Canadian Pacific Coast.................	" "	32
Map shewing part of Northern British Columbia and of Peace River District,—with author's route from Port Essington to Fort Edmonton	" "	56
Map shewing Southern portion of the North-West Territories,—with author's route from Fort Edmonton to Winnipeg	" "	252

ILLUSTRATIONS.

Indian Village, Queen Charlotte Islands	Frontispiece.	
Fraser River (18 miles above Yale).......................	To face page	28
Metlahkatlah..	" "	46
Junction of Nation and Parsnip...........................	" "	147
Mount Selwyn..	" "	153
Peace River (20 miles above the Canon)	" "	161
Fort Edmonton	" "	239
Prairie Carts *en route*	" "	255

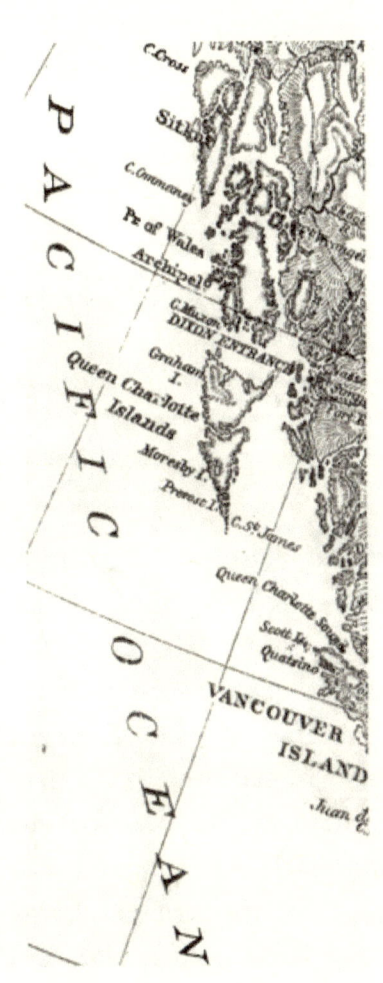

MOUNTAIN AND PRAIRIE.

CHAPTER I.

VANCOUVER ISLAND AND THE LOWER FRASER.

Ottawa to San Francisco.—Victoria.—Indian and Chinese Labourers.—Resources of British Columbia.—San Juan.—The Lower Fraser.—New Westminster.—Burrard Inlet.—Yale to Boston Bar.

From Ottawa to San Francisco by rail, thence by steamer to Victoria, V. I., a journey in all of about four thousand miles, was a requisite preliminary to our more interesting journey from Victoria across Northern British Columbia, through the Rocky Mountains, by the Peace River Pass, and over the prairies to Winnipeg.

The railway route across the Continent is so often traversed, so familiarly known, and has been so frequently described, that we need not linger long upon it.

Ontario was just bursting into leaf, for the season had been somewhat late, as we passed through on the 13th May, 1879. At Chicago we entered on the prairies of Illinois; prairies which to one who had not yet seen the Valley of the Saskatchewan or the farm lands of Manitoba, seemed rich beyond all rivals. The country is as fertile as it is flat, but it suffers from the biting north wind that sweeps down from Lake Michigan; therefore almost every homestead is guarded by a grove of Lombardy poplars, or other quickly grown trees. At Burlington we crossed the Mississippi and passed into Iowa, which seems like a continuation of Illinois, save that the soil is scarcely so rich, and occasional stretches of rolling country vary the monotony of the dead-level prairie. At Council Bluffs we crossed the Missouri and entered upon the plains of Nebraska, that look like a sea of grass, sometimes rimmed by low hills on the distant horizon, sometimes stretching away an unbroken level as far as the eye can reach, occasionally dotted with the bleached bones of cattle, or the herds of the ranchers, or the caravans of new immigrants. One of its towns, Sidney, the outlet of the Black Hills mining country, is a centre for those incidents and anecdotes that seem to British and New England ears characteristic of Western life. Here, and at almost any point between this and Ogden, you may hear stories of atrocities by Indians, and of worse atrocities by white men; of train robberies, murders, etc., by the ruffians who frequently gravitate towards gold and silver mines. Three days before we passed through, a murderer had been lynched, hung to the telegraph post nearest to the station, and the incident caused little comment and no enquiry. The mining districts, however, are gradually coming under law and order; vigilance committees have already done good work, as they did in the early days of San Francisco; and as capital is being largely invested, business and society are becoming more settled, so that life and property may soon be as safe here as they have long been in California and Montana.

We crossed the Rocky Mountains at a height of 8,000 feet above sea-level, more than 6,000 feet higher than where we expect to re-cross them at the Peace River Pass, and with no sign that we had reached such an altitude, save the stunted vegetation around us, the snowy peaks shimmering in the distance, and the more exact indications of railway-map and aneroid. We rattled along through the Echo and Weber Cañons, where the frowning and precipitous rocks alternate with snatches of scenery that remind one of some parts of Scotland, especially of the uplands of Galloway, though here the grass is not so rich and no sheep are seen grazing on the hill-sides. Then came the plains of Utah, part of the Great American Desert that lies between the Rocky Mountains and the Sierras of Nevada, where nothing grows without irrigation, but where, with this assistance, many dreary levels have been changed into smiling fields. Wearisome, at times, even to the traveller by rail, what must those alkali plains have been to the traveller by stage in the old coaching days?

or, still worse, to the earlier Mormons, many of whom traversed them on foot? It was a relief to pass from the Desert, over the snowy range of the Sierras, by many an abandoned gold claim—abandoned by whites, though now worked by Chinese—down to the smiling valley of the Sacramento. They had been ploughing in Ontario when we left a week ago; here in California they were reaping. Touching the sea at Oakland, we crossed, by a ferry of four miles, to San Francisco, arriving at the very hour we had hoped to do when leaving home seven days ago.

'Frisco—for life is too short, and business too pressing, to allow Californians to use, in common conversation, the full name San Francisco—was agitated about the new constitution which the State of California had recently adopted. Newspapers and people alike were full of it. How far it might conflict with the Federal authority, and how far it might fulfil the hopes of its advocates, still remained to be seen, for though passed it had not yet come into force. Its chief points are: the taxation of all manner of property, stocks, bonds, mining shares, etc., as well as real estate; the restraint of some huge monopolies, especially the Central Pacific Railroad; and the fulfilment of the maxim, "the Chinese must go." It was the boast of an American poet regarding his country, that

> "Her free latch-string never was drawn in
> Against the poorest child of Adam's kin";

but apparently California is prepared to repudiate this honourable claim.

Time did not admit of our seeing the city to advantage, though even a hurried visit to its **chief business** streets, its markets, its Chinese quarter and its wharves, give sufficient evidence that, though inferior to a number of cities in the East, San Francisco has many attractions. Its chief attraction, however, is its harbour. It is small praise to call this the finest harbour **on the** Pacific, **for** the North American Pacific is singularly destitute **of** good harbours. The next best are those **of British** Columbia, but they are scarcely worthy of mention in comparison. This is **one of** the finest harbours in **the** world.

At mid-day on Tuesday, the 20th May, we left it, **and** steamed out through the Golden Gate on to the blue waters of the Pacific. The *City of Chester*, on which we took passage for Victoria, was lightly laden, and seemed capable of more motion in the wrong direction than any other steamer afloat. The effect of **this on** the writer is seen from the following extracts from a brief journal. They are somewhat monotonous: "Tuesday **evening**, sea-sick; Wednesday, 21st, do.; Thursday, 22nd, do." To examine the life preservers, or the slats in the upper berth; to hear the gong call others to dinner; to listen day and night **for** the bell that each half hour marks off the time; to wonder if it would be well to take the medicine now that should have been taken last night; to hear the grinding of the shaft, varied by an occasional whirr as the screw rose out of the water; to leave unopened the books that were brought for reading by the way; to abandon all desire for a trip around the world; to feel thankful that the steamer is not bound for Yokohama or Honolulu; to question the boasted progress of medical science that has not found any remedy for seasickness; and to long for the fulfilment of the prophecy: "There shall be no more sea;" these were some of the lighter occupations that engaged attention when not engrossed with the more serious and painful duties of the situation; nor did it greatly lessen one's discomfort to know that others were similarly engaged.

It is about 750 miles from San Francisco to Victoria. On Friday, the 23rd, we rounded Cape Flattery and entered the Straits of San Juan de Fuca. We had some sixty-five miles more to run, and when we awoke on Saturday morning we found that we were safely moored at the wharf in Victoria.

Before starting for the Skeena, where we purposed leaving the coast on our journey eastward, we required to spend a few days in the southern part of the Province, which is, even yet, a comparative stranger to the sister Provinces east of the Rocky Mountains. Although Vancouver Island was constituted into a Crown colony in 1849, it really was little known outside of the ledgers of the Hudson's Bay Company and the official documents of Downing Street, until **1858, when the** discovery of gold on the Fraser attracted thousands to Victoria, and when the mainland portion of what is now the Province of British Columbia was first erected into a colony. The two colonies were united in 1866, the one giving the name to the united colony—British Columbia, the other giving the capital—Victoria. The old rivalry, however, between the two capitals still exists, **as New** Westminster has not yet abandoned her claim to present and prospective superiority to Victoria. On the **20th July,** 1871, the colony was **united to the other Provinces** of the Dominion, and Canada was thus **extended from the** Atlantic to the Pacific.

Victoria is British Columbia in much the same way as Paris is France. Originally an Indian village gathered around a post of the Hudson's Bay Company, then a small settlement of traders, etc., it sprang forward rapidly under successive waves of excitement: first, on the discovery of gold on the lower Fraser; again, in 1860, when new and most profitable gold **fields were** opened in Cariboo; and, subsequently, **on the discovery** of gold in Cassiar in 1873. **Its population** like its prosperity has fluctuated, at one **time swelling** to 12,000, but now shrunk to less than half that number. Although some parts of it, especially those occupied by the Chinese and the Indians, have a worn-out look, yet it is upon the whole a pretty little city, with delightful drives, tasteful gardens, comfortable homes, a charming public park, and views of the snow-capped Olympian range, the sight of which on a warm day is as refreshing as a breeze from the hill tops. The surroundings of the city are very attractive, the foliage being rich and varied, the shrubs including species seldom seen in the eastern Provinces, and not grown there as here in the open air, such as holly, ivy, arbutus, etc., while the yew and the scrub oak give additional attraction to the scenery. It is somewhat inconveniently situated for the capital of the Province, as the harbour is only a small bay with very limited accommodation, the true harbour being at Esquimault, some four miles distant. Esquimault, which was for a time supposed to be a suitable terminus for the Canadian Pacific Railway, is beautifully land-locked, and easy of access, but the harbour is very small—too small to allow a large vessel to enter under canvas and come to anchor, unless she had most of the harbour to herself. The road-stead outside of the harbour, however, known as the Royal Roads, is safe and commodious, and the value set upon Esquimault by the Imperial and Dominion authorities is seen in the fact that it is the site of a Government graving-dock now in course of completion.

Victoria is a focus for people from every land. Men of almost all nationalities rub shoulders here. There are

Indians, the old possessors of the soil, whose contact with city life has not yet greatly improved them; Spaniards, whose former influence along this coast is notched in many of the names of British Columbia, such as Quadra (the old name of Vancouver Island), Texada, Valdes, etc.; Chinese, who are rapidly becoming ubiquitous along the Pacific; Frenchmen; Russians; Americans; Jews; and Britons from almost every quarter of the Empire. Yet, though its population is thus mixed, there is a strong English tone in Victoria, and a deep attachment to the Empire. Unfortunately there is not yet the same strong attachment to the Dominion. The people hardly regard their Province as an integral portion of Canada, and still speak of Canadians as of a distant people, severed from them in life and purpose. Yet the same was the case in Nova Scotia for some years after Confederation. Along the Atlantic coast, as here, the communication was more frequent with the old country than with the interior Provinces; many doubted the wisdom of Confederation; some, even of its friends, considered it to be premature; some vehemently opposed it; but none would now undo it, or bring back the isolated life in which each of the Provinces formerly dwelt; and, naturally, as the intercourse of British Columbia with other parts of the Dominion becomes closer and more frequent, and as the construction of our Pacific Railway proceeds, loyalty to the Empire will develop loyalty to the commonweal of the Dominion, of which this Province forms a part. The people, however, thought that they had a grievance against the Dominion. When they entered Confederation, in 1871, it was agreed upon, as one of the articles of the union, that the Government of the Dominion should " undertake to secure the commencement, simultaneously, within two years of the date of union—of the construction of a railway from the Pacific to the Rocky Mountains, and from such point as may be selected, east of the Rocky Mountains, towards the Pacific, to connect the seaboard of British Columbia with the railway system of Canada—and, further, to secure the completion of such railway within ten years of the date of union." Nearly nine years have passed and construction is only now commencing. True, there was far more work involved than was at first anticipated, in the location of the line. Nearly four millions of dollars have been expended in the surveys, of which a large portion has been disbursed in British Columbia. Many routes had to be examined, amounting in the aggregate to 46,000 miles, of which one-fourth was measured, yard by yard, through forest, mountain and prairie; but these are facts of which an impatient people take little notice. Since, however, construction has been commenced, it may reasonably be expected that adverse criticism towards the Canadian Government, on the part of the people of British Columbia, will cease, and that they will recognise the earnestness of the Dominion authorities in fulfilling, as far as possible, the pledges given when British Columbia entered Confederation. Certainly, the people can hardly regard themselves as identified in interest with their fellow-Canadians until greater facilities for intercourse have been provided, and these can be most fully secured by the construction of the Canadian Pacific Railway.

Many causes have been at work to retard the progress of Victoria—causes that have similarly affected the welfare of the whole Province. It suffers, and has suffered, largely, from the fact that many of its temporary citizens have been only birds of passage, coming with the intention of leaving as soon as they had made their "pile," and therefore taking no interest in the settlement or development of the country. For this reason many, even of the better educated British Columbians, take no active part in the political or other public interests of the Province, and some are confirmed in this course by the condition of the franchise, which, being virtually that of manhood suffrage, places a large amount of power in the hands of the floating population. The mining excitement, too, has slackened. Men do not now come in from the gold-fields as they once did, so flush with money that they could throw a handful of $20 gold pieces at a saloon-keeper's mirror, and ask the proprietor to take the price of the shattered glass from the coins on the floor. More capital and cheaper labour are now required to work the gold-fields to advantage.

The extensive iron deposits of the Province are lying undisturbed. The great coal-fields are worked only in a very small degree, and mines that may yet give employment to many thousands now employ only a few hundreds. The agricultural capacity of many districts is but imperfectly known, and even the recognized officials can hardly tell the new immigrant where to go for the best unoccupied farm lands, for much fertile soil is still covered, or hemmed in, by forests of large timber.

Although forty millions of dollars have been taken out of the gold mines of British Columbia, there is very little in the Province to-day to represent that amount. Many have carried their money away; many others have left the country "dead broke"; and while in Ontario, and other Provinces, the fortunate remained on account of their success, and the disappointed also remained, because unable to get away; and while all thus settled, worked, and developed the resources of those Provinces, many who had been disappointed in British Columbia could easily move elsewhere, and they left the Province rather the worse for their having lived in it. It must be confessed, too, that Victoria suffers from saloons more perhaps than most of our cities, there being some sixty saloons for a population of about 5,000,—"an intolerable deal of sack to one half-penny worth of bread."

Copper currency is unknown, the smallest coin being a "bit"—that is, the English sixpence, whose nearest equivalent is the ten-cent piece. The **hotel** clerk smiles when you offer him three Canadian cents in payment of a three cent stamp, and suggests that he does not keep a museum of curiosities, while it is said that the presence in church of Canadians from the older Provinces can be sometimes detected by the discovery of copper coins in the collection.

Labour is still dear, notwithstanding the presence of a large Chinese element, against which the chief accusation laid by the anti-Chinese agitators is that it keeps down the price of labour, and so impoverishes white men. Labourers receive from $2 to $2.50 per day; mechanics, $4 to $5. Household servants receive from $15 to $30 per month, and farm servants $20 to $40 per month, with board and lodging, while other labour is paid in proportion, so that the country is a most expensive one for those on salaries, whose incomes are measured by the figures that prevail in other parts of Canada, or in England,—an attractive one for labourers who are willing to work, and for capitalists who have brains to guide their investments in mining, lumbering and fishing,—and a very paradise for domestic servants.

The two great classes of labourers, however, in Southern British Columbia, are the Indians and the Chinese. Many of the Indians work admirably on steamers, in saw-mills, in salmon-canneries, &c. They are active, strong, good-tempered, with very little self-restraint if liquor is within reach, and with a great contempt for Chinamen; some of them are excellent farmers, with very comfortable cottages; and a number of the Lillooet Indians along the Lower Fraser, who bear a specially good name, raise cattle and hay for market. White settlers find no trouble from them. One white settler reports regarding those in his neighbourhood: "The Indians go into farming; quite quiet; keep cats." The keeping of cats is a new test of civilization, although perhaps not much more reliable for that purpose than the use of suspenders.

It is not easy to map out, with accuracy, the different Indian tribes, or dialects, to be met with in the Province. The generic name is Siwash, a corruption, no doubt, of "sauvage," but when you try to define all the species of Siwash you are sure to run across some of the lines laid down by one or other of the writers on this subject. On Vancouver Island there are the Ahts, the Cowichans, the Comox and others. On the mainland, we have the Kootanies, the Lillooets, the Shuswaps, the Chilcotins, the Bellacoulas, the Tsimpseans, the Babines, the Sicanies, and others; and on Queen Charlotte Islands, the Haidahs. Their languages differ in much the same degree as the dialects of English from Cornwall to Caithness, although sometimes one might be tempted to include the varieties of Gaelic as well as of English in this comparison. A common medium of communication with most of them, however—at least, with those near the coast—is found in the Chinook jargon, which was originally the language of the Chinook Indians, near the mouth of the Columbia River, but which has been enriched and altered by the addition of words from the Spanish, French and other languages. It is easily acquired; it cannot be said to have any grammar; but it forms a most convenient means of intercourse with the Indians, from the Fraser to Alaska, being more profitable to the traveller in those regions than all other modern languages.

The other chief labourer of British Columbia is the Chinaman. It is not merely within recent years that men have come from the land of the Celestials, across the Pacific, to our own western coast. There is ample evidence that at some past period the blood of the Chinese, or of the Japanese, was blended with the blood of our Indians, for many of the Pacific Indians are of such a marked Mongolian type of face that you can scarcely tell them from the Chinamen except by the difference of dress, or of language, or by the absence of the pig-tail, which, however, the Chinaman often wears coiled up under his cap. As lately, indeed, as 1834, Japanese junks were found stranded on our western coast. Whether the coming of the Asiatics was the result of accident, or of set purpose, one consequence has been an infusion of Asiatic blood amongst some of our Indian tribes. The immigration, however, of Chinamen for trade and labour, is a thing of recent date. As yet their presence can hardly be said to have had any serious effect on the labour market of the Province, or to provoke much hostility; but as those who have already arrived may be only the advanced guard of a large army of workmen, it is possible that British Columbia may yet witness a strife between white and Chinese labour similar to that which has seriously disturbed the peace of California.

The Chinamen, as a class, are sober, diligent, frugal and trustworthy. They are objected to by the saloon-keeper, who gets no custom from them,—by the indolent, whom they prevent from exacting exorbitant wages for a minimum of work,—by agitators, who try to win the favour of the white working-man, and by others who are more or less influenced by those objectors. And yet remove the Chinamen and you disturb every industry in British Columbia; exclude their future immigration and you increase the cost of working your future factories. It is, of course, only fair that all citizens should contribute a due share to the good of the commonwealth. If, therefore, the Chinaman does not consume enough of our produce, preferring his rice to our wheat, if his work is not enough to entitle him to live among us, and if his labour precludes the employment of those who seem to have a prior claim upon the country, then regulations may be framed to lay upon him a more equitable share of the general burdens. But if it is objected that the Chinese come and work here only with the view of carrying their earnings out of the country, it may be asked, for what other purpose are hundreds of Britons now doing business in China, and with what other object, indeed, have many of the anti-Chinese agitators themselves gone to British Columbia? Or, if it be objected that our civilization, as well as our commerce, may suffer, that the Chinese lower the general tone—then surely we have little faith in our civilization and in our Christianity if we cannot hope rather to mould the Mongolian to a higher life. Even if we would we could not, with any consistency, close one of our ports against Chinese immigration, remembering the way in which the **ports of China were opened for the** commerce of our empire; and before any serious wish should be expressed, or serious attempt **be made, to** exclude them, some more vigorous efforts for their improvement, than have yet been witnessed, are required of us if we be a Christian people.

The development of the resources of British Columbia, however, may well call for the fullest possible supply of cheap labour from whatever quarter it may be derived, for there can be no doubt about the vast extent of the resources of this Province. Compared with Ontario, Manitoba, and other agricultural Provinces, it is an inferior farming country, although parts of the valley of the Fraser, and the valleys of some of its tributaries, as well as other southern portions of the Province, are rich in arable and in pasture lands, while, from the facilities that they afford for wintering cattle, without housing or home-feeding, many parts are specially adapted for stock-raising.

But, while the agricultural capacities of the Province are small, it is in other respects exceptionally wealthy. Its bituminous coal is of the best quality, in quantities that are practically inexhaustible, found close to the water's edge. The estimated coal-producing area of the Comox district alone is given in the *Geological Survey Report for* 1871-2 *(page* 80*)* as 300 square miles; where the estimated quantity of coal underlying the surface, is, on the same authority, set down as 25,000 tons per acre, or sixteen million of tons per square mile; and yet, as if this were not sufficient to warm the world for a while, and to enrich Vancouver for ages, the *Geological Survey Report* assures us that the coal measures " run " in a narrow trough, which may be said to extend to the " vicinity of Cape Mudge on the north-west, and to " approach within fifteen miles of Victoria on the south- " east, with a length of about 130 miles."

Even these areas do not exhaust the coal measures of the island. It was at Fort Rupert, near the northern extremity of Vancouver, a trading post of the Hudson's Bay Company, that coal was first found on the island, but while the Company were making all necessary preparations for mining and shipping coal here, the mines at Nanaimo were discovered, and being richer, more accessible, and more convenient for shipping, they have been opened and worked, while the coal fields at **Fort Rupert** have been allowed to lie idle. Coal from Nanaimo forces its way into San Francisco, notwithstanding the high duty against it. It is used on the Central Pacific **Railroad**, and it is regarded by the U. S. **War Department** as being 20 per cent. better than the best coal of the Pacific States. From Fort Rupert there is said to be a low flat country extending along the **north-western** portion of the island to Quatsino, another locality where coal has been found. Possibly this flat land **may over-lie** extensive beds of coal, and Quatsino **being directly accessible** from the Pacific, would be advantageously situated for large shipments. Moreover, it is at least possible that rich coal beds may yet be found underlying the timber lands, whose dense forests have hitherto prevented any thorough examination of the interior of the island ; and there are known to be extensive beds of anthracite coal in Queen Charlotte Islands.

In addition to the rich coal measures of Vancouver, there are abundant iron deposits. **The whole island of Texada**, not far from the coal-fields of Nanaimo and Comox, seems to be almost a mass of iron ore, easy of access for mining and smelting, and with facilities in the immediate vicinity for producing unlimited charcoal. The ore of Texada is reported, upon assay, to yield **80 per cent.** of pure iron of the best quality.

Silver and copper may be added to the list of mineral resources, while the gold fields of the Province, though ceasing to attract the large numbers that they once did, and being wrought at a great disadvantage, on account of the high price of provisions and of labour, still yield a large return, and may be expected to yield more when improved machinery and cheaper living are introduced; for even of Williams' Creek, one of the most paying in the Cariboo district, which was supposed to have been exhausted, Dr. G. M. Dawson, of the Geological Survey, states that "it would not be extravagant to say that the " quantity of gold still remaining in the bed of this creek, " which has been worked over, is about as great as that " which has already been obtained;" and the same may reasonably be supposed to be the case with other mines.

Its mineral resources, however, though so extensive, are but a portion of the wealth of this Province. Its fisheries are amongst the richest in the world. Salmon swarm in its rivers, in almost incredible numbers, so that the Indian, or any one else who may follow his example, can, in a few days, catch enough salmon to form his chief article of food for the year. The coast is rich with halibut, herring and cod. In the northern waters the seal and the otter abound, while in the river Nasse, and its neighbourhood, the Indians catch large numbers of oolachan, or candle-fish. This fish, which is about the size of the smelt, and considered by some a great delicacy, is so fat that by simply inserting a piece of pith, it serves as a candle, the pith burning like the wick of a well-filled lamp. One gets some idea of the abundance of the oolachan, and also of the herring, from the manner in which they are frequently caught. In a pole, about ten feet in length, nails are inserted, which are set about an inch and a half apart, like the teeth of a comb. When the fisherman in his canoe comes upon a shoal of fish, he draws the pole quickly through the water, and with a backward sweep impales several upon the sharp teeth. In two or three hours he may secure a boat load.

Added to its resources of the mine, and of the sea, this Province boasts the largest of all Canadian timber,—vast forests of Douglas pine. Excellent for ordinary use, this wood is specially suited for such purposes as ship-building, the manufacture of spars, etc., where toughness, lightness, and durability are essential qualities. Trees of Douglas pine sometimes grow to a gigantic size, being even 180 feet in length, and from nine to eleven feet in diameter at the base. Near the northern coast there are extensive forests of cedar and hemlock.

This enumeration of the chief resources of the Province may to some appear tiresome as an exhibition catalogue, but it is necessary in order to convey even a faint idea of the country's wealth. Only in respect to farming does British Columbia seem inferior to any of its sister Provinces. Its climate is much better than that along our Atlantic coast, for it has no cold stream from the Arctic flowing down upon it, and its shores are washed by a warm oceanic current, that keeps its ports open at all seasons, and that gives the southern parts of the Province a climate not unlike that of the south of England, while securing, even to the northern parts, at least near the sea, a temperature as moderate as that enjoyed 10 degrees further south on the Atlantic coast of America.

It would be unreasonable to question the future prosperity of such a Province. The tariffs of other countries may for a time delay its development; they cannot permanently prevent it. Its time must come, when the restless and speculative spirit created by the gold fever, and still too palpably present, shall give place to steady labour, when industry shall unfold the resources of which as yet only the outskirts have been grasped, and when possessions similar to those that secured the material prosperity of the Mother Country, shall make British Columbia one of the wealthiest Provinces of the Dominion.

While waiting for some of our party to complete their arrangements before starting for the Skeena, two of us visited the Fraser River. From Victoria we went by steamer to New Westminster, seventy miles distant, near the mouth of the Fraser, the capital of the old colony of British Columbia before its union with Vancouver. Our course lay through the Straits of San Juan de Fuca, thence across the Straits of Georgia into the broad and turbid Fraser.

The sight of the island of San Juan can hardly fail to arouse Canadians into indignation and regret at the way in which our rights have usually suffered in any controversy with our neighbours regarding our boundary line. A large portion of the State of Maine was lost through the reckless ignorance, it would seem, of some of those who were engaged in negotiating the Ashburton Treaty, or Ashburton Capitulation, as it has sometimes been called. Washington Territory and part of Oregon were lost to us, it appears, because the then Premier of England considered the country not worth contending for, basing his judgment on a report of his brother, who condemned it as useless because the salmon in the Columbia River would not rise to the fly. And, surely, there must have been serious carelessness in the wording of the Treaty, or some culpable deficiency in the evidence and arguments submitted to the Emperor of Germany, when, as arbitrator, he decided that the boundary line should run down the Haro Straits, instead of following either the Middle Channel or the Straits of Rosario, thus giving to the United States an island to which until recently they laid no claim.

Not long ago there died in San Juan an aged servant of the Hudson's Bay Company, a Scottish Highlander, who, with a brother and sister, had come there when the British title to the island was undisputed. It was the dying wish of the old man, as well as the desire of his only surviving relatives, that his remains should not lie in a foreign land. With some difficulty and expense they were removed to Victoria, where the brother and sister, who spoke very little English, told their story to the Rev. S. Macgregor, who could speak to them in their native Gaelic. The little funeral procession of two, accompanied by the clergyman, passed from the wharf to the graveyard, and there they left the bones of the old Loyalist beneath the protection of the flag he loved.

As it nears the sea, the Fraser flows, broad and slow, between low alluvial banks or tide-flats. It starts on its winding course some 800 miles above this, in the upper slopes of the Rocky Mountains, cleaving its way through many a wild cañon, skirting rich gold bars and fertile valleys, and receiving as its tributaries all the streams which flow from the Rockies through the Cascade Range to the sea. Other rivers, such as the Bellacoula, the Homathco, the Skeena, and the Nasse, rising in the interior plateau, flow through the Cascades to the Western Sea; others, again, both from the Cascades and the Rockies, swell the waters of the Peace in its northward flow to the Arctic Ocean; but the Fraser alone, rising in the Rockies, cuts its course through the high broken plateau that divides the Rocky Mountains from the Cascade or

Coast Range, and, forcing its way through this latter, finds rest at last in the Pacific.

Near the mouth of the Fraser is the little city of New Westminster, which was shorn of some of its pretensions and prospects when Victoria was chosen as the capital of the united colony, but which has now every chance of soon surpassing its old rival, as the neighbouring harbour of Burrard Inlet has been selected as the terminus of the Canadian Pacific Railway. Although the city can scarcely be said to have a harbour, it being little more than a river bank approached by the winding Fraser, yet it claims, as in some sense its own, the harbour of Burrard Inlet, about nine miles north,—a claim, perhaps, as valid as that on which Victoria prides itself on the possession of Esquimault.

Though smaller and less attractive than Victoria, with somewhat more of a backwoods appearance, it has a pulse of life and energy stronger in proportion to its population than is found in its rival. It is the centre towards which the lines of travel and of traffic from the interior converge. The herds of cattle from the ranches of Kamloops, the farm products of Sumas and Nicola, with similar returns from other districts, are brought here as to a common point of distribution.

Burrard Inlet is certainly the most suitable harbour in British Columbia for the terminus of our Pacific Railway. Only two others can be seriously compared with it,—

Port Simpson and Esquimault. Port Simpson, although in some respects suitable, especially if the convenience of the Asiatic trade were made a prominent consideration, is too far north to serve the general interests of the Province; while, at the same time, in approaching it from the east it would be necessary to traverse a large tract of country that, as far as known, is seriously deficient in resources.

Esquimault is smaller than Burrard Inlet, and, even with the roadstead of Royal Roads, would not give as much harbourage as Burrard with its roadstead, English Bay; while the enormous cost and practical inutility of a railway from Esquimault to Nanaimo, which would have been a necessity if Esquimault had been chosen as a terminus, as well as the great expense and other objections that might be urged against the Bute Inlet route, render Burrard Inlet much more eligible as the Pacific terminus of the line.

Objection has been taken against it on the ground that any vessels bound from the Pacific for Burrard Inlet might, in case of disturbance between Britain and the United States, be stopped by the batteries of San Juan; but there is little doubt that in the event of such disturbance the batteries of San Juan would soon be held by the British, or Vancouver be held by the States; that both islands, in short, would, in the event of war, fall to the power that held naval supremacy on the Pacific. At the same time, if a course north of that which runs by the valley of the Fraser to Burrard Inlet had been selected for our railway, much of the traffic of the southern part of the Province must inevitably have passed to any Northern Pacific railway that may be constructed through United States territory with a terminus in the neighbourhood of Puget Sound.

Burrard Inlet is already a busy place, for it is the centre of the British Columbia timber trade,—the manufacture and export of the Douglas pine, which grows in great excellence and abundance in this vicinity. Lumberers here work under great advantages as compared with those of our Eastern Provinces. The climate is so moderate, and the pine forests are so close to the water's edge, that men are at work in the woods all the year round felling trees and drawing them, by means of oxen, to the water, so that they can be easily rafted to the mills; while other gangs of men are at work throughout the whole year in the mills and on the docks, sawing and piling lumber and loading vessels, which have easy access to the mill-wharves at all seasons. The road from New Westminster to Burrard Inlet passes through a forest of Douglas pine, where on either side rise these giants, straight, lofty and almost branchless, waiting for the axe.

From New Westminster we went by steamer 100 miles to Yale, the head of navigation on the Fraser. There are navigable reaches of the river above Yale, but all progress by steamer from the sea beyond this point is prevented by the character of the river—wild, broken and rapid—and by the precipitous cañons through which it flows. From Yale, the one great highway to the interior is the waggon-road which was built by the Province at a very large cost when the Cariboo gold-fever was impelling thousands up the banks of the Fraser. It follows, for the most part, the course of the river, though taking sometimes the easier valleys of tributary streams, running northerly about 300 miles until it reaches Quesnel, and then striking east to the Cariboo district, one of the richest gold-mining fields ever known.

Anxious to see something of the cañons of the Fraser, we drove over this road as far as Boston Bar, a distance of 25 miles. For wild and startling scenery this drive has few equals. The road winds around high and precipitous hills, sometimes cut out of the rock, sometimes built up on crib-work at an altitude of several hundred feet above the river, while leaning over the side of the waggon you look down on the Fraser, at the foot of the sheer and rugged cliff, wild, masterful, turbulent, whirling and swirling in rapids and eddies that invariably prove fatal to any who fall within their grasp. Frequently one meets great ox-teams, dragging huge waggons, or extensive pack-trains of mules, well laden, carrying their cargoes to the interior. Only steady nerve and experience could enable a man to guide a span of horses at a rattling

From a Photo. by Dr. G. M. Dawson.

FRASER RIVER (18 miles above Yale).

pace, sometimes at full speed, over such a road, near the edge of those precipitous banks, and around corners where you know not what mule-train or ox-waggon you may meet; but the drivers on this line are men of nerve and experience. We were in the hands of such a Jehu, and although at times the driving was furious as that of the son of Nimshi, yet we had every confidence in him. What is life worth without faith in your fellow-man?

Often along this lower part of the river we passed " bars" that once attracted thousands—Emory Bar, Wellington Bar, Boston Bar, &c.,—for small grains of gold are commonly first detected at the head of a sand-bar, where the current of the river leaves only the heavier sand and the metallic particles that are borne down with it. Some of these bars are still worked by Indians and Chinamen, who make fair wages at them, but they do not yield enough to attract the more restless or more ambitious white man.

From the road one can see the old trail by which hundreds of gold-hunters travelled, through hardship and suffering, before the waggon-road was made, carrying, in many instances, provisions, blankets, mining tools, &c., a burden of some 120 lbs. per man, for nearly 400 miles. We hear of the handful of successful men, whose good fortune sends hundreds of others to the mines. We hear nothing of the thousands of unfortunates, broken in purse, broken in all sober industry that would fit them for steady labour, often broken in health, but still unbroken in hope, still strong in the gaming spirit that flings the past to the winds, and, with confident outlook, says, " better luck next time."

A rough crowd those miners often were; and yet, our knowledge of British Columbia to-day, small as it is, would be much smaller but for them. They opened up the country and made it known. The Indians could not, and the Hudson's Bay Company's officials would not, let the outside world learn from them about this land of cañon and of mountain. But the miner came, and he laughed at difficulties that would have made other men despair. He pierced the country from Kootenay to Cassiar. Railway explorers and surveyors followed, and now almost every available pass and road and stretch of farm land, at least in the southern portion of the Province, is mapped out. Few of the miners made fortunes, yet many helped to open the country for those who have come after them. They may rest in unknown and unhonoured graves, but their work, however different in aim, was in result not unlike that of an advanced guard in many an old conflict, who bridged the ditch with their bodies that others might pass over them to victory.

Frequently along the Fraser society was wild as the scenery, although, thanks to the prompt administration of justice by Sir Matthew Begbie and Judge Reilley, life and property were as safe in the mining districts as in the best regulated parts of the country. But the language was sometimes rough, very rough. A Canadian clergyman on one occasion visited Cariboo, and hearing occasional profanity, he attempted gently to remonstrate with the offenders. The miners could stand a good lecture on Sunday, but they did not relish reproofs of this kind through the week for what, after all, appeared to them little more than emphatic language; so they undertook to astonish his reverence. By pre-arrangement some of them, when within ear-shot of the Doctor, dropped into conversation, and interlarded their talk with such profanity as even they themselves had never heard before. No wonder that the good man was horrified and gave the miners of Cariboo a bad name, although, had he been behind the scenes, he would hardly have taken this as a specimen of their common conversation.

CHAPTER II.

VICTORIA TO THE SKEENA.

Along the Coast.—The Chain of Channels.—Nanaimo.—Bute Inlet and the Route of the Canadian Pacific Railway.—Port Essington and the Mouth of the Skeena.—Metlahkatlah.—Mission to the Indians.—Port Simpson.—Work Inlet.

Having returned to Victoria, and having completed all our preparations for our journey northward and across the mountains, we left there on Tuesday, the 3rd June, for Port Essington, at the mouth of the Skeena, in the commodious steamer *Olympia*, belonging to the Hudson's Bay Company.

As the *Olympia* was to go as far as Fort Wrangel, in Alaska, where travellers for the Cassiar gold fields leave the coast to ascend the Stickine, and was to call at Fort Masset, and at other intervening ports, before returning, and as she was incomparably more comfortable than the ordinary steamers on this route, there was a goodly number of passengers on board. We had a party of ladies and gentlemen from Victoria, who availed themselves of this opportunity of seeing a portion of our

Northern Pacific, of which Victorians, in **general**, know very little, **some** traders and **miners** for Cassiar, a staff **of** railway engineers, with assistants, axemen, voyageurs, etc., that were to be engaged during the summer in the upper part of the Province, and also a number of Haidah Indians, returning to their homes on the Queen Charlotte Islands, after **one of** those visits to Victoria, from which the morality, both of whites and Indians, suffers considerably.

Our course lay eastward through the Haro Straits, then northward between Vancouver and the **smaller islands** that stud the Straits of Georgia, until, leaving the northern extremity of Vancouver, we passed through the chain of channels that divide the mainland **from** the long succession of islands which fringe the coast, with scarcely any interruptions, as far as Alaska.

This land-locked strip of ocean that stretches almost unbroken along our Pacific coast from San Juan to Port Simpson, some 500 miles in length, **is** one of the most singular water-ways in the world. On the western side of Vancouver and of the line of islands lying to the north, the waves of the ocean break in an unceasing roll that, even in calm weather, strikes the shore as with the shock **of** battle; but here, inside of this breast-work of islands, between it and the mainland, the sea is, commonly, smooth as a canal. It is deep enough for the largest man-of-war, even within a few yards of almost any part of the shore, and yet the tiniest steam yacht runs no risk of rough water. For pleasure sailing, this deep, smooth, safe, spacious, land-locked channel, or series of channels, is probably without a rival. Now it broadens to a width of several miles, and again it narrows to the space of a few hundred yards; the number of islands enabling one to shape his course over calm water in almost any wind, while on every hand one is girt by varied and attractive scenery. For commercial purposes, when the mines along the sea-board become more fully developed, its forests more extensively utilized, and its coasting trade increased, the value of such a highway, possessing all the advantages of deep-sea navigation, yet protected by a line of break-waters from all the dangers of the sea, can hardly be over-estimated.

Only in two places is it exposed to the gales and the swell of the Pacific. First, from the north end of Vancouver Island, as you round Cape Caution, for a distance of about thirty miles; and, again, for less than ten miles, on passing Milbank Sound. Here, with a strong westerly wind, the sea runs high, but the surrounding land forms a barrier against all except westerly winds. At two places—Dodd's Narrows, near the entrance to Nanaimo, and at Seymour Narrows, between Vancouver and Valdes Islands,—there is, at certain conditions of the tide, a strong current, which might cause a delay of two hours, at the utmost, to an ordinary steamer, but the approaches to these Narrows are so straight and wide that they would offer no danger to navigation. For the rest, there is no more difficulty or cause of delay than would be met with in a deep, narrow lake.

The one discomfort, to which the traveller along this coast is most likely to be subjected, is the moist climate, which prevails when you pass beyond the protection of the mountains of **Vancouver.** Until you approach the northern extremity of that island, its lofty hills, some of which are over 7,000 feet in height, intercept the showers that drift landward from the Pacific, so that these **fall** upon the western slopes of the island. Hence the eastern coast, from Vancouver northward, enjoys a most delightful climate; but when you have passed Vancouver, the islands to the north, being less lofty, no longer serve in the same degree to intercept the clouds from the Pacific. These roll inland until they strike the lofty summits of the Coast Range, which run close to the sea-board along **its whole** length; **and** hence the northern part of the coast enjoys, or rather endures, a much greater rain-fall than either the east coast of Vancouver Island or the southern part of the mainland. In this respect it is not unlike some portions of the west of Scotland, where the **proverbial** relief from the rain is that " whiles it snaws."

After leaving Victoria, our first place of call was Departure Bay, a coaling station adjoining the extensive Nanaimo coal-fields. Nanaimo, however, is known in the

Eastern Provinces less by its coal-fields than by the much disputed project of a railway to connect it with Esquimault. Had it been absolutely necessary at any cost to build this railway, either as a separate line or as part of the Canadian Pacific Railway, there might have been some propriety in the proposal; but, apart from the fact that the country through which it would pass is one of the most difficult of countries for railway construction, even were it built and in working order, coal could be conveyed more cheaply from Nanaimo to Victoria by large barges than by rail. Fifty miles north of Nanaimo are the coal-fields of Comox. In the various mines of these districts Indians and Chinamen are employed, as well as white labourers. The wages of white men range from $2 to $5 per day; the others receive from $1 to $1.50.

The day continued clear and beautiful. Sometimes we passed close to the shore, and beneath the shadow of the hills; sometimes by low lying islands, well timbered with cedar; while on either hand rose a background of snow-capped mountains,—on one side those of Vancouver Island, which, however, will lose their snow ere the summer is ended, on the other hand the coast range of the mainland, some of whose peaks remain white throughout the year.

On Tuesday night we passed through the Seymour Narrows, that separate Valdes Island from Vancouver. This locality, like a number of others in British Columbia, has attracted attention chiefly through its connection with one of the proposed routes of the Pacific Railway, as any line by Bute Inlet would necessarily pass over, or near, Valdes Island; over it if the straits were to be bridged from the mainland to Vancouver, near it if a ferry should be used connecting Bute Inlet with Vancouver.

Like the other fiords that cut into this rough, mountainous coast, Bute Inlet, which is about fifty miles in length, is a narrow arm of the sea, hemmed in on either side by lofty banks of rock, in many places precipitous, in all places very steep, with no anchorage except a few chains at the head of the inlet, where the River Homathco flows into it. This limited anchorage has been designated Waddington Harbour. Near the mouth of the inlet is Valdes Island, which, though regarded as an isolated island until a thorough survey had been made, is really a group of islands, separated from each other and from the shores of the mainland and of Vancouver by wide channels.

If an unbroken line of railway coming from the east to Waddington Harbour were to pass over to Vancouver and so down to Victoria, it must skirt the precipitous side of Bute Inlet, cross by a succession of long-span bridges to Vancouver, and run about one hundred and seventy miles along the eastern coast of that island by Comox and Nanaimo to Esquimault, the true harbour of

Victoria. This line from Waddington to Vancouver would involve the construction of works so stupendous as to place it practically out of the question; although not, indeed, impossible to engineering science, the cost would be so enormous that it may well be regarded as financially impossible, and may therefore be abandoned. The alternative is a ferry from Waddington Harbour to Vancouver, forming a break of some seventy miles of steam navigation as a link between the line on the mainland and the line that would follow the coast of Vancouver to Esquimault, and even the latter section would be so costly, owing to the broken character of the country between Nanaimo and Esquimault, that its construction could not be justified unless this part of Vancouver were almost as thickly settled as the mining districts of England, or unless there were absolutely no other way of reaching a suitable harbour on the Pacific. A line from the east to the excellent harbour at Burrard Inlet will be less expensive and fifty miles shorter than one terminating at Waddington Harbour, and as Burrard Inlet is but seventy miles distant from Esquimault, while Waddington Harbour is about two hundred and fifty miles, these considerations amply justify the decision of the Government in selecting Burrard Inlet as the terminus.

We passed through the Seymour Narrows by night, so that we saw nothing of Valdes Island, nor of the neighbourhood of Bute Inlet. On Wednesday morning we drew away from Vancouver Island, and, crossing the entrance of Queen Charlotte Sound, we passed Cape Caution and entered Fitz-Hugh Sound, continuing our course through a succession of channels that render navigation here unusually safe and enjoyable. For a little we felt the roll of the Pacific when passing Cape Caution, but ere long we were in smooth water again, and even those most sensitive to sea-sickness soon recovered their confidence. We found, however, as we had expected, that when we left the shelter of the Vancouver Mountains the climate became much moister and a drizzling rain generally obscured our view. Sometimes, when the leaden mist would lift, we could see the hills, now bare and precipitous, now wooded and gently sloping, now rugged and snow-capped; sometimes presenting a wall of adamant, as if defying the attacks of the ocean, and sometimes cleft by a deep narrow gorge, or fiord, whose beetling sides had opened thus far to the inroads of the sea, but forbade any further advance.

The whole country appeared to be wrapped in silence; no sign of life could be seen except some salmon-canning establishment, such as that at Cardena Bay (now called Aberdeen), or an occasional Indian village that had grown up in some locality well favoured for shooting and fishing, or had clustered around some post of the Hudson's Bay Company.

Thursday dawned heavy and dull as the day before, but

in the course of the morning the clouds lifted, the drizzling rain ceased, and as we passed through Grenville Channel we were favoured with wider views of the scenery, which still continued to be most attractive. Sometimes the stretch of water broadened to several miles, its surface broken by wooded islands, whose foliage seems to be freshened and preserved by the moisture to which it is exposed; sometimes it narrows to a few hundred yards, bound on either hand by hills, whose valleys and ravines are channels for foaming torrents that are fed by the snow fields above them.

About mid-day on Thursday we reached Port Essington (formerly called Spucksute), at the mouth of the Skeena. Port Essington has not many attractions. The village consists of some fifteen or twenty houses, the best of which is occupied by the solitary white trader of the place, the others by Indians. The chief staple of trade, which is also the chief article of food, is salmon, for here as elsewhere along the coast, salmon is found in extraordinary abundance, and during the fishing season there is a ready market for them at the small cannery, a little north of this, known as Willaclach, called also Woodcock's Landing, or Inverness. There is very little land in the vicinity fit for cultivation, the country being for the most part rugged and mountainous; but there are excellent cedar forests close at hand, a fact that induced an enterprising firm to build a steamer here some years ago, as it was possible to bring the engines, etc., here more easily than cedar could be conveyed to Victoria, but the price of labour made the venture a costly and unprofitable one.

For some distance from the mouth of the river the clear sea-water is discoloured by the dark waters of the Skeena; indeed, the river seems to push back the sea rather than to blend with it, for though there are the usual tidal variations, exposing at low water a rough beach in front of the village, yet the water near the shore is almost perfectly fresh, and is constantly used for cooking and other domestic purposes. The large bay that receives the waters of the river affords good anchorage, but it cannot be called a good harbour, for not only is the access from the sea somewhat intricate, but during the winter season it is blocked with ice brought down by the Skeena. Adjacent islands prevent the waters of the Pacific from having much effect upon the bay, except in the rise and fall of the tide, and as it receives the waters of a large river that in winter are ice-cold, and frequently blocked with ice floes, this bay, unlike the great majority of the bays on the Pacific coast, is ice-bound for a part of the year.

We were to leave the coast at Port Essington on our journey towards the Peace River district, but before doing so it was necessary for us to go as far as Port Simpson and Work Inlet; so, having landed a party of engineers and their assistants, who were to work in this neighbourhood and up the river during the summer, we steamed northward, arriving a little before sunset at Metlahkatlah, where it was necessary for us to call in order to secure Indians and canoes for our journey up the Skeena, and where we were all anxious to visit Mr. Duncan and his most interesting Mission-station.

Almost every one who takes any interest in Missions to the Indians of British Columbia knows something about Metlahkatlah; but, although we had heard and expected much, our information and our expectations alike fell short of the reality. There are active missions to the Indians maintained by the Methodist Church at Victoria and at Port Simpson. There are missions of the Anglican Church at Lytton and elsewhere. There are several missions maintained by the Roman Catholic Church. But it is no injustice to these others to say that none of them have been so singularly successful as that which is conducted by Mr. Duncan at Metlahkatlah. It is in connection with the Anglican Church, in so far as Mr. Duncan is a member of that communion and loyal to her teaching; but, not being an ordained clergyman, he is not subject to direct ecclesiastical authority in the management of the mission, and is thus perfectly free to exercise his own judgment and energy.

Though now a very active and thriving community, Metlahkatlah must have presented a most uninviting appearance when Mr. Duncan commenced his work there, seventeen years ago. The Tsimpseans, as the Indians of this district are called, were at that time as fierce, turbulent, and unchaste as any of the other coast tribes, not excepting the Haidahs. Everything had to be done, and it was difficult to see where the work of reformation should begin; and it required a man with strong faith in God, and in the possibilities of human nature, to undertake the work. Necessarily, Mr. Duncan set himself to acquire the language of the people to whom he had come, and he was himself the first to make Tsimpsean a written language, or to translate into it any portion of the Scriptures; but, while teaching them in their own tongue, he endeavours also to secure that they all, and more particularly the young among them, shall learn English.

It has, from the first, been a leading object with him to draw in the Indians from their scattered settlements towards one or more centres, and this has been simplified by the fact that they live largely upon fish, of which, at any point along the coast, they can procure an abundant supply. Hence, when the mission had been once established, the determination of any Indian to go and make his home at Metlahkatlah was almost equivalent to a profession of his conversion to Christianity, or at least of his desire for Christian instruction.

One of the first reforms effected among them was in the character of their dwellings, and the need of this is seen from the fact that although the Indians in and around Victoria were, when Mr. Duncan came to Metlahkatlah, nominally Christian, yet, largely on account of the slums in which they have been allowed to live, they have made but little progress in cleanliness, and in some other virtues that are closely allied to godliness. Indeed, one does not need to go among Indians for illustrations of this. Anyone who has been much among the lapsed classes of our large cities must know that much of their degradation is caused, or is at least increased, by their surroundings; and it must be so with savages. Let grown-up members of one or more families be huddled together in the same sleeping apartments, and purity becomes impossible. All the vices among the Indians have not been introduced by the rough characters that hang on the outskirts of civilization, although no doubt many of their worst vices have been strengthened by intercourse with whites.

To give them homes for huts was one of Mr. Duncan's first objects, and it is surprising how much has been effected in this respect. Not only have their original huts given place to better houses, but these again, through the educating influence of this improvement, have stimulated the people to take advantage of Mr. Duncan's plan to provide still better dwellings. He desires, as far as possible, to secure uniformity in the character of the houses, and many of the Indians, at his suggestion, have built comfortable dwellings on the following plan:—the houses are built in pairs, which are connected by one common room that serves as a guest-chamber for both families, where they may entertain their heathen friends who have not yet fallen into their own ways. Each house consists of two rooms on the ground floor and of three bedrooms upstairs, one for the parents, one for the sons, a third for the daughters. There is of course no constraint put upon the people to make them build houses of this kind, but they are educated into the desire for comfortable homes, and when they have secured a certain proportion of the cost, Mr. Duncan advances the remainder, allowing them sawn cedar lumber at $7.00 per thousand feet. Already the result is a degree of neatness, cleanliness and uniformity seldom found in any of our eastern villages.

To have a busy, industrious and prosperous community there must be men of different trades. Mr. Duncan found these Indians skilful in certain arts, such as weaving and carving. They weave mats from rushes or from cedar bark, which is sometimes simply cut into strips or sometimes passed through the more elaborate process of being soaked, beaten and twisted into threads. Out of this matting they make baskets, floor-cloths, cargo-covers, etc., for it is so closely woven that it is impervious to water. They carve wood and silver with considerable ingenuity, the former chiefly for door-posts and other ornaments in connection with their houses, the latter principally for bracelets, the favourite pattern being the beaver, though they sometimes adopt the pattern of the eagle from the United States half-dollar piece. These bracelets are frequently purchased and worn as *curios* by white visitors.

While maintaining the arts and trades which he found in existence among them, Mr. Duncan introduced the ordinary trades of Anglo-Saxon communities, some of which he learned in order that he might instruct the Indians, while in others he has secured instruction for his flock by sending some of their own number to Victoria to be taught. For the greater convenience and better training of these, a series of excellent workshops has been erected, where the smiths, coopers, carpenters, weavers, shoemakers, etc., ply their trades, and a good saw-mill provides all the sawn lumber used by the people.

There is a large, commodious and well-arranged schoolhouse; a town hall, to which a reading-room is attached, and in which justice is administered; a good jail, to which any offenders, their number being very small, are taken and imprisoned by Indian policemen; while prominent for situation as for influence is the church, a building that can comfortably accommodate 1,000 people. The edifice is most tastefully constructed, Gothic in architecture, plain and substantial, an enduring testimony to the skill and energy of the missionary, who was architect, clerk of works, and chief builder. In

From a Photo. by Dr. G. M. Dawson. METLAHKATLAH.

the religious services there is an utter lack of outward show,—none of those appeals to the senses which many regard as essential to any effective mission work among Indians. It is the reality and not the mere ritual of religion that the missionary tries to impress upon the people. The service of the Church of England is used; the most simple and popular hymns are sung; and evidence of the genuine grasp which the people take of the instruction imparted to them is found in their diligence and trustworthiness, which cause them to be employed in preference to any others by those who require men to convey goods to the interior, in their careful observance of the Sabbath, whether at home or in the country, and in the ability with which the better educated among them are able to conduct services in some of the Indian settlements which Mr. Duncan is unable to visit.

Their chief source of food and of wealth is found in the abundance of fish,—of salmon, halibut, whales, fur-seal, sea-otter, etc.,—which are obtained around the coast. These they exchange for goods or money at the store in the village, or with traders from other parts of the country. Formerly they used to go in large numbers to Victoria to sell and buy, and these visits frequently proved injurious to the virtue of both men and women. It was necessary, if possible, to remove this temptation, and therefore Mr. Duncan established a store at Metlah-katlah, where all that the community could require might be purchased as reasonably as at Victoria. The necessity for their annual visits to the temptations of the capital has thus been removed, and, although some critics have found fault with Mr. Duncan for engaging thus far in mercantile pursuits, yet anyone who understands the circumstances can see that the step was necessary in the interests of his mission.

Other centres besides Metlahkatlah have been chosen for similar mission work, and there are at present, in connection with this mission, stations at Fort Rupert, V.I., at Masset in Queen Charlotte Islands, and on the River Nasse.

Considering the former state of affairs among the Tsimpseans, as illustrated in what has until recently prevailed, and even to a great degree still prevails among the Haidahs, and contrasting with that their present condition,—the chastity of the women, the steady, honest industry of the men, the thrift and cleanliness of all,—it is not to be wondered at that the people are intensely attached to Mr. Duncan, or that every visitor speaks with cordial praise of this indefatigable missionary, and of the success with which God has crowned his devoted and stout-hearted labours.

Around Metlahkatlah some attempts have been made at gardening. Vegetables are grown with fair success, especially potatoes, but, with the exception of a few occasional patches of tolerable soil, the country in this neighbourhood is unfit for cultivation, and, beyond the resources of the fisheries and of the **cedar** forests, offers few inducements to settlers.

We had had rain for the two preceding days, but our evening at Metlahkatlah was fair. Mr. Duncan kept a weather record for one season, from October till April, and found that for those seven months only an average of seven days per month were fair, and, after a residence of seventeen years in this locality, he thinks that **this is a** fair average proportion of fine weather for that part of the year, but that the proportion of wet weather during **the** remaining months is not so large. Yet, although the rainfall is apparently heavy, the climate seems to be healthy, if one may judge from the fresh and vigorous appearance of the people, and those resident here say that the cold is not more severe than in the southern parts of the Province.

To Canadians along the Atlantic seaboard it may seem strange that the climate on our Pacific Coast should be so mild—that the harbour of Port Simpson, for **instance,** in latitude 54° 30′, is never frozen—and that it enjoys a climate as mild as that of Halifax, although ten degrees north of Halifax, that is, as much further **north of Halifax** as Halifax is of the lower part of North Carolina. The climate of this whole coast, however, is made much more temperate than that of the same latitude on the Atlantic by reason of the *Kuro-Siwa,* or warm oceanic current, which, flowing northward along the coast of Japan, washes the shores of the Aleutian Islands and sends its influence as far as the coast of British Columbia; while, at the same time, there is no Arctic current flowing down our Pacific seaboard as there is along our Atlantic shores.

Before leaving Metlahkatlah we arranged for the employment of two canoes and two crews of Indians for our trip up the Skeena, Mr. Duncan's Indians, as they are commonly called, being most reliable. At daybreak on Friday morning we continued our journey to Port Simpson, about twenty-five miles north of Metlahkatlah, which we approached by Cunningham Passage, between Finlayson Island and the mainland, and entered through Dodd's Channel.

Port Simpson is a small village that has gathered around an old Hudson's Bay Company's post (from which it is sometimes called Fort Simpson), occupied almost entirely by Indians. Here, as at many points along the coast, the Indians have become accustomed to cash payments in trade, although in the interior they generally adhere to the old system of barter. At one time articles were valued here according to the number of seals that they were worth, or the number of them that a seal might be worth, just as the Indians of the Peace River district still measure the value of an article by beaver skins. At a later period the blanket was the chief currency, and a canoe or seal skin was worth so many blankets or fractions of a blanket. **Now**, however, the Indians of the coast, like the U. S. Government, have come down to specie payment.

The harbour of Port Simpson is easy of access for **steam** navigation from the south through the channel by **which** we approached it, and easy of access to sailing ships or steamers approaching it from the **west** through Dixon's Straits, that separate the Queen Charlotte Islands from Alaska; **and it is as safe as it is accessible.** Facing the west it has two approaches: **Dodd's** Passage, between the southern extremity of the harbour and a reef of rocks, and Inskip Passage, which separates this reef of rocks on its northern side from Birnie Island; while, between Birnie Island and the northern extremity of the harbour there is a choked passage, unfit for any navigation except that of canoes or other light craft. The reef of rocks, although hidden at high tide, is traceable at low water on account of the kelp attached to it. It serves as a partial breakwater for any sea that might roll in from the Pacific, while Birnie Island further protects the harbour **on the** western side. Its only exposure is in the direction of the approach known as Inskip Passage, but no severe gales ever visit it from that quarter. Finlayson Island and the Dundas Islands protect it to the south-west and south, while any gales from the north-east, east, or south-east, (the prevailing quarters for high winds in this locality), can scarcely have any influence upon it, as it is so well defended on those sides by the high surrounding land. The extent of the harbour may be set down at not less than three miles in length, with an average breadth of one mile. Its anchorage is reported to be excellent by Captain Lewis of the *Olympia*, one of the most experienced navigators of those waters.

Port Simpson was, until the recent decision of the Government, considered by some a possible terminus of the Canadian Pacific Railway. If trade with Asia were the chief consideration in the selection of an ocean terminus, Port Simpson must unquestionably be preferred to either Burrard Inlet or Esquimault, as it is easier of access than Esquimault, as large as Burrard Inlet, if not larger, and as safe as either of them; while, in point of latitude, it is much to be preferred, as a vessel sailing from this port could at once take advantage of the northern circle and so shorten the distance very greatly in crossing to the coast of Japan or China, and the same advantage would be enjoyed by any vessel bound for this port from the western coast of the Pacific. At the same time, the chain of channels that stretches from Victoria to Port Simpson affords remarkable facilities for coast navigation, and brings Port Simpson within comparatively easy access of the southern parts of the Province. Indeed, in view of the difficulties, amounting almost to impossibilities, that would have to be encountered in the construction of a line by Bute Inlet to Esquimault, Burrard Inlet and Port Simpson may fairly be regarded as the only two points worthy of serious consideration in the selection of a Pacific terminus for our Canadian Pacific Railway. But, while probably fewer engineering difficulties would be experienced in reaching Port Simpson from the east by way of Pine River Pass than must be encountered in reaching Burrard Inlet by the Yellow Head Pass, yet, as the resources of British Columbia are confined almost entirely to the southern part of the Province, as the country between Pine River and Port Simpson seems to be generally deficient in resources, as the selection of Port Simpson would necessarily throw the traffic of Southern British Columbia into the United States railways, and as the interests of the country on the eastern side of the Rocky Mountains will be better served by a line running through Edmonton and the Yellow Head Pass than by one through the Peace River district (by either Pine River or Peace River Pass) to the Pacific, the weight of argument is in favour of the decision already arrived at by the Government in the selection of Burrard Inlet as the Pacific terminus of the railway.

From Port Simpson we steamed around by Cape Maskelyne into Work Channel, which runs in a south-easterly direction nearly parallel to the Pacific for about thirty miles, thus forming the Tsimpsean Peninsula. This peninsula is about twelve miles in width from near the mouth of the Skeena to Cape Maskelyne. Work Channel has never been fully surveyed. It seems to be similar to many others of the deep inlets that run into the mountains along this coast, and that have often been likened to the fiords of Norway. The banks are precipitous, although along the south-westerly shore there runs for the most part a ledge or bench, while, near Port Simpson, the land dips, so that from the head of the inlet a road might be constructed without extreme difficulty along the south-westerly shore of the inlet and through this valley to Port Simpson. At the head, or south-eastern extremity of the inlet, a stream enters from the south, and up the valley of this stream there is a pass at low altitude connecting by a few miles Work Inlet with the river Skeena.

As we were returning to Port Simpson, the drizzling rain, which had fallen more or less steadily since Wednesday morning, ceased; the clouds broke away; the sky grew clear, and the day became bright and fair as an English May day. Steaming around Cape Maskelyne, we could see along the coast of Alaska for many miles, and as we turned south and passed Port Simpson, the harbour and its surroundings appeared to great advantage. The sea was calm; the rugged hills were purpled by the light of the westering sun, as we ran down along the coast past Metlahkatlah and Willaclach to Port Essington, where we landed on the afternoon of Friday, the 6th June. Before leaving the *Olympia* we wrote to our friends in the east, thinking that this might be the last chance we could have of sending word to them before reaching the telegraph station at Edmonton, east of the Rocky Mountains. The engineering party, who had landed at Port Essington the day before, were already under canvas. They asked us to share their camp, for they were "on hospitable thoughts in-tent," and we gladly availed ourselves of the offer. Next day we were to commence our journey up the Skeena.

CHAPTER III.

UP THE SKEENA.

Leave Port Essington.—Canoes, Crews, and Stores.—No Trout.—Tracking and Poling.—Indian Watch-tower.—Catching and Curing Salmon.—Carved Posts.—Burial Customs.—The Sweating-booth.—Height of Steam Navigation.—Division of Coast and Cascade Range.—Indian Villages.—Gold-washing.—Medicine-man.—The Forks of Skeena.—Lip-ornaments and Nose-rings.—Mosquitoes.

We left Port Essington on Saturday, 7th June, eastward bound, our proposed route being up the Skeena, to the village of Hazelton; thence on foot to Babine; up Lake Babine; down Stewart's Lake to Fort St. James; across country with a mule train to Fort McLeod; down the Parsnip and Peace Rivers to Dunvegan; thence on to Edmonton, and across the prairies to Winnipeg.

We were not in search of adventure, and the work in which we were engaged was not one that would naturally involve us in thrilling episodes or hair-breadth escapes, while we had large enough crews and sufficient creature-comforts to spare us any real hardship. Yet our journey had the attraction of novelty. We would

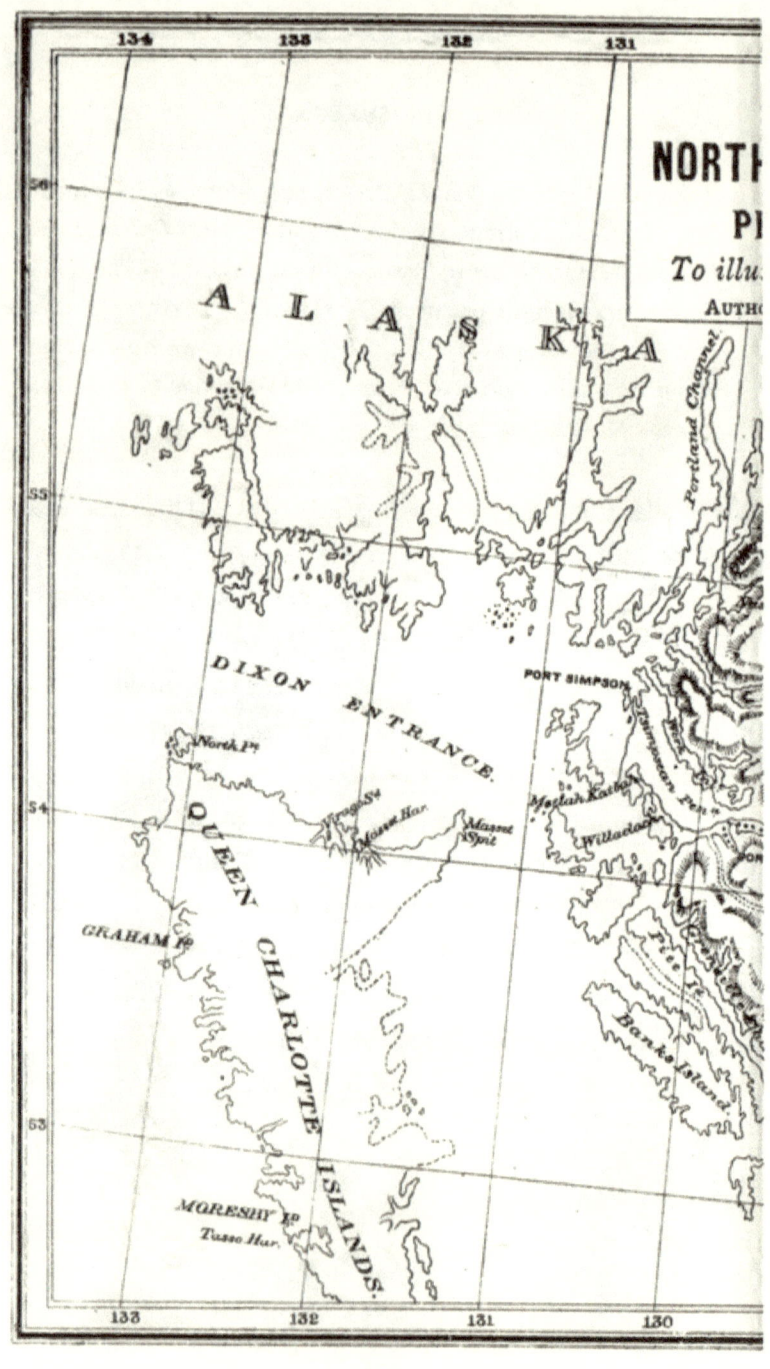

see the country; our engineers would examine its fitness for railway construction; our geologist would take note of its mineral and agricultural resources; and we would learn something of the character and life of the inhabitants. Indeed, from the mouth of the Skeena to Fort St. James the country was so little known that any information we could obtain beforehand was most fragmentary, while of a large portion of it there was not even a correct map to be had, the best, Trutch's, requiring considerable alteration so far as this northern part of the Province is concerned.

Our first duty, preparatory to leaving the coast, was to examine our canoes, make the acquaintance of the crews, and see that all our stores were safely on board. The boats are spoken of as canoes, but they are very different from the birch-bark canoes of the eastern Provinces, as they are made of wood, sound and firm, capable of as rough usage as any wooden boat. They are, however, neither carvel nor clinker-built, but simply "dug-outs," each one being made of a cedar log. When the log has been shaped and hollowed, it is filled with water into which highly heated stones are dropped. The wood is thus steamed, the steaming process being sometimes assisted by a gentle fire beneath the boat; the sides in this way become pliable and are extended; the seats are forced in; and the thin, tough shell of cedar, retaining the shape which it has thus received, serves as an excellent boat. Sometimes these canoes are as much as sixty feet long, and capable of carrying several tons of freight, and are so safe that the Indians of Queen Charlotte Islands use them in whale-fishing and in making long journeys down the coast. They are usually modelled with taste and skill. Before the Indians had iron tools they used to make their canoes, carve their door-posts, and do all their other work in wood with such rude instruments as a chisel of flint or of elk-horn, fastened in a wooden handle or held by a haft of twigs, a stone mallet, a mussel-shell adze and a gimlet of bone; and yet, with these and with the assistance of fire they produced excellent work.

We had two canoes, twenty-five feet keel and of about four feet eight inches beam, with five of a crew in each, irrespective of our foreman and our cook. They were capital fellows as indeed the Metlahkatlah Indians generally are. Some of them had retained their old Indian names, some had received " Boston " names, as English words are commonly called by the Coast Indians, probably from the fact that the first vessels navigated by white men sailing to the Columbia River hailed from Boston. In one boat were Yilmauksh, Matthias, Reuben, Theodore, and Christopher; in the other Kamigham, Highsh, Charles, Henry and Oswald.

Our most essential stores were flour, bacon, beans and tea, which form the staple food of travelling parties throughout the interior of **British Columbia**. Of these it was necessary for us to take a goodly quantity, as we could not expect to add to our supplies before reaching Fort St. James, which might possibly take five or six weeks. Not only are extra stores valuable in case of delay, but they are also of great use in dealing with the Indians, a little flour, tea, or tobacco, being more serviceable than money in purchasing salmon or such other commodities as the Indians might have to barter. Our crews, who would be fed from our stores, took with them as delicacies a quantity of dried oolachans and of dried herring spawn with dulse,—delicacies that we had no desire to share with them.

For several miles before it reaches the sea the Skeena is nearly two miles in width. Its banks are lofty, the hills on the north side sloping gently to the water, which is so shallow that at low tide a great breadth of beach is laid bare. In passing up we could see on either side of Work Channel some of the hills that we had been admiring the day before, as a narrow neck of land, not more than three hundred feet in height divides the waters of the river from those of the inlet.

As we started up the river we had the tide in our favour, for the tide makes itself felt for over twenty miles above Port Essington, and as there was a light breeze blowing up stream we set the small sprit-sails, thus making easily about eighteen miles before we pitched camp for the night. When camp had been pitched and supper ended, we observed that, in one respect at least, our men were more luxurious than ourselves. They were all provided with feather pillows, though for each of us a coat was a soft enough substitute. Their tents gave but a partial protection against the weather, being simply the two boat-sails spread like an awning, beneath which they slept five in a row; their blankets were so short that their feet remained uncovered; but of this one comfort they made sure, each head with its mass of dense black hair was softly pillowed.

We camped near a stream that looked as if it might be well stocked with trout, but an hour's careful fishing failed to secure a single rise. Indeed this was the case with every tributary of the Skeena on which we cast a fly; tempting and likely as the stream might appear, we could never find the slightest indication of fish. The morning had been dull and overcast, but the afternoon and evening were beautifully clear. The light of the setting sun lingered on the snow-clad peaks; gradually the tints of the clear sky changed; the stars appeared, and after a long "confab" around the camp-fire,—the first of many camp-fires around which the evening hours were spent,—all was silent and still.

The next day, like all our Sundays, was a day of rest. The Indians joined in our service, and, though unaccustomed to converse in English, they united audibly in the

Lord's Prayer, and sang a number of English hymns, which they had been in the habit of singing at Metlahkatlah. Some of them had excellent voices, and they had been trained to sing in parts. The bass was particularly good; and as we listened to them, or joined with them, we felt that it would be very difficult to find a congregation in our eastern Provinces from which we could select, at random, ten such good singers as our canoemen.

Next morning we found the proverbial difficulty, which many travelling parties have experienced, of making an early start on the Monday, as if all were anxious to enjoy a continuance of the Sabbath rest. Our canoeing hours were from 7 A.M. till 4 P.M., with an hour at mid-day for lunch and as the Skeena, like all the rivers along the Canadian Pacific coast, is very rapid, our ascent was slow, usually averaging about eleven miles a day.

Various means, besides the ordinary use of the paddles, were necessary for propelling the canoes. Sometimes, when a favourable beach gave the opportunity, the men "tracked"—that is, dragged the canoe by a tow-rope, in the same way as is done with ordinary canal boats,—but frequently, where the bank was too precipitous, or the overhanging woods were too dense to allow tracking, "poling" became necessary. Each man is provided with a hemlock pole, from ten to fourteen feet in length, some extra ones being kept on hand in case of loss or breakage. A strong steering oar has been lashed to the cross-bar at the stern, for in some places a paddle for steering purposes would be as feeble as a feather, and if the canoe were to sheer it might involve an upset. The men lay themselves to their work, poling against the stream as if they were straining their strength to the utmost, and the poles seem to grip the gravelly bottom, while the current makes them quiver and rattle against the side of the canoe. Foot after foot is gained, but the current grows stronger, for we are nearing a rapid. With that powerful spurt for which the Indian is remarkable, each man draws on his reserve strength, and, as he bends to the gunwale, he lays out every ounce of his force upon the pole, as if the pole were a spear transfixing a dragon more formidable than any that St. George ever encountered. Perhaps it may be necessary for the men to spring out and seize the canoe; this they do most nimbly, and then fairly lift her up as they press forward, although themselves nearly overborne by the rushing water. If a strong breeze be blowing in our favour, we hoist our sail; then, at it we go,—sail, wind, and poles against the force of the river. The wind scatters the spindrift from the rough water around us, as it does in a storm at sea. The mast and sails seem to be strained to the uttermost, although, perhaps, these, like their owners, have a reserve supply of strength, which only a further necessity can disclose. Even the Indians appear excited, while to us the situation has at least the charm of novelty. Up, up, we go, each moment expecting that something will give way, until we have passed the rapid. Then it may be necessary to cross the river. The poles are dropped; the paddles are snatched, and flash out like sword-blades. For a few moments we are borne backwards, but the calmer water which tempted us across is soon reached, and each man gives a hearty "ho! ho!" and braces himself for another pull, or to fight the next rapid that may be waiting for us in this up-hill navigation.

For about eighty miles from the coast, the river is dotted with islands that have been formed by the rich alluvial deposits borne down by the stream, and that are now covered by a luxuriant growth of timber, chiefly cotton-wood, spruce,—which sometimes measures six feet in diameter,—aspen, willow, with occasional hemlock and cedar. We frequently followed the narrow channels between these islands, where the water is calmer than in the open current, or, if swift, is more easily mastered than the full force of the river. The foliage on either side, which sometimes almost met in an arch above us, was rich and varied, and the sun-light streaming through the trees burnished the leaves and cast a network of shade on the water that swept beneath them.

The banks were rich with crab-apple trees, currant, cranberry and raspberry bushes, and strawberries in blossom, etc., and vegetation appeared to be at least as far advanced as it is at the same date in Ontario. The hills on both sides become more precipitous as we ascend, being generally covered to the snow line with spruce and cedar, except where an avalanche of snow or a landslide has swept away all the timber, and exposed the bare rocks. The river, from bank to bank, often widening to a span of a mile, is fringed with well-wooded flats, which, like the numerous islands, though apparently fertile, are liable to inundation every year. If any object, such as the reclamation of land, or the construction of a road, were to be served by it, the bed of the river might at many points be narrowed with no great difficulty by blocking up the channels between the norther. ore and the nearest islands, where the water is usually very shallow.

About thirty-six miles from the sea stands a rocky bluff, some eighty feet in height, in front of a precipitous hill, to which our attention was directed by one of our men, whose father had bidden him look for it, as historic memories were connected with it. For years it had been used as a watch-tower by the Indians of this district, from which to see the approach of the Haidahs, who made plundering visits to the mainland from their ocean homes on the Queen Charlotte Islands, and who frequently extended their raids for some distance into the interior. On a narrow level surface, at the top of the bluff, we found a small hollow, or basin, perfectly circular, a foot in diameter, and five inches in depth, which had been hewn out of the rock, and had no doubt been used in olden times as a bowl in which to grind "wundah." Wundah is a plant which the Indians use for chewing, as many use tobacco, and is much relished by the coast tribes. In many a house among the Tsimpseans, one may find a curiously carved stone bowl, made specially for this purpose, and each evening the Indian's wife, in token of her affection for, or subjection to, her lord, grinds up and prepares his "quid" of wundah. Among the earth near the summit of the bluff we found some charcoal. This and the wundah-mortar were the only relics of the people that may, from this rocky eminence, frequently have watched the approach of their foes, and met their onsets in days of yore.

Looking around from this height we seemed to be girt about by an amphitheatre of hills, for we were already well into the Coast Range. Indeed, all along the Skeena the views are very striking. Some of the summits are snow-capped, some are wooded, and some expose peaks of bare gray rock. In the foreground are islands of rich and varied foliage, and a broad strong river that now flows gently by some quiet reach, and now rushes rapidly on in a masterful current, while the birds fill the air with melody such as one never hears in the woods of Ontario. One becomes so accustomed to these views that after a few days they almost lose their impressiveness, and yet could any of the scenes through which we were passing from day to day be transferred to our eastern Provinces, it would be the object of many a pilgrimage on the part of tourists and of artists.

In our course we passed Indians engaged in fishing, for the first run of salmon had already begun, and salmon swarm in the Skeena, as in other rivers of British Columbia, in almost incredible numbers. Different families, or rather, different settlements and villages, along the river, seem to have their separate fishing grounds, with which others must not interfere, and in three or four weeks the villagers may secure a sufficient supply of salmon to serve as their chief article of food for the whole year. These salmon may be speared, they may be caught with scoop-net or with gill-net, but, unlike those on the Atlantic coast, they cannot be persuaded to rise to the fly. Whether from the turbid character of the rivers, or from some peculiarity in the species, or from unguessed causes, the salmon in these waters give no response to the angler, let him cast his flies never so skilfully. In another respect also they differ from the salmon in our eastern streams. It seems that when they once return to the rivers to spawn, they never go back to the ocean. Descending to the sea when a year old they are full-grown before they return to the rivers, and they only return to spawn. Having spawned once they die. This, at least, is the commonly accepted theory among those that have most carefully examined the subject; but it has not yet been clearly proven that they do not descend to the sea under the ice in winter, though it is manifest, from various experiments and many observations, that they do not return while the rivers are still free from ice.

The Indians preserve their salmon after they have cleaned them simply by drying them in the sun, and as the curing ground is usually near the beach, quantities of sand are commonly blown over the fish while they are being dried. One result of this is that the teeth of the Indians are gradually ground down by the sand, which has thus been incorporated with their food, so that you can approximately tell the age of an Indian by "mark of mouth," the teeth of the young being but slightly affected, while those of the aged have in some cases disappeared altogether, being worn down to the gums.

Occasionally we passed an Indian village on the banks of the river, consisting of a few rude houses made of rough cedar boards. Attached to some of these houses are small potato patches, but the amount of cultivable soil here is very limited. Each house accommodates two or more families, and in the villages along the upper part of the river, as in those of the Haidahs on the Queen Charlotte Islands, almost every house is adorned by a curiously carved door-post. The figures ingeniously cut upon these door-posts are supposed to be the heraldic bearings of the family—the *totem*, as it is sometimes called, which is occasionally tattooed upon the arm or chest of the Indian; but as heraldry among the Indians is almost as complicated as among the nobility of England, it is difficult for the uninitiated to understand all that is intended by these figures. Frogs, bears, beavers, whales, seals, eagles, men, sometimes men tapering off into fish, like the fabulous merman, are the figures most frequently seen. Several of these may be found on each post, the post being about thirty feet high and two feet in diameter, the carving being executed with remarkable skill, and wonderful expression being thrown into the faces. In some instances the post is large enough to admit of a hole being made through it sufficient to serve as the door-way of the house, and this opening is usually, by a quaint conceit, the mouth of one of the carved figures. In many cases more labour is expended on this post than upon all the rest of the house, and although it often serves a useful purpose as part of the dwelling, it is sometimes quite distinct, standing in front of it like a flag-staff.

Not far from any of these villages may be seen the little cemetery, with its carved and painted monuments. Frequently, however, the grave of the Indian is separate from the graves of his kinsmen, and is commonly marked by his canoe and his gun, or in the southern part of the Province by the hide of his horse, his own remains being enclosed in a rough box, which is sometimes laid upon the ground, and sometimes interred a few feet beneath the surface. Among some of the Skeena Indians the remains of the dead are cremated, the charred bones and ashes being enclosed in a box which is left in the ground near the outskirts of the village, or sometimes attached to the carved door-posts. This practice of cremation, however, is now dying out, being more observed among the Haidahs of Queen Charlotte Islands than among any others. With them, it is said, the idea prevails that if their enemies should secure the dead body of any one of their tribe, they would make charms which would render them irresistible in battle. They are, therefore, careful to prevent the possibility of their being conquered by any charms or influences furnished by themselves, or of meeting the fate of the eagle who has nursed the pinion that impels the shaft now reddened with his life-blood. Among the Indians of the Stickine tribe, near the Alaska boundary, the obsequies have in some instances assumed a more serious aspect. It is said that on the occasion of a chief's death among them, not many years ago, twelve slaves were executed in order that they might accompany their master and serve him in the spirit world; and the slaves submitted willingly, as they preferred death, with the prospect of continuing in the service of the old chief, to life with the prospect of serving his successor. Where the Indians are becoming Christians, however, the remains of the dead are interred in ordinary graves.

Frequently, near the villages, and sometimes, too, in solitary and secluded spots, we passed the remains of a "sweating-booth," the Indian's substitute for a vapour-bath. A few branches are fastened together like a hen-coop, giving space for a man to sit and turn round in; these are covered with blankets; stones are heated and placed inside this enclosure; the bather, in nature's bathing costume, creeps in, taking with him a can of water, which he pours upon the stones. If he has supplied himself with a sufficient number of heated stones, and a sufficient quantity of water, or if friends will supply these for him while he continues his bath, he may remain there, enjoying the steaming until he is almost exhausted by the process. The use of the sweating-booth prevails amongst many of the North American Indians. This and the "pot-latch," or grand feast, at which some generous spend-thrift or some aspirant for the chiefship spends his little all in banqueting his friends, are the supreme luxuries of an Indian's life.

About seventy miles from the sea stands the little village of Kitsumgallum, the highest point ever reached by steamer on the Skeena. In 1866, the stern-wheel steamer *Mumford* came up thus far with supplies for those engaged in constructing the telegraph line which was projected from the United States, through British Columbia and Alaska, to the northern parts of Asia. In 1865 the Western Union Telegraph Company of the United States, probably the most powerful corporation of the kind in the world, commenced explorations with a view towards the construction of an overland telegraph, which, by way of Behring Straits, was to unite the old and new worlds. After the expenditure of three millions of dollars, the scheme was abandoned, owing to the success of the Atlantic cable. To construct and maintain this telegraph it was necessary to clear a wide track on either side of the proposed line, which is now known as the "telegraph trail," running from Quesnel by Fort Fraser and the valley of the Watsonquah, near the Forks of the Skeena, as far north as Fort Stager, some forty miles beyond Hazelton. Before the project was abandoned the line had been completed as far north as Quesnel, and this portion became eventually the property of the Government of British Columbia, and was by them transferred to the Dominion Government; but beyond Quesnel the only remnant of this expensive undertaking is the trail which was cut in connection with the work of construction.

A little beyond the point where the *Mumford* was compelled to stop, we were able, from a hill some 250 feet in height, to trace, for some distance, a valley which encloses Lake Lakelse, to the south of the Skeena, and which leads through from the Skeena to Kitimat, at the head of

Douglas Channel, an arm of Gardner Inlet. This pass would connect the waters of the Skeena at this point with the tide-waters of the Pacific, by a much nearer route than that which we had followed; but the harbour at Kitimat is much inferior to that of Port Simpson, and its approach from the ocean is more difficult. Indeed, a general depression may be traced in a direction somewhat similar to that of the coast line along the valley of the upper waters of the Nasse River, and by the streams and lakes which at Kitsumgallum connect it with the Skeena, thence by the valley just mentioned to Kitimat, on the northern arm of Gardner Inlet, down to the south arm of that inlet, and from that point to the head of Dean Channel, and even to the southern extremity of Bentinck Arm. This depression is not clearly indicated in the published maps of British Columbia. It cannot properly be called a valley, but if we may suppose the general level of the land to be lowered by, say, 1,500 feet,—and the average level of British Columbia, exclusive of any portion of the Peace River district, is estimated at little short of 3,000 feet above the sea,—there would be traceable among the remaining elevated ridges a valley or chain of valleys in the direction indicated. This depression seems to mark off the mountains between it and the coast as somewhat distinct from those lying to the east of it, which are more properly known as the Cascade Range. A fuller examination than has yet been made, both geological and topographical, would, however, be required before this distinction could be decidedly drawn between the so-called Coast and Cascade Ranges. At the same time, it may be noticed that in going up the Skeena the highest mountains east of this line have a somewhat different appearance from those west of it, the summits being loftier and more peaked than those nearer the coast.

At two places in our ascent of the river it was necessary for us to make a portage—first, at the Tsipkeagh Falls, or Rapids, a little above Kitsumgallum, and again at Kitsilas, some miles further on. At Tsipkeagh we required not only to carry our cargo, but also to drag our canoes overland some thirty or forty yards to the calmer water above. The river as it passes over these falls is not more than 500 yards wide, hemmed in by a ledge of rock on either shore, and with wooded islands in the broad reaches above and below. On the southern ledge, as at the upper end of almost every island that is exposed to the main current of the river, there are huge piles of worn and shattered trees, the accumulated drift of years, borne down by freshets and left stranded by the receding waters.

At Kitsilas, when the water is high, a portage of nearly a quarter of a mile is necessary, but in moderate water such as we experienced, the portage can be taken in two instalments of twenty or thirty yards each, connected by a bay of the river. Here there is a small Indian village, and as we approached it we saw several persons catching salmon with scoop-nets. We bought three twenty-five pounders, **paying** seventy-five cents each for them, an exorbitant price, but even here the first of the season sell at fancy figures. Two or three days later, a small piece of tobacco would be sufficient to buy the largest salmon on the Skeena. But prices vary, depending not so much on the supply or the demand as on the Indian's need of what you offer in exchange, or on the price that he received from his last customer. Unless he happens to want what you offer it makes little difference to him whether he sells or not, and if any traveller going before you has paid high **prices,** whether for salmon or for the hire of men or of canoes, you need not expect to pay less.

On a nameless stream near Kitsilas some gold miners had been prospecting shortly before we passed. They found little more than the " colour " of gold—that is, the small sand-like particles which, though of no great value in themselves, indicate the presence of gold, in greater or less quantities, in the rock from which these particles have been washed down. Gold " colour" may be obtained in almost any river of British Columbia by washing the dark sand to be seen at the upper extremities of the sand-bars, the darkest sand being that of the magnetic iron ore which has been borne down from some of the rocky beds, or sides, of the river. When any quantity of earth is washed in a pan exposed to the current, this dark sand, being heavy, sinks to the bottom of the pan, and all else can be gradually separated from it, while, if there is any gold dust, it will sink in the washing and be found in the dark sand, where it may be readily detected. Should this " colour " be plentiful, it may lead to further exploring, and perhaps to successful mining. No success, however, has hitherto attended the efforts of miners on the Skeena.

Above this the river becomes narrower, for the most part not more than from 300 to 500 yards in width. The banks are still fringed by flats, but there are fewer islands dotting the surface of the river, so that the landscape loses, to some degree, the attraction of the rich groves of cotton-wood with which for a few days we had been familiar. Sometimes these flats, or plateaux, which are several hundred yards in width, and which are here exposed to inundation, are heavily timbered, and their number and extent increase as we ascend the river, the timber including spruce, hemlock, cedar, aspen, and, less frequently, Douglas pine, birch and mountain ash.

Nearer the river-banks, where the soil has probably been cleared of its timber through fire set by the Indians in order to secure a larger growth of berries, the flats are usually rich with pea-vine, strawberries, raspberries, gooseberries, and with a great variety of wild flowers, such as the rose, columbine, linnea, violet, anemone, etc.

Some of these flats appear well fitted for cultivation. They are of light loam, covering a sandy soil about two or three feet in depth upon a gravel bed, and wherever cultivated, as at the scattered Indian villages along the river side, they yield good crops of potatoes, nothing else apparently being attempted.

We passed through the narrows known as Quotsalix Cañon on the afternoon of Wednesday, 18th June. As we approached the cañon, our attention was attracted by a glacier which we saw up the course of a tributary stream that flows in on the north bank. It was too far away, however, to admit of close examination. There are several scattered houses at this narrow part of the river, and rocky ledges running down to the water's edge give it the character of a cañon, though only on a small scale. Above these, the nearer hills are, for the most part, rounded, with gentle slopes towards the flats that fringe the river, while the remoter hills are lofty, with rugged, serrated, snow-capped peaks. One of these summits, named Ishganisht, which approaches the river bank more closely than the others, is the grandest we saw in our course up the Skeena. It terminates in a cluster of snow-clad peaks, whose valleys, forming a semi-circle, enclose a glacier. Beyond this are some distinctly marked benches, or terraces, while, further up, the country appears more open, until on reaching Kitwongah we found a wide stretch on either side, apparently suitable for cultivation.

Kitwongah, about forty miles above Kitsilas, is a little Indian village containing about twenty houses, each house representing several families, and distinguished chiefly for its numerous and curiously carved door-posts. Attached to one of these posts we saw a rude box, about the size of an ordinary tool-chest, said to contain the cremated remains of an old Indian, and outside of the village several such boxes may be seen left on the ground and exposed to the weather. From Kitwongah there is a trail running northerly to the Nasse River, which meets one running in from Kitsigeuchlah, and, further on, one running in from Kispy-ox. Near the junction of these trails the Rev. Mr. Tomlinson is establishing a mission connected with the mission at Metlahkatlah. The place is well suited for such a purpose, as there is a great deal of traffic along these trails, and many others besides the residents in these localities might thus come under the missionary's influence; while, at the same time, the neighbourhood is said to be better suited for farming than any other locality in this district.

Camping on the plateau opposite Kitwongah we heard at night, when retiring, a tum-tumming as if on some sort of tambourine, accompanied by a chanting sound, as of the human voice. We thought that the natives might be having a dance, but on hearing the same sounds next morning, from the time we rose until we left camp, we fancied that even Indian dissipation would not keep up such revelry all night. We found on enquiry that it was the work of the medicine-man, who was practising on some sick person according to the usual method of the native doctors. They do not prescribe any medicine; they simply rattle sticks upon a small drum, or tambourine, and howl in a most melancholy manner, thinking that by such means they can banish the evil spirit by whom they suppose the disease to have been caused. After the medicine-man leaves, some old woman may administer a preparation of herbs, which has possibly a healing effect, but if the patient recovers it is not the nurse, but the medicine-man, who receives the credit, whereas if the patient dies the medicine-man is praised for his bravery in attacking so formidable a spirit. In either case it is for him a game in which he may win, but cannot lose, while the sufferer might well pray for death to release him from the torment of such an attendant.

The next village reached by us was Kitsigeuchlah. Approaching it we had an exceedingly tough stretch of tracking for a mile and a half, and then crossed the river just below the village where it is about 150 yards wide and where the water is very wild and the current strong, rolling like the sea in a storm. In such a place a false move on the part of the steersman would speedily send each man struggling with the stream on his own account; but we were in the hands of skilful canoemen. Seven years ago Kitsigeuchlah was burnt down, the fire having spread from a mining camp in the neighbourhood at a time when the Indians were away salmon-fishing. They suffered severely for a season through this disaster, but the Government allowed them some $500 damages, and the village has recently been rebuilt. Just beyond the village is the river of the same name that flows in from the south, and above its entrance, on both banks of the Skeena, there is a vein of carbonaceous slate, with sandstone, iron-stone and clay. We found a small quantity of inferior coal cropping out of the surface, but further examination would be requisite to ascertain if there is any large deposit in this vicinity.

From Kitwongah to the Forks, on the north side of the river, a distance of about twenty miles, there is an almost continuous stretch of plateau, broken only by occasional ridges, while apparently a valley runs in a direct line between these two points, some distance back from the winding valley of the river. The district enclosed between these two valleys, with the exception of a hill rising out of the centre of it, seems to be suitable for cultivation. Possibly this upper part of the Skeena may compare favourably in point of agricultural resources with some of the restricted cultivable southern portions of the Province, but as yet there has been scarcely anything done here by white men in the way of farming, and the small potato-patches of the Indians do not supply sufficient data to warrant any decided opinion.

Working up the river above Kitsigeuchlah, and passing several rich flats, similar to those we had already seen, we reached the Forks of the Skeena on the afternoon of Saturday the 21st June. The village stands at the junction of the Skeena and Watsonquah; hence its name of " the Forks." Its Indian name is Kitunmax ; its more recent name Hazelton. In front of it flows the strong rapid river; immediately adjoining it is a stretch of excellent land, which, where cultivated, yields abundant crops, especially of roots and oats, though as yet no wheat has been tried ; and, where left uncultivated, the land is covered by luxuriant herbage. In rear of the village, and surrounding this rich, flat, low land, as well as on the opposite, or northern, bank of the river, there are plateaux of light soil partly wooded, which give every promise of good returns if cultivated; and in the distance in several directions, beyond the lower wooded hills, there are snow-clad peaks and ranges.

At a little distance back from the village stands a cluster of peaks which the Indians call Nilkiawdah, known commonly by the name Roche-Deboulé, a name which more correctly belongs to a broken mass of rock at its base, in the cañon of the Watsonquah. It is the most striking feature of the surrounding landscape, standing 5,955 feet above the level of the village, that is, about 6,600 feet above the level of the sea.

The population of the village consists of about 250

individuals, with three white families, the only whites found on the river with the exception of one family at Port Essington. The Indians here consider themselves quite distinct from the Coast Indians; indeed, each village along the river is the centre, if not of a separate tribe, at least of a separate division of a tribe, sufficiently important to regard itself as distinct from others, with tribal rights on land and water. It is not easy to ascertain with any accuracy the population along the valley of the river, but it may approximately be set down at about two thousand, including in that number some settlements adjacent to the Skeena.

For a time the "Forks" was looked on as a promising village, it being the point from which a large proportion of the supplies was portaged to the mining district of Omenica, 200 miles east of this. Had the mines turned out as well as was at first expected, the promised growth and importance of the village might have been realised, but as the Cassiar gold-fields drew away the miners, the glory departed from Omenica, and though there are still some fifty white men, and a smaller number of Chinamen there, yet they are meeting with so little success that the mines will probably ere long be abandoned.

The Indians here live in low houses, several families in one dwelling, most of them, like the majority of those on the Skeena, being still Pagan, though an increasing number are Christians. There was for a time a teacher among them nominally Christian, and during his residence here many professed Christianity; but the teacher abandoned his work, became careless, left for the mines, and thereupon many of the Indians went back to their old ways, and the Chief brought his Bible to one of the white residents, saying that he did not want it any longer if it taught men to act as the teacher had done. If a mission station be established, as proposed, somewhere in this vicinity, it is to be hoped that the success which has placed Metlahkatlah foremost among the missions to the Indians of North America, may be repeated among the Indians of the interior. It is manifestly necessary not only to instruct these men in the truths of Christianity, but to train them in trades, in agriculture, and in habits of settled industry. For the most part they are peaceable and well disposed, although they are apt to take advantage of an employer if they find him at all in their power,—perhaps to desert him in an emergency if he will not accede to their demands. The Achwilgates, for instance, on the Watsonquah, sometimes ask exorbitant charges for the privilege of crossing the river, giving the use of their canoes as an excuse for levying heavy toll; and their neighbours, the Kispyox Indians, imposed such tolls on those passing through their territory as to stop for a time the cattle traffic which had been carried on extensively for some years, by drovers taking cattle from the Fraser River District, by way of Watsonquah and the Upper Skeena, to the mines of Cassiar. Physically these Indians of the interior are as active as the Coast Indians, not apparently as strong, yet capable of carrying heavier burdens. Mentally they seem quite equal to them, and it may reasonably be hoped that, if similar privileges of instruction be given them, they may soon equal the Indians of Metlahkatlah in industry and in general good conduct.

The climate of the Skeena valley is by no means as pleasant as that of the southern part of the Province, though much better than its latitude and the physical characteristics of the country might lead one to expect. During our course from Port Essington to the Forks,—that is, from the 7th until the 21st June,—we had most enjoyable weather; on four days we had slight rain; for the remainder, though the sky was frequently overcast, the weather was fine. The proportion of rain diminishes towards the interior, and the snow-fall, which in some seasons is seven or eight feet near the coast, does not exceed three feet at the Forks. Horses have been wintered out here, though it was necessary to shovel away a quantity of snow in order that they might be able to feed on the grass beneath. The cold of winter is severe, the thermometer falling frequently to 30° below zero for several consecutive days, and sometimes as low as 45°, while it rises in summer to 90° in the shade, and sometimes higher, a variation very much greater than that of the southern part of the Province. At the same time the climate of the Forks is said by the white residents to be very healthy, and the number of thriving children to be met with seems to confirm this. The most frequent complaint is ophthalmia, which prevails in almost every Indian village, caused no doubt, or, at any rate, increased, by the smoke of the camp-fire and of their houses.

After our tents had been pitched, near the river's edge, a large proportion of the inhabitants came to inspect our premises, watching with special curiosity the labours of the cook, as if they all expected an invitation to a grand pot-latch. Among our visitors were some women who wore a kind of lip ornament, which used to be much more common among them than it now is. It consists of a piece of wood passed through the lower lip. At first the hole is made in the lip with a needle, and a proportionately small piece of wood, about half an inch in length, is inserted and left there. Gradually this hole is made larger, and, while the length of the "ornament" remains about the same, its diameter is increased, the desire of the wearer being apparently to make it as large as possible. Others of our visitors had adorned themselves with nose-rings, a favourite ornament with savages.

One of our party, who had been a great deal among the Indians of British Columbia, showed a looking-glass, on one occasion, to some young women who had adorned themselves with nose-rings. Apparently, though familiar with the sight of nose-rings on each other, none of them realized until then what they looked like on themselves, and the effect of this disclosure was that very soon afterwards they appeared without them. These intended ornaments are, as may be imagined, a serious disfigurement, though, as with some absurd decorations worn by their civilized sisters, the Indians usually regard them as things of beauty.

Among others who came to interview us was the son of the chief of the Achwilgate tribe. He was not dressed in the traditional picturesque attire of an Indian chief; one sees little of that phase of Indian life outside of Cooper's novels; nor had he come to question our right of way through the country. He was anxious simply to hire as one of those who should "pack" for us—that is, carry our impedimenta, consisting of tents, blankets, baggage, provisions, etc., across to Lake Babine. We left the management, however, of this, as of most details of a similar nature, to our excellent foreman, McNeill, who had long been familiar with the Indians of this part of the Province, and who had spent two years at Fort Stager, some distance north of this, in charge of the supplies left there by the Western Union Telegraph Company before they finally abandoned their project of a great overland line between America and Europe.

We spent a Sunday at the Forks, and had service in

the school-house with some of the villagers, as well as with our own crews. Throughout the day we were more troubled with mosquitoes than during any other part of our journey. It is a common belief among the people of Victoria that there are no mosquitoes in the Province. We found them, however, as active and powerful as we had ever known them in Ontario. If, as is said, it is the female mosquito that stings, this is the only instance in which there appears to be a superabundance of female labour in British Columbia.

CHAPTER IV.

FORKS OF SKEENA TO LAKE BABINE.

Our Packers.—The Trail.—Up the Susqua.—Coal.—Women Packing and Nursing.—Skilokiss Suspension Bridge.—The Ooatzanli.—The Nataltsul.—Cascade Range compared with Swiss Alps.—Indian Legends. — Taim-Shin. — Scene on the Summit.—Approach Lake Babine.—Engage Crews.—Offended Chief.—Babine Indians.—Neighbourhood of Lake

On the 23rd June we left the Forks for Lake Babine. Early that morning we paid off our crews, and saw them start for home. They would go down in two and a-half days the distance that it had taken us thirteen working days to ascend. We had found them capital fellows,—active, industrious and thoroughly reliable. We gave them a cheer as they left, which was heartily returned by them, and we then began acquainting ourselves with our new hands. We required a considerable number to portage our stores, etc., across to Babine, for although the trail is sufficiently good for mules, yet there was only one mule in the village.

Having collected those who had engaged to go, it was no easy matter to apportion their packs, as each one seemed to think he had the heaviest, and to regard himself as the most ill-used labourer in the company. Among our packers was the Achwilgate prince, as we called him,—the son and heir-apparent of the chief of the tribe, — with his wife, who, like many of the native women of the district, can carry a very heavy pack without a murmur, and whom none of us was gallant enough to relieve of her burden. We had also the medicine-man, a strapping, sinewy fellow, with his wife, and a number of others. Nowadays each of the Indians of this neighbourhood restricts himself to the possession of one wife, but formerly polygamy was common among them; yet with them, as with the Mormons and Turks, the number of their wives depended pretty much upon their wealth. If a man was able to support more than one, his ideas of propriety did not prevent him from having several dear ones; but, as a rule, his means were not sufficient to meet such increase of responsibilities. Polygamy seems to have been more common among the Coast Indians, who, from the varied and abundant supply of fish at their doors, were more amply furnished with the means of supporting a family than the less favoured tribes of the interior.

The trail which we followed is a portion of the route which leads from the Skeena, by Babine, the Frying-pan Pass and Lake Tatla, to the Omenica district, 200 miles from the Forks; and, as the only rival route to Omenica from the coast is the more expensive one of the waggon road along the Fraser River, and the trail from Quesnel, this trail from the Skeena has been for some years the highway for a good deal of traffic. Following it we ascended at once to the plateau in rear of the village, from which we had extensive views of the surrounding country, and specially fine views of the Roche-deboulé.

About two and a half miles from the Forks we struck the old telegraph trail which runs through the valley of the Watsonquah to Fort Stager, about forty miles beyond this, and after following it for a mile we turned up the valley of the Susquah, a tributary of the Watsonquah, passing over low rolling hills that are separated by narrow valleys, the channels of wild and precipitous streams. On the banks of one of these streams we found a vein of carbonaceous shale, in which a small quantity of true coal could be detected,—another indication of the possibility of finding coal measures in this part of the country. Here and there we saw small patches that might be cultivated, and the hill slopes, where clear of timber, abound in pea-vine and wild grass, which afford excellent pasture. The valley of the Susquah, however, is not as rich as the valley of the Watsonquah. There the grass is particularly good, but with the exception of that, and of the land around the Forks, there seems to be very little throughout this district that is fit for cultivation, while even of this one cannot speak with much confidence on account of the limited efforts hitherto made in farming, and the probable climatic difficulties. The wood with which hill and valley are timbered is chiefly poplar and small-sized spruce.

We pitched camp about six miles from the Forks, after half a day's march, it being slow work for the packers, each with his burden of at least 100 lbs. One of our packers was the owner of the only mule kept at the Forks, so he took the mule to carry his burden, while he himself walked at ease like a gentleman, the object of general envy. Some of the other packers used their dogs to assist them, the dog trotting along gaily with his balanced burden on either side. Their day's work did not prevent these dogs from barking as vigorously as two others, idler and more indulged, that accompanied us, and judging by the muzzles that were put on them before the provision boxes were opened, their reputation for honesty was of a low order.

Most of the men who packed for us belong to the Achwilgate tribe, and are accustomed to attend the services of the Roman Catholic Mission which has for some time been established among them. It was gratifying to notice that they had prayers each evening, one of their own number leading their service. It is surprising how these men pack as well as they do, and more surprising how their wives endure such toil. They do not look very robust, though they must be sinewy to stand it at all.

Some of them were well up in years, having been long accustomed to such labour; and it is quite common to see an Indian woman carry her young child on the top of a heavy pack, while, after climbing a hill that prostrates others for a little with fatigue, the first thing she may have to do is to nurse her infant. Indeed they require to nurse their children much longer than is necessary in civilized communities on account of the scarcity of suitable food for the young, their chief article of diet being dried salmon. Their capacity for carrying heavy burdens lies in their ability to preserve an accurate balance rather than in any great muscular strength. The pack rests on the back, chiefly between the shoulders, supported by a tump-line which passes in a broad band across the forehead, and secured by the ends of the line being tied across the chest. Sometimes the packer may have difficulty in raising his pack, or rather in raising himself with his pack from the sitting posture in which it is fastened on, but once erect he moves off nimbly with it. His ability for this kind of work is developed from childhood, for even the little ones are trained to carry some of the family goods and chattels almost as soon as they can walk by themselves.

Although the walk was tiresome to the burden-bearers, to us it was very enjoyable, our only discomfort being caused by occasional rain, when one was forced to recognize the strides that civilization has made in mastering the difficulties which climate and temperature may cast across the path of the traveller. Foot-travel, buck-board, covered coach, and railway-car mark stages of progress in the conquest of such difficulties.

On our second day from the Forks our cook, a Lillooet Indian from the Lower Fraser, who had been with us all the way from Port Essington, returned to the Forks, partly in order to join another party there, but partly also because he felt somewhat afraid to accompany us further with the prospect of returning alone among the Kispyox Indians, through whose territory we were travelling; for there is still among the Indians of one tribe a lingering jealousy, if not a positive enmity, towards those of another, often preventing them, unless when under the protection of white men, from crossing into each other's territory. In view of the necessity of his leaving us we had secured another at the Forks, a good-humoured, active fellow; and indeed he required to be active, for he had a large family to cook for, as the Indians received food from us in addition to wages, and they are as capable as most men for discharging the duties of the table.

About seventeen miles from the Forks we crossed the Skilokiss by an Indian suspension bridge ingeniously made. Four large cotton-wood trees had been felled and trimmed, two on each side of the stream. These projected from the banks until they met and overlapped.

They were then lashed together midway across the stream, the lower portions, lying on the bank, having been heavily weighted with logs and stones to prevent the bridge from sagging; a rail and platform were added, and the whole structure completed without a nail or spike, the fastenings being of roots and of tough inner bark. This is a common Indian method of constructing bridges, although sometimes the trees that form the main supports instead of being placed level are set at an angle from the banks so as to form an arch from which girders are suspended that serve as supports for a level platform.

After following for some distance the valley of the Susquah the trail leads up the valley of a tributary stream, the Ooatzanli, running along the face of a low range of hills. Ascending we found that the views, looking westwards along the course we had traversed, grew more and more attractive. On the opposite side of the river stands the Nataltsul, a cluster of peaks, the loftiest of which cannot be less than seven or eight thousand feet in height, enclosing a small glacier in a shell-shaped valley that receives the snow and rivulets from their scarped and rugged sides.

From this westward there is a range of snow-capped peaks and serrated ridges along the line of the Susquah, while the view is closed by the Roche-deboulé that stands massive, compact, well-defined, the sentinel of the Skeena. Sometimes the scenery becomes almost Alpine in character, although it has not the sustained grandeur of the heights of Switzerland. Anyone who has looked from the Righi-Kulm, upon the cloud-raked, snow-capped summits of the Oberland Alps, or from the Görner-Grat on the Matterhorn, Monte Rosa, and other peaks that encircle Zermatt, will seek in vain for similar effects among our Canadian Alps. And yet it is not so much great height that they lack, for beyond a certain point the eye does not readily detect additional height; and, besides, the contour and surroundings of a mountain may be such as to make it more impressive than some loftier summit, as the Matterhorn is more impressive than Mont Blanc. They seem to lose in comparison with their European rivals rather in the distance that divides their loftier peaks and clusters, for these are not massed as closely as are the heights of Switzerland. As you look upon them you think that you can grasp their details, and this impression weakens their effect upon you. They lose still more in this comparison, by the fact that the low ranges of intervening hills are commonly covered by burnt and branchless trees—rampikes, as they are called, —which have, in part, been strewn by the wind, but which, for the most part, stand, weathering the storm, blackened by the flames, or else bleached by sun and rain, a picture of desolation without sublimity, and of barrenness without relief.

Each day's march usually began for us about 8.30 a.m.,

our pack-train having started an hour earlier. To us the walk, or rather the leisurely stroll, was very enjoyable, as it did not need much exertion for us to keep up with our pack-bearers, who required the relief of a frequent halt, and we would gain nothing by going away in advance of tents and provisions. Indeed our daily walk was little over ten miles, broken by numerous stoppages to sketch, botanize, geologize, philosophize, and get-up-to-our-eyes in admiration of the valley that was gradually stretching behind us.

While thus enjoying the scenery one could not help speculating as to the possible thoughts that might flit through the minds of our Indian fellow-travellers, marching over the country of their fathers with the burdens of the white man. The scientist sees everywhere something to remind him of the laws of nature, and of prehistoric changes on the surface of the earth;—the pietist may pass through the study of these same laws to Him who first appointed them;—the poet can find, even in the meanest flower that blows, " thoughts that do often lie too deep for tears." Is the Indian never awakened to reflection by the hills and streams and forests, or is he thinking only of the weight of his pack, and of the supper in store for him when the burden of the day shall drop from his weary shoulders? He knows little about the laws of nature, little at least that would serve him in a competitive examination, that favorite modern test of knowledge, although he may know much that might enable him, in certain cases, to distance his examiners. His poetry and his religion are of a vague, indefinite character, not easily ascertained except where he has received the teaching of the white man. And yet he retains some of the traditional beliefs of his forefathers, which he may possibly tell you if your acquaintance with him is sufficiently long and intimate.

You may get from him, for instance, some of the legends about Taim-Shin. He may tell you how this supernatural being made the branches of the spruce trees. Taim-Shin can assume what disguise he chooses. On one occasion he appeared as a little boy, in the hut of an old woman, and asked her to let him eat and rest. She gave him food and shelter on condition that he would not look at what she did. His curiosity was awakened by this demand, and, though he pretended to be asleep, he watched her. When she thought herself unobserved she went out to a little spring not far from her hut, walked around it once or twice, crooning an old song. Then, from the clear water of the spring there arose, in the form of white strips or ribbons, something that she ate with evident relish. She did this several times, each time securing a new supply of food, and then returned to her hut. Taim-Shin had followed her unseen, and when she was returning homeward he ran ahead of her, and lay down, so that when she came in she thought that his sleep had been unbroken. Then she slept, and he went out to the spring. He tried to repeat her incantations, and in response, the white substance rose from the water, but when he attempted to eat it he found it hard as wood. Again and again he tried, but with the same result. Then, seizing some of the white strips, he flung them in his disappointment at a spruce tree,—which, like all spruce trees up to that time, had been as bare of twig or foliage as a hewn log,—saying that they were fit only for the woods. The ribbons hung on the trees and became branches, and, ever since, the spruce tree has been as it is now.

If a thunder-shower is passing the Indian's thoughts may turn to the thunder-bird, the belief in which appears to be common to all the Indians of the northern part of the Province, especially to the coast tribes. The general idea seems to be that there is a supernatural being residing among the mountains who sometimes sallies forth in search of food, covering himself with wings and feathers as one puts on a coat. His body is so large that it darkens the heavens, and the rustling of his wings produces thunder. Sometimes he seizes small fish, as an eagle would, by suddenly darting down to the sea, then he hides them under his feathers, and, in catching a whale, he darts one of these captured fish down with great velocity, and thus produces the lightning.

If he hears the dismal cry of the loon, he has for that

also a legend. The story is that two Indians were out fishing; the success of one provoked the jealousy of the other to such a degree that the unsuccessful fisherman stunned his companion, stole his fish, and then cut out his tongue, that he might tell no tales. In answer to any questions the mutilated man could only give a low wail. The supernatural being who is concerned in human affairs, known by some of the coast Indians as Quawteaht, and by others as Taim-Shin, changed the injured man into a loon, his assailant being changed into a crow; and hence the dreary cry of the loon, as if it were the wail of the tongueless.*

Perhaps some legends like these, which are common among the Indians, may flit through their minds as they traverse the woods and the hill sides. It is questionable whether, apart from their Christian teaching, they had any higher conception of a Supreme Being than that which these legends illustrate, although, as their burial rites and customs prove, they have always had a strong belief in a future life. They have also a strong belief in ghosts, and especially in the deep interest taken by departed friends, such as husband or wife, in the affairs of those left behind. But it is really difficult to ascertain, with any clearness or accuracy, the ideas of the

---

* For this legend I am indebted to Mr. G. M. Sproat's interesting book, "Scenes and Studies of Savage Life." There seem to be several versions of the legend of the thunder-bird.

Indians in regard to the supernatural, partly because their conceptions on these subjects are at best vague and shadowy, and partly because they are very reticent in speaking about them to those outside of their own tribe.

Moving along the trail at much the same pace with ourselves was another pack-train, consisting apparently of two native families on their way to trade with some of the Indians of the interior in dulse and other commodities of the coast, which they might exchange either for money or for furs. Money is much more current now among the Indians here than it was some years ago, numbers of them having earned considerable sums by packing supplies for the miners and others to Omenica, so that now, whatever they are being paid for, whether labour, furs or other marketable commodity, they generally like to receive their pay in coin.

Frequently we met parties of Indians on their return trip, and observed that most of the women had their faces smeared with black grease, as a precaution against mosquitoes and black-flies, perhaps also as a beautifying cosmetic. Whatever its value for defensive purposes, it was not a success as an ornament; but the mosquitoes and black-flies along some parts of this trail were troublesome enough to justify almost any expedient that might render them harmless.

We did not reach the summit between the Skeena and

Babine, until the afternoon of Thursday, the 26th. On the way we observed a profusion of wild flowers,—lupin, violet, forget-me-not, etc.—and on the opposite side of the Ooatzanli we saw some small grassy meadows. The highest point crossed by the trail is about 4,500 feet above sea-level, or 3,850 feet above the Forks. But about 750 feet below this there is a small lake from which flow the waters of the Ooatzanli westwards, and also those of a small stream that flows eastwards into Lake Babine; the level of this lake, which is about 3,100 feet above the Forks, and about 1,550 feet above Lake Babine, is the lowest altitude of the pass.

Each evening after camp had been pitched and the vigorous appetite of the whole party had been appeased, the scene was usually one of life and animation for a little while; and it was especially so on the evening on which we reached the summit, as our up-hill tramp of forty miles from the Forks was over, and from that point to Babine, a distance of about ten miles, was all down grade; so that on this evening in particular all seemed in good humour. If any member of our party happened to take an observation with a sextant, or if some were comparing their aneroids, the men would crowd around as if hungering and thirsting after knowledge; and, although accustomed to conceal their feelings, they could not help expressing their surprise when any explanation was given of the use of the instruments. One of the men, Yessen, who continued in our employ as far as Dunvegan, succeeded so well in noting with accuracy the readings of the aneroid, that he was frequently afterwards spoken of as "the astronomer." In addition to the pursuit of knowledge, the men employed the leisure of the evening in drying their clothes, which had been drenched with perspiration, and cooling themselves off after their day's work. The cooling process was conducted in much the same way as it is with a race-horse when bridle and saddle are taken off, and a blanket is thrown over him. Commonly the Indian has no change of suit, but he has a blanket, and that serves the same purpose. At these evening halts there was usually some repairing to be done; moccasins required mending; rents had been made in nether garments; some of the packs had caused blisters, so that even backs required repairs; while, if there was nothing else to attract attention, all could find an unfailing source of interest, if not of information, in watching the cook baking bread for the next day's use. Gradually, however, these details are completed; the long northern twilight and a comfortable camp fire tempt one to linger yet awhile under the clear sky, but the blankets spread on the spruce boughs have strong attractions after a day in the open air. The Christian Indians have had prayers, conducted by one of themselves in their own language, for they have no knowledge of ours. We too have joined in a similar service; and soon all are sleeping as soundly as if death reigned in the camp.

Having spent a night at the summit we left next morning with the prospect of an easy forenoon's work; and after the dogs had ended their morning fight,—in which they usually indulged in the interval between the removal of their muzzles and the adjustment of their packs,—our train started down-hill to Lake Babine. Our cook, Charley, whom we had hired at the Forks, a jovial fat fellow, was the last of the train to leave. The morning start had each day been for him a busy time, as he felt himself possessed of a petty brief authority, which he was careful to exercise to the utmost, and he fairly bristled with business until all were on the move. The personal habits of an Indian cook are not such as to prepossess one in favour of his cooking, but fresh air and hunger destroy many scruples, and we were in hopes that Charley might have a bath at Lake Babine, even though it could have no retroactive influence.

We were struck with the absence of life on the hills that we had been traversing; with the exception of insect life, which was painfully abundant, a few small birds and an occasional partridge were the only creatures that disturbed the otherwise unbroken silence, though later on in the season bears or cariboo might be found here. It may be, however, that game is more frequently found in this vicinity than our own experience would lead us to suppose; and it is manifest from the frequent remains of old camp fires that the trail is often travelled.

Soon after leaving the summit we caught, through the burnt timber, glimpses of Lake Babine stretching away below us, for the one redeeming feature of rampikes is that you can see further through them than through leafy woods. Near the end of the hill we crossed a stream which flows into Lake Babine from the little lake that at its western extremity supplies the Ooatzanli, and on the bank of this stream we found some coal. From this stream to the edge of the lake there is a meadow more than half a mile in length, slightly wooded with groves of poplar and spruce, and rich with wild hay, vetches, etc. If the climate permitted, a good farm or at least good grazing-land might be made of this meadow, but as we had frost two nights between the Skeena and Lake Babine, it would seem that the climate is too severe for farming, while the long winter, during which cattle would require to be housed and fed, would render stock-raising unprofitable.

Nearing the lake, on the afternoon of the 27th, we heard from the little Indian village at the head of it the barking of dogs, a sound frequent in every Indian village, but notoriously frequent here. Babine has quite a reputation in this respect. We knew the locality by sound, before we could detect it by sight. Ask any Skeena Indian for information about **Babine**, and the first item he will mention, the one of which he feels absolutely certain, is—" Many dogs there!"

We had no desire to visit the village, which is situated near the lower end of the lake on its eastern bank, and preferred camping on the western side, as the village and its inhabitants are such as to remind one of the answer given by a British resident in India, when asked for information regarding the manners and customs of the people around him:—"Manners none, customs nasty." Before our tents were pitched, however, we had a host of visitors from the village, and among others the chief, whom we unfortunately failed to recognize. The curiosity of each of them seemed limitless. They would stand or sit at the door of each tent in turns, scrutinizing the proprietor and his baggage, and watching all his movements. Even a heavy thunder-shower that swept over us failed to damp the ardour of their investigations.

Having paid off the men that came with us from the Skeena with the exception of two, Yessen and Jim, who had proved themselves specially useful, we proceeded to engage others to accompany us up the lake, and across from Babine to Stewart Lake. Babine Lake discharges its waters into the Skeena by Babine River, which is seventy miles in length, flowing for the most part between precipitous banks, with an elevated plateau along the southern side, and joining the Skeena near Fort Stager.

The lower end of the Lake and Babine River abound in salmon: indeed the fishery here is known as one of the best in the northern part of the Province.

The work of engaging crews to take us to the upper end of the lake, and to pack for us across the eight mile portage that connects Lake Babine with Lake Stewart, was not as easy as we had at first expected. The chief, whose dignity may have been offended by our failure to recognize him, but whose appearance was a valid excuse for our oversight, had returned to the village, while we deferentially smiled at and nodded to one of his men, who wore a coat of many buttons. We soon discovered that we had been bowing to the wrong man, for, when we tried to make terms for two crews and their canoes, we found that the chief had issued an edict that none were to go with us except at an exorbitant figure on which he had decided. To accede to his terms would not only be a serious matter for ourselves, but it would also be a serious matter for a surveying party that was expected soon to visit this lake, as well as for any subsequent visitors, for the prices we paid would regulate the price for the rest of the season. Rather therefore than agree to their demand we would make canoes, paddle down the lake twenty-five miles to the H. B. Company's post at Fort Babine, and try to secure men there. However, before deciding on our further course, we determined to interview the chief. A deputation went over to the village, and ventured through the accumulation of sickening odours to his house, where he received them with the dignity of one who feels that his rights have been overlooked and that now his turn has come; but by a little gentleness and flattery, applied through the aid of a friendly interpreter, and by the offer of a special rate for the use of his own canoe, the chief was soon brought to terms, amicable relations were resumed, and the utmost cordiality marked the rest of our intercourse with him. Later on in the evening he paid us a second visit, told us that he had been sick, and, with child-like confidence, put himself into our hands for treatment. A consultation was held, medical stores were examined, and a liberal allowance of pills, accompanied with some tobacco, was dealt out to him, it is to be hoped with good effect. The Indians very frequently ask travellers for medicine, and seem grateful for the smallest favours in this line, so far as any of them will allow themselves to show their gratitude.

When mention is made of the chief of an Indian tribe it must not be supposed that the chief is by any means the influential person that the ordinary imagination pictures. He has not the absolute authority with which he is credited. Indeed he has very little authority; his proposals are loyally followed by the men when approved by them, as was the case when the Babine villagers were told to insist upon our paying them an exorbitant rate, but they are rigidly ignored **when not in harmony with** their own wishes. Sometimes to English, and even to Canadian ears, it sounds well when a settler reports his marriage to the daughter of an Indian chief. A young Englishman, well-connected at home, who has been for some years a resident in the wilds of British Columbia, wrote to his friends that he had formed such an alliance. His mother, thinking that his marriage was somewhat similar to that of Smith with the daughter of Pocahontas, and regarding her daughter-in-law **as a native** princess, sent out to her a beautiful satin dress as a wedding **present.** The poor squaw could hardly understand its use, and had no conception of **its value.** A pair of blankets would really have been a more appropriate gift.

The Indians of Babine, though nominally Christian, have the poorest reputation for honesty of any of the British Columbian tribes. It is a cardinal article of an Indian's creed and practice not to tamper with anything entrusted to his care. Such a charge he considers sacred; but, in regard to this doctrine, the **chief** of the Babines and some of his men have, on more than one occasion, been guilty of heresy, having taken serious liberties with provisions of which they had somewhat imprudently been appointed guardians; and, in their general dealings with us, they were more ready to prove exorbitant, wayward, and unreliable than any others whom we employed. The H. B. Company's agent at Fort Babine says of them, that "they won't take what they can't reach, but that they can reach very far;" while they seem idle enough to realize the miner's description of an indolent acquaintance, who "had been born tired, and was unable to do any work between meals."

Some years ago, before the present Roman Catholic Mission was established here, after the brief visit of a Christian Brother to the village, one of the Babine Indians constituted himself priest for the tribe, manufactured his own vestments, baptised the people, pretended to receive revelations from heaven, and acquired for a time great influence over the others. He used to feign that he was dead, and that he came to life again, saying that during the interval he had passed into the spirit world. After one such experience, he said he had been at the gate of heaven, and being asked why he did not go in, he replied, that St. Peter, of whom he had heard the Christian Brother speak, was away at the salmon-fishing, and that the gate was shut. At another time he declared that he had been dead, and had passed right into heaven, but had come back to teach the tribe. They asked him what heaven was like: "Oh very like one of the Company's Forts," he said, "and the men were launching the boats to go and set their nets."

Even after the old chief had relaxed his terms, we found some difficulty in getting trustworthy crews. One man, Jacimo, who had been previously out with a party of surveyors, was anxious to go with us in any capacity. He told us he had been through the Peace and Pine River country, and as we were going in that direction, we agreed to take him. He then thought himself indispensable, and so at once demanded that his pay should be increased, and his work diminished. "Well, what can you do? Cook?" "No." "Cut trail?" "No;" he "was not good with an axe." "Pack?" "No;" he had "hurt his back some time ago and it was not quite well." "Paddle?" "No;" his back was too "stiff for paddling." Apparently Jacimo wished to go as "guide, philosopher and friend," but as we did not require him in that capacity, we allowed him to remain. Then he would have come gladly at any wages, but of course had we taken him he would have been ready to desert us, or to demand exorbitant wages, on the first emergency.

Even after our crews had been secured we were delayed for a day by strong wind, which made the lake so rough as to be unsafe for the cotton-wood canoes. These canoes, or dug-outs, are much narrower than the cedar canoes of the coast, or the birch-bark canoes of the east. They look like elongated horse-troughs pointed at each end; yet they are very much safer and swifter than their appearance would lead one to suppose. They are made in the same manner as the cedar canoes which we had used coming up the Skeena, but with much less taste, and on account of the small size of the cotton-wood as compared with the cedar, they are very much smaller than the coast canoes.

A day's detention in the midst of Babine Indians is not pleasant, but in travelling through a country where facilities of conveyance are still of the most primitive character, one is exposed to delays and disappointments. We had to accept this detention with all available grace as one of the enforced pauses of life, and utilized our delay to examine some parts of the neighbourhood. Near the village starts the trail to Lake Tatla, which leads over low rolling hills eastward, by the Frying Pan, or Firepan Pass, through snow-clad ranges, towards Omenica, 150 miles from Babine. Following this trail for a short distance as it gently ascends a low ridge that skirts the Lake, we had an extensive view of the country east and west,—of the Cascade Range through which we had come, and of lofty snow-capped peaks and ranges that lie between this and the Omenica district. But although, both east and west, there are high mountains in the distance, the nearer country is gently rolling, and seems as if it might be easily traversed in almost any direction.

This district, like many other parts of British Columbia, was almost unknown, except to Indians and H. B. Company's officials, until it was explored by miners in search of gold. Gold was discovered in Omenica in 1872, and for a time the new mines attracted a good deal of attention. A gold commissioner was stationed there by the British

Columbia Government; men crowded in under the excitement that is always aroused by the discovery of new diggings; supplies were required; Indians were employed as porters, and times were brisk about Babine. But the glory has to a great extent departed; the mines have not realized the expectations formed of them; only a few of the eager crowd are left there now; capitalists have not thought it worth while to begin quartz-crushing, and the whole district seems to be falling back into the silence and stillness of former years.

Although, however, gold-mining has slackened, it seems probable that something may yet be realized out of the argentiferous galena which is known to exist in this district As yet the region has not been examined by any of the Geologica Survey staff, but valuable specimens of this galena have been found, and although, under the present difficulties of access to Omenica, the production of silver and lead would not be remunerative, yet, if the facilities for communication were increased there might perhaps be a profitable industry established here. Occasional indications, too, of coal, or at least of lignite, have been discovered in this northern part of the Province in rock formations which are said to be somewhat similar to those in which the coal-fields of Vancouver Island are found.

This can never be a good farming country, for, although potatoes and barley may be cultivated in some measure around Babine, and although there are small pasture lands near the borders of the lake, yet the climate is too severe, and the summer too short for farming. It is true that at this elevation, in some portions of the interior plateau of the southern part of the Province between the Rocky Mountains and the Cascade Range, arable farming and stock-raising are successfully carried on, but, on account of the difference of latitude, and the small proportion of land fit either for the plough or for pasture, farming cannot be as successfully carried on in these northern districts. Indeed, unless some valuable mineral resources be developed here, in sufficient quantity to be remunerative notwithstanding the difficulty of access and cost of labour, this portion of the Province must continue for some time to come, as in the past, valuable chiefly for its fur-bearing animals.

CHAPTER V.

BABINE TO FORT MCLEOD.

Up Lake Babine.—Fort Babine.—Indian Farming.—Indian Reserves in British Columbia.—Reluctance to mention names.—Lake Stewart.—R. C. Missions.—Fort St. James.—Home-sick Indian.—Mule train.—Following Trail.—Fort McLeod.—Attractions of the H. B. C. Service.

We left the lower end of Lake Babine on the evening of the 30th, a number of villagers having gathered to see us off, perhaps attracted to our camp by the prospect of a possible breakfast. Our crews were much inferior to the Metlahkatlah men, and were ready to slacken their feeble efforts on the least provocation. If we spoke to one of them he immediately ceased paddling, as if to do justice to the subject of enquiry, and the others stopped out of sympathy. Sometimes they used English expressions which they had picked up at random from the miners, by whom they had been employed, and such phrases as "Go ahead," "All right," "You bet your life," etc., were made to do duty on many occasions without the least regard for the fitness of things.

The lake from the village to Fort Babine, some twenty-five miles, has an average width of about a mile. The banks rise very gently, with a good deal of low-lying land fringing the lake. There is no timber along its sides except small poplar and spruce, and the lightly wooded slopes, backed by undulating hills, give place occasionally to tracts of excellent pasture. Were it not for the lofty summits that here and there stretch up in the back ground, one would have little idea that he was in a country that has, for the most part, been fitly described as a "sea of mountains."

Our bowman, in one of those periods of loquacity with which he relieved the monotony of paddling, informed us that there was a "large town" at the Fort. We found it to be an ordinary Indian village, built like the one at Babine, a few yards from the lake shore, while between the dwellings and the water's edge stand a row of fish caches, or small huts supported by poles, six feet in height, in which the year's supply of dried salmon is stored. This, with potatoes that can easily be raised around the village, forms the staple article of food. Should the salmon fail great destitution and distress are the result. Instances have been known in which through this cause many Indian families were forced to subsist for weeks upon bark and berries, when even the dogs lived by browsing. Only such dogs as were absolutely necessary had been spared, for some must be kept as hauling dogs for the winter; all others had been eaten. When provision is plentiful dogs are sometimes fattened for food, and when the stores are reduced the dogs grow thin, and then at the touch of the knife they fill the platters that they once had licked. One Indian, who, with his dog, had been reduced to extreme hunger, cut off the dog's tail, cooked it, dined off it, and then gave the bone to its original owner.

As we landed near the Fort, or rather immediately after we were first sighted, and as we approached the land, the host of unemployed men and boys about the village rushed down to see and to scrutinize. Their curiosity on such occasions is intense. You may fix on them a reproving stare as steady as the head-light of a locomotive, but they will meet you with a gaze as calm and unflinching as your own. You long in vain for privacy however, as no unkindness is intended it would be foolish to take offence.

Following a trail that leaves the lake-side near the Fort, Messrs. Cambie and Macleod examined the country for some distance east of Babine to ascertain its fitness for railway construction. Were it necessary to locate a line across this northern part of the Province more than one favourable route might be found connecting Port Simpson with the Pine River Pass. Probably the best of them would be that by the valleys of the Skeena and the Watsonquah and Lakes Fraser, Stewart and McLeod. Any northern route, however, whether by way of Pine

River or of Peace River, must touch the sea at Port Simpson, and there are conclusive reasons against making that the Pacific terminus of our transcontinental road.

Soon after leaving the bay on which Fort Babine is situated, we had an almost unbroken view to the head of the lake, or rather, to an horizon where no land was visible, while on either side the low purple hills slope gently down, ridge after ridge, to the water's edge. The banks in some places are more precipitous than those near the lower end of the lake, but, for the most part, the scenery is similar in character, though with more numerous islands fringing the shores. About twenty miles from its upper extremity the lake bends suddenly eastward, and here the banks on the north shore become precipitous and rocky, while granite and marble bluffs and basaltic columns are visible at some points, the hills on either side being higher than those near Babine village. There is no good timber near the lake shore, but some timber of fair size is found between the lake and the Watsonquah Valley.

We did not reach the head of the lake, which is about a hundred miles in length, until the forenoon of Thursday, 3rd July, and owing to a thunder-storm and to the great unwillingness and delay of our canoemen in portaging our tents, baggage, etc., we did not reach Lake Stewart till the next day, although the portage is only about eight miles in length. A waggon-road, fit for ox-carts, connects the two lakes, and the country on either side affords good pasture. We were surprised to find, at the head of Stewart Lake, a well-stocked farm, owned and worked by the Indian "tyhee," or chief, who raises excellent cattle, as well as good crops of hay and vegetables, lives in a cottage, and wears an air of respectability.

There are frequent stretches of undulating country and of plateau fringing the numerous lakes, from which arable farms might on a small scale be formed, and which already afford abundance of rich pasture. In the valley of the Nechaco and along the borders of Fraser and Francois Lakes, a little south of Lake Stewart, there are considerable areas well fitted for stock-raising, and some that would be suited for the growth of hardy cereals and roots. With few exceptions, however, an elevation of 2,000 feet above the sea-level may be regarded as the maximum altitude of cultivable land in British Columbia, whereas Babine and Stewart Lakes are 2,200 feet above the sea. The backward seasons incidental to such an elevation in this latitude, the long winter during which cattle require to be housed and fed, and the summer frosts which prevent the cultivation of wheat, although admitting the successful growth of barley and roots, render these northern districts much less inviting than some of the southern parts of the Province. At the same time, if the Indians here were as good farmers as the Lillooets in the valley of the Fraser, or if the country were more easily accessible and facilities of intercourse more abundant, so that a market might be supplied for farm produce, this northern plateau, if it may be so called, between the Cascade Range and the Rocky Mountains could sustain a considerable population.

The limited extent of farm-lands throughout British Columbia has led to a different policy, in the allotment of Indian reserves, from that which has prevailed in the other Provinces. In the North-West Territories, for instance, where, of late years, treaties have been made with large tribes of natives, the Government recognized from the first the Indian title to the whole territory, and did not offer a single acre for settlement until that title had been extinguished by treaty. In British Columbia, however the Indian title to the soil has never been so fully recognized. In all negotiations with the Indians the Government allowed them whatever reserves they asked for, but proceeded on the principle that the Indians had no right to any land beyond what was necessary for their maintenance, a principle in which the natives themselves seem always to have acquiesced.

These reserves were by no means as large as those allowed in the other Provinces, nor was it practicable that they should be; for had they been extended to eighty acres per family, as the Dominion Government desired that they should, the result would have been, in many cases, the sacrifice of large tracts of land to Indians who would not utilize them and the exclusion of many white settlers. Besides, the reserves could not equitably be of uniform size, for some parts of the Province being well suited for farming admitted of larger reserves of arable and of grazing lands than others; while, at the same time those tribes that lived chiefly by fishing did not require large reserves of land, and could be more appropriately assisted or compensated by the whites in other ways, such as by instruction in trades or by the supply of increased facilities for traffic.

Through their intercourse with the whites, especially in the southern parts of the Province, the Indians have already very materially advanced. When labour was scarce, in the early days of gold-mining, many of them were employed by the miners, and many also by farmers and others who soon followed on the track of the miners. They enjoyed almost equal rights with the white settlers; they were, for the most part, industrious and trustworthy; and so they became boatmen, porters, herders, and in a number of cases independent farmers and stockraisers. Whether from superior natural ability, or from their intimate contact and partial competition with the whites, or from the Government policy that regarded them not as minors in a state of tutelage but as responsible citizens, it is manifest that the Indians of British

Columbia are as a rule in a better, more self-reliant, and more hopeful condition than those of the other Provinces, and more clearly destined to blend with the whites in the ordinary avocations of civilized communities. Some of them have been a little irritated on learning, through the representations of designing men, that the Indians of the other Provinces had been more liberally dealt with than they had themselves been, but there is reasonable ground for expecting that the Indian Commissioner of the Province with his official assistants will allot the reserves on an equitable and satisfactory basis, so that although the policy pursued in the other Provinces has not been, and cannot now be, adopted in British Columbia, yet the true object of the Government in dealing with the Indians,—their material, intellectual and moral elevation,—will probably be as fully realized here as in any other part of the Dominion.

At the head of Stewart Lake we paid off the crews who had come with us from Babine, with the exception of two, Jim and Yessen, who had accompanied us from the Forks and had been faithful among the faithless. When the others, who were anxious to be re-engaged, found their offers of service refused, they tried hard to dissuade these two from coming with us, as much from jealousy towards them as from the desire to inconvenience us. They have little union among themselves, and will seldom make common cause with each other. Perhaps it is this lack of unity, combined with a dread of the indefinite power of the whites, that has prevented them from giving much trouble to travellers or settlers. We, at least, had no more difficulty with them than we might have expected with white labourers if similarly situated, though we found them inclined to be more indolent if treated with special kindness and leniency.

When paying off the men we had occasion to notice what we had observed on previous occasions, a great reluctance on their part to tell their names, a reluctance amounting almost to a superstitious dread. When asked their names they usually request some companion to reply for them; and even in referring to each other, they will often use a roundabout description rather than the appropriate name. A woman in speaking of her husband will sometimes point to her son and refer to her husband as "that boy's father," rather than mention his name. One of our men, Jim, was so called by us because we could not ascertain his correct name, and we required some way by which to distinguish him from the others.

Is not this reluctance to utter names a common characteristic of primitive people? May it not be traced to the idea that a man's name should be something more than a mere word-of-call by which to distinguish him from his fellows; that it should be, in some sense, expressive of his character or of his influence, and that, therefore, to tell one's name would be to disclose the secret of his power? Among the Scandinavians of old it was commonly thought that to utter aloud the name of a fighting warrior would infallibly strip him of his strength, and probably it is to this that we must attribute the practice still prevalent in the British and Canadian Parliaments of referring to members not by name but by their constituencies, while, if any member is guilty of a breach of discipline, the Speaker of the House threatens to "name" him. At any rate, whatever be the origin of this reluctance to disclose the name, or whatever be its connection with the practice of people elsewhere, it seems to prevail generally among the Indians.

Our camp was pitched near the lake, by the bank of a little stream called the Yekootchee, which rises near the streams that flow through Lake Babine and the Skeena to the sea, and flows through Lake Stewart and the Fraser to the Pacific, nearly five hundred miles from the Skeena. A little to the north of this there is a chain, or rather, a network of lakes, some of which discharge their waters through the Peace to the Arctic Sea, others through the Skeena or the Fraser to the Pacific, while one small lake near Fort Connolly drains both ways, at one end into a tributary of the Skeena, at the other into a tributary of the Peace.

We expected to meet, somewhere on Stewart Lake, probably at Fort St. James, Mr. G. Major, who had left Victoria shortly before we had, intending to come by the road along the Fraser Valley, with mule-train and supplies for our journey eastward from Fort St. James. Great was our joy on the night after we reached Lake Stewart to be roused up by his arrival, and to find that he had brought a large sail-boat from the Fort which would save us the necessity of paddling down the lake. Next morning the camp was early astir, and we were soon under sail, gladly discarding the canoes that we had conditionally engaged, which were smaller and more cranky even than those on Lake Babine.

On our way we met Père Lejacques, the missionary of this district, whose charge embraces the whole territory between the Forks of Skeena and Fort McLeod, east and west, and between Fort Connolly and Fort St. George, north and south. After leaving the valley of the Skeena and of the Nasse all the Christian Indians of the interior throughout this northern district are Roman Catholic. The mission is under the direction of the Oblate Fathers, and the missionaries, if all are like the devoted Père Lejacques, are "in journeyings often and in labours abundant."

Lake Stewart is forty miles in length, ranging from one to six miles in width; the scenery is bolder than that of Lake Babine. If the latter might be compared to Loch Lomond, Lake Stewart might be not unfitly regarded as the Loch Katrine of British Columbia.

As our progress down the Lake was interrupted for a

time by head wind, it took us the whole day to make the distance, but we reached Fort St. James that evening, 5th July, the very day on which, when leaving Victoria, we thought we might possibly arrive there if we were favoured by the weather and by absence of unforeseen accidents. The distance travelled had not been great, yet as one is exposed to many delays and disappointments in such a country, where the means of communication are of a very primitive kind and where, as far as travel is concerned, almost everything is uncertain except the flight of time, we felt peculiarly thankful that this stage of our journey had been brought so successfully and pleasantly to a close.

The day after our arrival was one of rest, a Sabbath for which all felt thankful. The men who had accompanied our pack-train from Yale, as well as some H. B. C. officials, with ourselves, formed a goodly congregation at our service, which in the morning was conducted in the open air, and in the evening, in a large room of the Fort. After evening service we enjoyed an hour or two of sacred music, for here, nearly 400 miles from the nearest town, we found that Mr. Alexander, the factor, had an excellent organ, which he played with much taste and ability. Years of life in these wilds had failed to rob him of his love of music, or of his artistic touch of the keys. The evening was very beautiful, passing as it seemed that such a day should do, not into darkness, but into the calm radiance of a northern midsummer night.

Fort St. James, the centre of the H. B. Company's posts of northern British Columbia is beautifully situated on a broad flat about twenty feet above the beach, with a commanding outlook, and with views of scenery that remind one greatly of the Scottish Highlands. There are no snow-capped summits visible from the Fort, but look in any direction you may, there is a back-ground of hills which in some parts border the lake, and in others are separated from it by wooded plateaux or by gently undulating slopes, while, under the prevailing westerly winds, the waters of the lake break upon the beach with the musical monotone of the sea.

Like many of the H. B. Company's posts, the Fort consists of a few subtantial wooden buildings, surrounded by a stockade. The houses are ranged in shape nearly resembling the letter H, with the factor's dwelling as the cross-bar of the letter. It is one of the oldest trading posts of the country, and is the central depôt for a large district which includes Forts Babine, Connolly, McLeod, George and Fraser, a district formerly known as New Caledonia, and no doubt so named by the Scottish officers of the old North-West Company on account of its general resemblance to some parts of Scotland. About a mile above the Fort there is an Indian village possessing a pretty little church, and houses which have an air of neatness and cleanliness not always found among the Indians, while between the Fort and the village there is an excellent saw-mill, and immediately adjoining the Fort is a large garden, in which onions, carrots, lettuce and other vegetables are successfully grown.

From Fort St. James the trail leads to Omenica, and during the first years of the mining excitement there, many came up by the waggon route from Yale to Quesnel, which is the great arterial highway of British Columbia, and by the trail from Quesnel, so that for several seasons there was considerable traffic at this place. During the influx of the miners there was a tavern close to the Fort, but that establishment, which is often regarded as a sort of *avant courier* of western civilization, has been closed, probably from want of patronage rather than from pressure of principle, as few now go by this route to Omenica.

Monday was devoted to the examination of our stores and to writing letters to friends in the east, which would go by way of Victoria, this being the last chance we would have of sending them any word until reaching the telegraph station at Edmonton, in the valley of the Saskatchewan. We were to travel with a mule-train as far as Fort McLeod, about seventy miles from Fort St. James, intending there to divide our party, some to go with the mule-train through Pine River Pass, others by boat down the Parsnip and Peace River, through the Rocky Mountains to Dunvegan.

In making preparations for such a journey, it was necessary to select men suitable, not only for accompanying the packers, who had the management of the mule-train, but some also that would be suited for the trip down Peace River. Our old friends, Jim and Yessen, who had come all the way from the Skeena, were re-engaged, at their own request, to accompany us to Dunvegan. At first they seemed happy at the prospect of visiting an unknown land, but after a little Jim's heart failed him. He grew terribly home-sick. He had already come to the most distant place that he knew, and when the men spoke to him about the world beyond Fort St. James, he lost faith in the possibility of his return if he should venture further. Suddenly he remembered that his wife and children had no food, that they could not fish, that they would starve if he remained away. What was the white man's gold when weighed in the balance against the tender, clinging affection of squaw and papooses, and the unspeakable charms of home? Yessen might remain if he would, but not Jim. Stolidly he stood the chaffing of all around, and very soon after we left Stewart Lake he would be in the bosom of his family, with strange tales to tell of all the wonders he had seen, and of the offers of gain that he had resisted. This may seem singular in people so little given to express their feelings, but it is quite a common thing for an Indian to treat his employer as Jim treated us.

Yessen, whom by way of honourable distinction we called the "astronomer," clung to us and proved himself diligent and trustworthy. He had probably never seen a horse until this trip. Once when he was offered the chance of relieving a heavy day's march by an hour in the saddle, and was asked if he could ride, he answered "Perhaps." He made the attempt, but having forgotten, or rather having never learned, to tighten the girth, he soon rolled off, and for some weeks afterwards preferred going on foot. The other men whom we required, in addition to our foreman McNeill, and those who had to take charge of the pack-train, we had no difficulty in procuring at Fort St. James.

On Tuesday, the 8th July, we left Fort St. James for Fort McLeod, seventy miles distant, where our journey down Peace River would begin. This portion of the country, with the exception of the gold-mining district of Omenica, a little to the north, is probably in much the same condition as it was when these fur-trading posts were established. The trails may be a little better and more frequently traversed; land has been cleared here and there by forest fires; but the habitations of white men are still confined almost exclusively to the Hudson's Bay Company's forts. The Indians shift their wigwams as frequently as ever, not growing, it would seem, nor declining, in numbers; the foliage comes and goes unobserved; the silence of hill and forest is little more disturbed than

PEACE RIVER.

From a Photo by C. HORETZKY.

if the voice of man had never broken in upon their primeval repose. Even yet the facilities of communication are few, though somewhat improved of recent years. A gentleman still living in Victoria, who was clerk at one of these northern posts in the days of Napoleon, did not hear of the battle of Waterloo until two years after it had been fought; but although the only white man in the district, he took down his old flint-lock and fired a *feu-de-joie*.

The only route connecting Fort St. James and Fort McLeod is a bridle-path which leads sometimes over low hills, or by the margin of small lakes, sometimes through thick woods, or over treacherous swamps, where we were frequently delayed by the necessity of "brushing" the trail, that is, of laying large branches crosswise upon the path, to afford sure footing for the mules that carried our supplies, and for the horses that carried ourselves.

As there are many parts of British Columbia to which goods can be transported only by means of mule-trains, this mode of conveyance is very frequently adopted. The best breeds of mules have been brought to the Province from the Pacific States, and the Mexicans, who first introduced them from Europe, are the most experienced mule-drivers and packers. To one who sees it for the first time the packing of a mule-train is interesting as well as novel. Very early in the morning, perhaps by three o'clock, the men start out to fetch the mules from the pasture where they have been feeding over night, and as they are very gregarious, following the bell-mare as closely as a flock of sheep follow the bell-wether, a protracted search for the mules is seldom necessary when once the bell-mare has been found. Before five o'clock all are collected, and the work of packing begins. The *apparaho*, or pack-saddle, which is made of strips of wood, leather and padding, as carefully as an ordinary riding-saddle, is first secured by a broad, firm girth, which is bound or "sinched," as tightly as two men can pull, each pressing his knee or foot against the animal's side to gain increased leverage, a blinder having been previously placed across the mule's eyes, to prevent all movement on his part, as this temporary sightlessness secures perfect stillness. Then the packers pile up the load, which has been already arranged in two large bundles. These are placed one on each side of the apparaho, and are bound on or sinched as securely as possible, the rope being fastened in a manner peculiar to this process. The blinder is then removed, and the mule is turned free to reconcile itself to its burden of two or three hundred pounds, and the process is repeated until the whole train is prepared to start. While the train is in motion some of the packers are continually passing to and fro, to see that each mule's pack is quite secure. Should it begin to loosen, and be allowed to jolt and sway, it would soon cause trouble, and when the slightest indication of this is detected the pack is at once sinched up afresh. Heavily laden mules seldom go at any other pace than a walk, and as they cannot bear the burden of their packs very long, fifteen miles a day is considered on the average good travelling for a mule-train.

Being well mounted on horses we greatly enjoyed our ride to Fort McLeod, even though our daily progress was slow, and though the woods were sometimes so thick that both hands were required for pressing aside the branches that would otherwise strike against the face. The fresh morning air, the peeps through the timber, the profusion of wild flowers, the broad views, when, from some rising ground which the fire had cleared we could see a wide sweep of country, the glimpses of stream or lakelet, partly flashing in the sun and partly shaded by the over-hanging trees, an occasional snatch of song, trolled out by some of the company, the procession of riders moving Indian file, now slowly and carefully over bog, or rock, or wind-fall, now breaking into a canter where the trail permits this freedom, now halting to examine some curious rock formation, or peculiar plant, or some trace of a far past glacial period,—these and similar elements were sufficient to render our morning rides pleasant in the extreme. For the sake of our mules we usually camped soon after mid-day.

The country presents few features of interest. It seems here to be utterly unfit for agriculture, both from the character of the soil and from its altitude, which ranges from 2,200 feet to 2,700 feet above sea level. The timber where it has been spared by fire, is of a poor quality, and there are few signs of mineral resources. There is still, however, a considerable annual yield of furs, bear and beaver being the most abundant. Indeed often along this trail that we were traversing we saw traces of beaver in the stubs of trees, that had been cut by their teeth as well as they could have been cut by the axe, in the regularly-built barriers or dams, and in their cunningly contrived houses, which rise like small islands near the shore of pond or lake, arched above with no visible outlet, the entrance being from beneath.

Passing from Carp Lake to Long Lake, the two chief sheets of water between Fort St. James and Fort McLeod, we crossed the "divide" that separates the waters flowing into the Pacific from those that flow through the Peace River into the Arctic Sea. From Long Lake an excellent trout stream, known as Long Lake River, flows into McLeod Lake. Its descent is very rapid, and in its course there is a water-fall of great beauty, estimated at 130 feet in height. A little further on is Iroquois Creek, near which there is abundance of pasture, and a few miles further, in the course of which the trail passes over a ridge about 150 feet above McLeod Lake, we reach Fort McLeod. Having rested near Iroquois Creek on the 13th, we did not reach Fort McLeod until Monday the 14th,—seventy miles in seven days.

Fort McLeod is beautifully situated at the lower end of McLeod Lake, whose waters are emptied by the Pack River into the Peace. There is abundance of excellent pasture on the plateau around it, and it boasts a small garden that seems capable of raising anything that can withstand occasional summer frosts. Indeed there is sufficient good land in this immediate neighbourhood for a large farm, if the climate were only suitable.

Some have supposed that wherever an abundance of the service-berry is to be found it indicates a climate fit for the growth of grain, but this seems to be as great a mistake as to imagine that the presence of the humming-bird argues an equable and genial climate; for the humming-bird may be seen around the banks of Babine Lake, and as far north as the Stickine, while the service-berry grows in abundance near Fort McLeod; yet Babine, Stickine, and McLeod are all unfit localities for the growth of grain.

The snow-fall here is heavier than at Fort St. James, averaging about five feet, and gardening is about three weeks later. The lake usually freezes about the middle of November, and opens about the middle of May. All the traffic between Peace River and Fraser River passes this way, as the route from the Parsnip (as the southern branch of the Peace is called) by the Pack River, Lake McLeod, Summit Lake, and the Giscombe Portage to the Fraser, is much shorter than the route by the head-waters of the Parsnip and the head-waters of the Fraser.

Near the Fort there is a plain little church used by the R. C. Mission, and a small grave-yard, kept with great neatness. The graves are in almost every case covered by small houses of squared timber, although the bodies have been interred at the usual depth of six feet. In the church we saw a large heavy whip, which is used for punishing those whom the priest condemns, one man being specially set apart to administer the lash. At the time of our visit no Indians were to be seen around the Fort, but in the early part of June, and of October, they swarm in for a few days to sell their furs, and to procure another season's supplies, dividing their leisure time between listening to the priest and rattling their gambling-sticks, for all Indians seem to be born gamblers. They appear to be throughout this district quiet, trustworthy and industrious. The only act of violence recorded against any of them in this neighbourhood was the murder of a clerk of the Company many years ago, under somewhat peculiar provocation. The clerk had been irritated by the Indian, and said to him by way of intimidation, " Your wife and child will be dead before your next visit to this Fort." By a strange coincidence the poor man's wife and child died that winter in the woods. He at once attributed their death to the secret influence of the clerk, whose random words had been remembered and regarded as a threat of coming doom. Soon after, he appeared at the Fort, and deliberately shot the clerk, supposing him to be the murderer of his family. In old days it was thought expedient to keep not less than three white men at even the smallest trading post in New Caledonia, but of late years this has been found unnecessary, partly because the Indians are so quiet, and partly because one or two Indians, or half-breeds, are found to be quite as serviceable as white men for all ordinary purposes around the Fort.

The name "Fort" applied to these posts of the H. B. Company is frequently imposing in more ways than one. It naturally suggests walls, bastions, loop-holes, formidable gateways, a fortified residence, palisades, etc; but frequently, as in the case of Fort McLeod, the reality is very different from the vision. A small single-storied dwelling made of hewn logs, little better than the rude farm-house of a Canadian backwoodsman, a trading-store as plain as the dwelling, a smoke-house for curing and storing fish and meat, and a stable constitute the whole establishment.

This Fort is said to have had its days of greatness, when it was surrounded by a palisade, and had other visible signs of importance, but it is now one of the smallest posts in British Columbia. The manager, a young English gentleman, who has whiled away some of his lonely hours by sketching for the *Graphic*, has named it "Fort Misery," a name indicative of many a dreary day. Indeed it is difficult to discover what attractions many of the agents of the Hudson's Bay Company find in their secluded and lonely life. Familiar in many instances in earlier days with comfortable and even luxurious homes, and able to procure positions in civilised life where a competence, if not a fortune, was assured, they have chosen instead a life that in many cases cuts them off for a large portion of the year from any intercourse with the outer world or any companionship worthy of the name, and from all or almost all that we are accustomed to regard as the advantages of civilization. When sickness comes they are dependent upon themselves, or on their Indian neighbours. When their children grow up they must send them away to school, often at an expense which their incomes cannot well afford. Their promotion comes slowly at the best, for it is a service in which men live long, and promotion may mean the charge of a post further away from civilization, while the prospect of becoming a chief-factor, or of being able to retire with a competence, is distant and shadowy. Missionaries will undergo all this, and more than this, but they are animated by a clear and lofty purpose, that nerves them for exile and hardship if they can but fulfil their aim. Gold-hunters will undergo much, but they too have a definite object before them; but the spell of the H. B. C. service seems as vague, though it be as powerful, as that which binds the sailor to his sea-faring life, which he may often abuse, but which he cannot abandon.

Its agents may be attracted by the utter freedom which it gives them from the conventionalities and artificial restraints of society, by the authority which they enjoy over Indians and half-breeds, or by the scope for adventure and the opportunity for sport which most of them delight in. Ask them what fascination they find in it, and they can hardly tell you. Listen to them when several of them are together "talking muskrat," (to use their own term for discussing the business of the Company,) and they have scarcely a good word for the service; only when an outsider finds fault with it, will they speak in its defence; and yet let them leave it for a time and they long to come back to it. One of them, a young Irish gentleman who had spent years in the service on the Upper Ottawa and had returned to Ireland, informed some of his Canadian friends that he "found Dublin awfully dull after Temiscamingue." But withal, among the officers of the Hudson's Bay Company you find many men of education and refinement, competent to fill places of importance in society had they chosen the more settled walks of life. Of late their prospects have been considerably reduced, as the fur-trade of the Company has, since 1871, been entirely separated from its landed estates, the profits of the latter going entirely to the English shareholders, while all the officers, engaged in trading, are paid exclusively from the proceeds of the fur sales. Two-fifths of the profits of the fur-trade are divided, according to rank, among the commissioned officers, who are known as junior chief traders, chief traders, factors and chief factors. As, however, the land held by the company must be its great and increasing source of wealth in the future, whereas the prospects of the fur trade must naturally diminish with the advance of civilization and of settlement, the Service is even less attractive than it once was.

CHAPTER VI.

THROUGH THE MOUNTAINS BY BOAT.

Explorers of Peace River.—Division of Party.—Leave Fort McLeod.—The Parsnip.—Fur Traders and Gold Hunters.—Mining.—The Nation River.—Pete Toy and Nigger Dan.—Finlay River and Rapids.—The Unchagah.—Peace River Pass.—Parle-pas Rapid.—Moose Hunting.—Buffalo Tracks.—Terraces.—The Canon Coal.—Navigable Extent of River.—Indian Hunters.—Charlie's Yarns.

In 1793 Sir Alexander Mackenzie, the intrepid explorer who was the first to cross this northern part of the continent, having made a previous journey from Montreal to the mouth of the great river since known by his name, that flows into the Arctic Sea, passed through the Rocky Mountains by way of Peace River to the Pacific. He touched the western ocean at Dean Inlet, where he left upon the rock the inscription, "Alexander Mackenzie, from Canada, by land, 22nd July, 1793.' There by a strange coincidence he almost met another daring traveller, Capt. Vancouver, who was then cruising along the coast, and who had passed Dean Inlet but a short time before his arrival. After spending a night within sound of the sea, he retraced his course by the Valley of the

Peace. His purpose was partly to explore the country and partly to extend the fur trade of the North West Company, with which he was connected and which was subsequently amalgamated with the Hudson's Bay Company; and, through his influence, fur-trading posts were planted, ere the close of the century, in this remote land west of the mountains, Fort St. James being then, as now, the central depôt of the district. Mr. Mackenzie's narrative of his journey contains the earliest account we have of any portion of that country, on which we were now entering, that is unwatered by the Peace; for, though the so-called Peace River country lies east of the Rocky Mountains, yet at Fort McLeod we stepped into the boat in which we were to be borne by tributary streams to the Peace and by it through the Mountain Range. Others, whose journeys have been recorded for us, have since traversed the same country. Sir George Simpson, then Governor of the Hudson's Bay Company, passed by this route to the Pacific in 1828, taking his canoe from York Factory, on Hudson's Bay, to the mouth of the Fraser River.* But, of recent accounts, the most detailed and interesting is that given in the Report of the Geological Survey of Canada for 1875-76, which contains the record of a journey by Messrs. Selwyn and Macoun in the interests of the Geological Survey in 1875.

---

* Butler's *Wild North Land* and Horetzky's *Canada on the Pacific*, containing narratives of ourneys by way of Peace River to the western sea, are familiarly known to many readers.

Indeed very much is due to the staff of the Geological Survey and to the engineers of the Canadian Pacific Railway for the knowledge that we possess of British Columbia and of the Rocky Mountains, as well as of our vast Prairie Region. Exposed, in many instances, to hardship, cut off for months at a time from intercourse with any whites except those of their own party, pursuing unweariedly their examination of the country to ascertain its physical features, the character and extent of its resources, and its facilities for railway construction, they have acquired a mass of information which is to a large degree stored up in blue-books, but which forms the basis of many a grave decision and important undertaking of Government as well as of many a venture of private enterprise.

At Fort McLeod our party was divided, some, under the direction of Dr. Dawson, proceeding through the Rocky Mountains by way of Pine River Pass, accompanied by the mule-train with supplies for continued explorations east of the mountains, while Messrs. Cambie, McLeod, Major and I with four of a crew descended Peace River by boat, all expecting to rendezvous at Dunvegan, the central H. B. C. Depôt of the Peace River District east of the Rockies. We were fortunate enough to procure at Fort McLeod a capacious boat, forty feet keel, nine feet beam, which, although old and well-worn, was by a few repairs and by frequent pumping fit for our purpose.

Our departure from the Fort was somewhat delayed by the work of trail-making, as all the available men had to assist in clearing the trail for the mule-train, from Fort McLeod to the crossing of the Parsnip, at the mouth of the Misinchinca. At that point those who were to proceed by Pine River Pass had the benefit of the boat in crossing the Parsnip ere we continued our course down stream. The same trail had been followed some years before by an exploring party, but a good deal of labour was necessary in cutting a course through the accumulated windfalls of several seasons. One of our Indians, an excellent fellow whom we had engaged for the trip down the Peace River, while employed in trail-making cut his right ankle so badly that he had to be carried back to Fort McLeod. He at once gave up hope, not only of being able to accompany us, but also of ever recovering from the effects of the accident, for it is characteristic of Indians under any sickness or accident to grow despondent, and to take a most hopeless view of the situation. Although enduring pain without a murmur, they very quickly despair of all recovery. Perhaps they have good reason for this habitual despondency in sickness, as the sick and wounded are very readily left behind by the others, and from lack of care a slight accident or illness may in many cases prove most serious.

Passing from Lake McLeod down Pack River, which

is about seventeen miles in length, we entered the Parsnip, the great southern tributary of the Peace, whose sources lie near the upper waters of the Fraser on the western slopes of the mountains. It was by way of this river that McKenzie's course lay when, after reaching its head waters, he carried his canoe, as Simpson did half a century later, to the great northern bend of the Fraser, a route much more circuitous than that which connects the two rivers by way of Lake McLeod, Summit Lake and the Giscombe Portage.

The Parsnip, so called from the abundance of cow-parsnip that grows near its banks, maintains pretty evenly a width of about five hundred feet, and a current of about three or four miles an hour. It is dotted by numerous islands, at the upper end of which it sometimes divides so evenly that it is difficult to distinguish the main channel, while at the same time there are many sloughs, or "slews" so-called, where part of the river flows by some devious and half-hidden course, that might, when they blend again with the main current, be mistaken for tributary streams. The banks are sometimes bare and steep, with exposures of sand, clay and gravel, and with occasional croppings of sandstone and of limestone; sometimes they are pleasantly varied by levels of pasture land, or by low wooded hills.

The voyageurs observe changes in the river, from year to year. The soil being light and sandy is easily washed down by the current in the spring, when the river rises fifteen or twenty feet above its lowest summer level; the shores are cast into new curves; bars of sand and gravel are removed from one locality, and built up in another; the islands are worn away above, and increased by deposits further down; and the slopes and bushes along the banks have, in some places, been stripped by fire of much of their foliage, while in others they have been covered by new growths of bush or tree.

Borne steadily and pleasantly along by the current we met some fur-traders, struggling up stream with their cargoes *en route* to Victoria, engaged in the precarious task of competing with the Hudson's Bay Company. Such competition is no safe nor easy work unless one can bring large capital into it, and conduct business at many different stations, for the Company may gain largely at some of its posts although losing at others, and can thus average a fair rate of profit, whereas "free traders," as their rivals are called, if dependent only on one or two posts, may be ruined in a single season. Besides, the Company have usually to pay less for their furs than others do, as the Indians are not readily seduced from a service which has always been faithfully and honestly conducted, and which has witnessed the rise and fall of many rivals, while it still remains a strong, successful and useful corporation.

We met also straggling miners engaged in prospecting; in one case, a solitary Frenchman, in another, three Scotchmen. Many a time the miner will start off alone to prospect new districts, trusting to his own brain, bone and sinew, taking some small supplies to stand between him and starvation if he should find no game nor human habitation in his wandering. Onward he goes, washing a pan-full of sand from this stream, and then passing on to the next, until he finds sufficient gold to tempt him to prolong his search at some particular point. Smiling at dangers that would make less resolute men despair, restless in his rambling as the wandering Jew, broken perhaps in fortune, sometimes broken in health, but never broken in hope, the miner has pierced almost every part of the country, opening the gates to let in the outer world, toiling with a degree of patience and of energy that would soon have enriched him if he could have practised the same virtues in some of the more settled walks of life. Weeks may be spent by him upon some promising "bar," where the stream has deposited the precious particles far from the vein that once held them; or he may trace the gold to the alluvial deposits of some older water-courses, and may find rich "pay-dirt" on levels far above the present rivers. Or, to vary the excitement, he may seek for the channel of some ancient stream far below the depth of the present water-course, and may find there the deposits of past ages. This latter, which is called "deep-digging," has in British Columbia as in California, frequently proved most profitable. By regular mining operations the course of the older stream is followed, at a depth perhaps of from thirty to a hundred feet below the surface, the buried channel being traceable by the rocks and gravel of its bed. Tunnels are formed; timbers are introduced to support the sides and roof; and the miner, standing ankle-deep in wet sand and gravel, beneath the continuous dripping that percolates through from above, carries on his laborious search. What cares he for cramps, discomfort, rheumatism, or other ills that flesh is heir to, when sudden wealth seems always close at hand?

Quartz-mining has as yet received little attention in British Columbia, the alluvial deposits whether on the surface or along the buried channels,—known generally as placer-mining,—having hitherto absorbed the energy of miners. These deposits, however, must in course of time become exhausted, while an important source of wealth may remain to be developed in the gold-bearing rocks from which at some period, recent or more remote, the alluvial gold has been borne down by the current. Quartz-crushing may require more capital and cheaper labour than are at present available, but when developed it is likely to prove a much more valuable and more permanent industry than placer-mining. Many more have lost than have gained by gold-mining, and yet

From a Photo. by A. R. C. Selwyn, Esq.　　JUNCTION OF NATION AND PARSNIP.

although field after field may prove unprofitable there are thousands along the Pacific for whom the mines have all the fascination that the dice have for the gambler, and who are ready with one accord to rush towards the newest "diggings." Let the solitary Frenchman or the three Scots whom we met on the Parsnip find a rich gold-field and make it known, and the news would spread like wild-fire; men would gather from every centre of population between Cassiar and San Francisco; and these unpeopled solitudes would soon become familiar to many thousands.

The Nation River joins the Parsnip from the west about thirty-two miles below the mouth of Pack River, after receiving the waters of numerous lakes that lie to the south of the Omenica district, between Lake Babine and the Parsnip, a region not yet surveyed, hardly even explored, and little known except to the Indians. From the mouth of the Misinchinca, twelve miles above Pack River, to the mouth of the Nation, traces of lignite have been found, regarding which Mr. Selwyn says,—"Some of the blocks found along the shores of the Parsnip were of large size, and sufficiently pure and compact to be of value as fuel if found in thick seams." Landing nearly opposite the mouth of the Nation we found the soil good, the ground undulating, covered with a rich crop of wild hay and pea-vine, from which it may reasonably be inferred that many of the flats and slopes along the river, and perhaps also the upper plateaux, would afford excellent and abundant pasturage.

Between the Nation and the Finlay we passed bars where gold has been found year after year, though not in very large quantities, probably borne down from the rocks in the neighbourhood of Omenica. On this part of the river there lived at some distance from each other, for several years, two men familiar by name, if not in person, to every traveller throughout this region, and whom the readers of Butler's *Wild North Land* will remember,—Pete Toy and Nigger Dan. Both gave attention to trapping and mining. In winter they searched for game, and in summer for gold. The neighbouring woods and hills supplied them with moose, bear, beaver and marten,—provisions and furs,—while the sand-bars gladdened and enriched them with gold. Over and over, year after year, they washed the silt brought down by the river at the spring flood and deposited along the margin of some particular bar, finding at each returning summer that from the territory drained by its western tributaries the river had rolled along new particles of gold, to leave them where it had left a similar precious burden the preceding year. They knew the river with all its swirls and rapids, its ice-jams and freshets, as well as they knew their own cabins. Each kept his own territory and held on his own course as if utterly independent of the outside world, although the desire for its luxuries may first have incited them to search for gold in this voluntary exile.

Pete would face almost any current, would dare the waters in any condition of day or night, of frost or flood but he launched his frail dug-out once too often. Though frequently upset, and seemingly like the beaver formed to live on land or water, the river at last received him that he rose no more. For some years he had an old chum, Joe Dates, that lived with him; and both bore a good name for honesty and hospitality. Joe was said to have made a goodly "pile," which he kept hid in some spot known only to himself, but death called him away, as he had called Pete, and as he calls most men, unexpectedly; and the place that contains the hidden treasure is now a sealed secret, to be sought for, perhaps, at some future day, with as much eagerness, and as little success, as the reported treasures of Captain Kidd, near the shores of the Bay of Fundy. Nigger Dan, who came to British Columbia as cook for Captain Palliser, still lives, but he has exchanged the freedom of the woods and mountains for the confinement of a police-station. He has been known for years as Nigger Dan. Negro he is, or at least mulatto, and his name is Daniel Williams, but miners and trappers are seldom called by their surnames. Enquire at any diggings for John McDonald, a man whose lithe form was familiar in many of the mining districts, and no one seems to have ever heard of him; but ask for Cariboo Jack, and you find that almost every miner from Kootenay to Cassiar knows him;—and so with Grey John, Dancing Bill, Yankee Jim, and the rest of the wild, roving "boys," who have sought their fortunes amongst the crowd, from the lower bends of the Fraser to the banks of the Stickine, and beyond the mountains of Alaska.

Nigger Dan had but a poor reputation. Rumours dark as his own skin were current regarding him. The distinction between "mine" and "thine" was too subtle for him, or if he knew it, it was only to ignore it. He moved down from the banks of the Parsnip to the neighbourhood of Fort St. John, near Dunvegan. There he waged war like a son of Ishmael instead of a descendant of Ham, the outer world being represented by the H. B. Company, while Dan's hand was against the Company and the Company's against him. He had a garden which was unfenced, and, because the Company's horses, cattle, and dogs made a free pasture and highway of his open garden, he treated them to poison and lead. All know the value of horses and cattle, and some set a fancy price on a favourite dog, but in this region good dogs have a recognized, market value on account of the extensive use made of them in winter in hauling toboggans. Sometimes four moose-skins, worth $40, have been given for one dog. And not only did this hermit distinguish himself by general acts of slaughter;—he had threatened the life of one or two men, and rumour gave him the credit of having executed years ago a similar threat;— and he had set fire to a store of the H. B. Company, so that the time had come when something must be done. The Company are not given to lynching, but yet law must be administered even on the remote banks of the Peace River, so by a skilful piece of strategy Dan was seized, a warrant having been issued for his apprehension, and was taken off to Edmonton to be tried; but it is now ascertained that the trial must be conducted at Victoria, as Fort St. John is in British Columbia, not in the North-West Territories. In a country where the inhabitants are few, and where crime is but little known, one man may acquire considerable importance and give great annoyance, and so during 1879 Peace River district was more concerned about this one individual than it could be over the rise and fall of Governments or the fate of empires.

On approaching the "Forks" where the Finlay and Parsnip meet, some seventy-seven miles below Pack River, we caught to the north-east the first glimpse, high up among the hill tops, of the gap between the mountains through which the Peace River carves its way. The hills are here rugged and densely massed, with occasional snow-peaks glistening amongst them.

The Finlay, so named from its first white explorer, drains a great portion of Omenica by one branch, while by another it receives the waters of an unexplored region to the north of Omenica. For fully 300 miles before it joins the Parsnip it has twisted and coiled itself by many a rugged mountain range, and through many a rocky cañon, receiving, as its tributaries, streams whose sands glitter with gold. Here its flow is gentle, but thirty miles off we could see bold snow-capped mountains that tell of the character of the country through which it carves its way. And the Parsnip, ere the two rivers blend, has flowed nearly as far as the Finlay, by many a curve from the uplands where its sources lie near the head-waters of the Fraser. As they meet, their waters broaden into a small smooth lake, and then rush down in a rough and stormy current, nearly half a mile in length and some two hundred and fifty yards in width, known as the Finlay Rapids. Here the names Parsnip and Finlay are dropped, and from this onward until it meets near Fort Chipewyan the waters that empty Lake Athabasca, a thousand miles away, the united river is known as the Peace. The Sicanies of northern British Columbia call it the Tsetaikah,—"the river that goes into the mountain." The Beavers, who live east of the Rocky Mountains, call it the Unchagah,—that is, "the Peace"—for on its banks was settled once for all a feud that had long been waged between them and the Crees. About a mile below the rapids the river, with its forces now united from the south and west, turns suddenly

From a Photo. by A. R. C. Selwyn, Esq.   MOUNT SELWYN, PEACE RIVER PASS.

eastward. At this bend it is fringed on both banks by gentle slopes and irregular benches, beyond which rise the hills, at first not more than 2,000 to 2,500 feet in height, some scarped by ravines, some castellated with regular strata of rock, but for the most part lightly wooded. This is the beginning of the Peace River Pass.

Our progress was delayed for a little by a heavy thunder-shower, and being anxious to see this part of the river to advantage, we waited under shelter until the rain had ceased. The storm soon spent itself, the sun came out with splendour, and large white billowy clouds, floating across the sky, made the deep blue beyond seem further away than ever. Almost immediately below the entrance to the Pass, Mount Selwyn rises to the right, 4,570 feet above the river, 6,220 feet above the sea. It is a massive pyramid, flanked by a ridge of rock on either side, its lower slopes formed by the detritus washed down from side and summit, partly covered by burnt timber, and tinted by frequent patches of grass; its upper slopes in part moss-covered, in part bare as polished granite, broken and irregular as if shattered by fire and frost; its sides now shelving, now precipitous, grooved and seamed by torrent and by avalanche; its edge ragged and serrated, until it terminates in a solitary snow-clad peak. Along the northern bank of the river the hills are grouped in endless variety of form, the irregular masses looking as if they had been flung there at some terrible convulsion of nature, to show into how many different shapes mountains can be cast.

Nearly opposite Mount Selwyn the Wicked River, a stream clear as crystal and noisy as a cascade, falls in on the left bank through a gorge between the hills. To the right and left, alternately, sweep the broad curves of the main river, which is here from 200 to 250 yards in width, while the ridges, between which it winds, appear to be dove-tailed as you look down the Pass. The view changes with each bend of the current. Here a rugged shoulder bare and hard as adamant, butting upward for recognition, there a frowning precipice, with no trace of vegetation, or a wooded knoll, solid beneath but with a fair green surface, here a wild ravine, there a great shell-shaped valley, while stretching far up are the peaks that form a resting place for the eagle and the cloud.

The day being fine there was a perpetual play of light and shade on river and hill, and so as we were swept on by the current, cloud, mountain and river, peak, bluff, and wooded banks were woven into countless and ever-changing combinations. Sketches, photographs and words alike fail to give an adequate picture of this part of our journey. Even could one thus convey any clear conception of separate parts of the Pass, yet it is impossible to reproduce that sequence and blending of views that was wrought by our own motion down the river as it ceaselessly shifted the scenes.

There was little snow to be seen even on the highest peaks, much less than we had expected. Indeed, in this respect the Rocky Mountains are less Alpine in appearance than the Cascade Range through which we came when ascending the Skeena; but here the Rockies are much lower than they are further south, while the peaks are clustered much more closely than on the Skeena.

Gradually, as we were borne onward, we found the character of the hills changing. Instead of being bold and peaked and serrated, they are covered with woods to the summit. The valley begins to widen. To the right rises Mount Garnet Wolseley, so named by Butler, the last of the range that seem with sharp edges to cleave the sky. Though the width of the river continues much the same, yet the plateaux on either side broaden until the hills are set about two miles apart, from north to south, summit from summit. We recognise that we have pierced, from west to east, the Range of the Rocky Mountains, through a pass about twenty-two miles in length, borne pleasantly along in a large boat upon the waters of the great Unchagah.

Passing the Clearwater and other small tributaries, whose crystal purity is in marked contrast with the turbid, grayish colour of the Peace, we ran with safety the Parle-pas rapid, so called because it is not heard far up the river, and may be closely approached before it is recognised as a strong rough rapid, although it speaks loudly enough when you are once in its grasp and cannot retrace your course. Our pilot, Charlie Favel, who had gone forward to examine it before venturing to run it, held the long "sweep" that was lashed astern to serve as the steering oar, for an ordinary rudder would be useless here; the four oars were vigorously manned, and then into the boiling current we went. We had taken the first plunge, when mid-way we were caught by an eddy; the bow swung around a little; had it swung much further we must have been swamped, for the waves were angry as in a storm at sea; the men bent themselves to their oars; the helmsman let out some of his reserve strength; it was only the work of an instant; the boat swung back into its true course, and the next moment we were in calm water, wishing we had another rapid to run.

We passed a number of small streams, but below the mouth of the Finlay the tributary streams are not as large nor as frequent as one would expect in a land of mountains. Indeed, until it receives the Pine River the united waters of the streams on the eastern slopes scarcely make any perceptible difference in the volume of the main river. This may perhaps be due to the reduced rain-fall on the eastern, as compared with that on the western side of the mountains.

We were being borne pleasantly along by the strong and steady current when, hush!—" there's a moose," said Charlie, and no one dared to distrust the old man's keen vision. The splashing oars are silenced; all eyes are turned away from stream, and hill, and wood, and are focussed in one direction. Sure enough, there it is at some distance down the river's bank, close by the water's edge. Eager hands grasp the rifles, for we have been hoping for a chance like this. The boat drops quietly down the current, each head is bent low, we draw nearer and nearer, we will soon be within safe and easy range. No! surely, it cannot be! Yes, it is,—a great brown rock! A growl of disappointment, then a general roar, and a proposal to present the too blind, and too blindly trusted, Charlie with a pair of spectacles,—and our solitary moose-hunt is over.

Continuing down stream we find flats and benches in almost unbroken succession, stretching between the river and the now receding hills, some of them half a mile in width, and less than thirty feet above the water's edge, with rich soil and luxuriant pasture. The banks, where not broken by the water that in places has exposed the sand, clay, or gravel bed, are green with grass, kinnikinnick, juniper, low red cedar, vetches, and the beautiful silverberry plant. Along both sides of the river there are terraces, in tier upon tier, some with their edges as clearly cut as if they had been meant for fortresses, others distinctly marked, but wooded; indeed these terraces continue for many miles, a striking and beautiful feature of the landscape, giving it an appearance of cultivation. Those on the right bank are almost uniformly timbered, those on the north bank are grassy and smooth. Their sides are occasionally seamed by old buffalo trails, for though the buffalo has not been seen on the banks of the Peace for many years, this was once the pasture land for large herds that found here their western limit. They wandered over a vast expanse of country " in herds upon an endless plain." Prairie and hill-side furnished them with unlimited supplies of food, for even in winter by pawing away the light snow they could always find plenty of grass upon the plains. The bow and spear and rifle of the Indian long made little inroad upon their numbers, while the reduction thus caused would in the course of nature be soon repaired; and it required but a small proportion of them to enable the Indian to supply his own wants. The buffalo fed him, clothed him, housed him, for his flesh was the Indian's food, and his hide gave him clothes and tent. But the trader came wanting buffalo robes. The skill of the Indian soon thinned out the herds, and the French half-breeds carried on a still more successful war of extermination against them. Fabulous numbers were slain annually until, by degrees, the vast herds were reduced, and now their number is so rapidly diminishing that on all the Canadian plains the buffalo will soon be extinct.

Gradually the valley widens, sometimes from bank to

bank the river is not more than 500 feet, though it usually spreads out its waters to twice that width. The flats are frequently covered with aspens that seem here to take, in part at least, the place which the cotton-wood holds on the flats and islands of the Skeena and of the Parsnip, indicating it is said a drier soil, if not also a drier climate. Along the hill sides, on the northern bank, the stratification of the rock can be very clearly seen, traceable even below the grass, the lines running in various directions, though never much crumpled nor abruptly broken. Throughout the Rocky Mountains, indeed, the strata of the rocks, which are chiefly limestone and sand-stone, are easily discernible, while in the Cascade Range, composed of rocks of an earlier formation, scarcely any sign of stratification can be detected.

The general appearance of the country upon either side between the river and the now receding hills, and particularly on the north side, is that of a pastoral district. Some of the flats and lower slopes might furnish arable farms; others, at least in the summer season, appear suited for stock raising, while the low grassy hills resemble some of the sheep-farming portions of Scotland. Mile after mile extend the terraces, sometimes as regular as if cut by square and rule, now smooth as a lawn, now lightly wooded, cleft here and there by ravines.

Have the Indians no legends connected with these

terraces? They remind one somewhat of the "parallel roads" of Glen Roy, but are as much greater in extent as our Canadian North-West is more extensive than Scotland. The Scottish Highlander has his legend, or as he regards it, his true history of these parallel roads. Tell him about the glacial period, when the whole land was rasped by icebergs, or about ancient water-levels that once stood high up along the slopes of Ben-Nevis, and he smiles at your foolish fancies. Does he not know, for did not his father tell him, that Fingal made those parallel roads that he might hunt down the red-deer, when, with the dogs, of whose prowess Ossian has sung, he coursed the antlered game along the hill side? Has the Indian no legends, no traditions of paths cleft by the heroes of old for the chase of moose, buffalo or grizzly? Is there nothing in the beliefs and byegone history of the Indians of this northern land worthy of some antiquary's time and study,—worthy even of some small place in our English literature?

Were it necessary to find a course for a railway as far north as the Peace River Pass, a comparatively easy route through the mountains is offered in this direction, for even at the wildest and most rugged parts of the Pass the mountains are almost invariably fringed by flats, or by gentle slopes of varying width. One or two avalanche courses, a few ravines and occasional projections of rock would form the chief difficulties, which are apparently much less serious than many obstacles that have been overcome on other Canadian railways. At its higher, or western, extremity the Pass is not more than 1650 feet above the sea level, and the current of the river, which is very equable, is about four or five miles an hour where it cuts through the mountain range. East of the Pass, for fifty miles, until the Cañon is reached, the engineering difficulties would probably be not much greater than those presented by an open prairie, but the chief difficulty on this route would be found at the Cañon, where the river sweeps around the base of a solitary, massive hill known as the Mountain of Rocks, or Portage Mountain, just above Hudson's Hope. Yet even here, though the work would be heavy, the difficulties would not be insuperable. For any railway line, however, that would pass by a northern route through the Rocky Mountains to the Pacific, the Pine River Pass, a little to the south of this, which is known to be practicable, would be preferable to the route by way of Peace River.

The Cañon of the Peace River, which at its upper extremity is about fifty miles east of the Rocky Mountains, is about twenty-five miles in length, and the river is here a wild broken torrent, some 200 feet in width, which, so far as known, has never been navigated except by the dauntless Iroquois crew that accompanied Sir George Simpson on his expedition to the Pacific, in 1828. Its rocky sides have been rent and peeled by the current, here scooped into great pot-holes, there seamed with broad fissures, now broken into jagged edges, now worn into smooth curves. The cliffs have in some places been levelled into terraces, in others they rise sheer and precipitous over 250 feet. Clambering along the face of the cliff where a foothold was possible we found a narrow seam of coal, about 150 feet above the river. A weather-worn piece, which was the best specimen that the situation allowed us to procure, when tested at the camp-fire burned with a bright flame but with a large proportion of ash. Another seam was observed, about two feet thick where exposed, and also a seam of lignite. The course of the river here is always curved as it dashes alternately to the right and left, while from end to end the Cañon forms one great curve around the base of Portage Mountain.

This Cañon is the only obstruction to the navigation of the river for several hundreds of miles. From the head of the Cañon to the mouth of Pack River, that empties the waters of Lake McLeod, that is, about 150 miles, or even further up the Parsnip, the river is navigable, except at low water, for steamers of light draught. The Parle-pas and Finlay Rapids are the only rapids of any importance. These can be run with ease and safety, and could be surmounted without much difficulty by warping the steamer against the current, as is done on the heavier and more tortuous rapids of the Fraser and the Columbia. From Hudson's Hope, at the lower end of the Cañon, it flows full-fed and strong with no hindrance to steam navigation for nearly five hundred miles when it leaps over the Vermilion Falls. Another break, requiring a few miles of land communication occurs at the Five Portages, on Slave River. Beyond that there is no further obstacle; the river is open to large steamers down to the Arctic Ocean. There would thus be but three breaks in the connection of continuous steam navigation from the mouth of Pack River down the Parsnip, the Peace, the Slave and the Mackenzie,—different names for one continuous water-course,—that is, from **Northern British Columbia, through the Rocky Mountains, by the fertile Peace River District, to the Northern Sea**, a distance in all, by water, of not less than 2500 miles.

We were forced to abandon our boat at the head of the Cañon, but were fortunate enough to procure the horses of some Indian hunters from Hudson's Hope to convey our supplies, baggage, etc., across the twelve mile Portage to the foot of the Cañon. At the Hope as elsewhere throughout these northern districts the agent employs two hunters to supply the Post with provisions. These men, accompanied by their families and by two grown lads who go with them to bring home the game, are employed during most of the year in hunting. They confine their attention almost entirely to moose and bear, and scorn such small game as ducks and prairie-chicken, however abundant. Each hunter gets ten dollars worth of ammunition in spring, and the same in autumn, a pound of tea, of sugar and of tobacco each month, and he is paid from five to ten "skins" for each moose, according to size, the "skin" being the chief currency of the district, equivalent here to about $1.50. We fortunately met the hunters of the Hope near the Cañon, and were thus spared the dreary toil of portaging our tents, supplies, etc., twelve miles. As their horses were employed to convey the slaughtered game to the trading-post their harness was of the rudest kind, especially when compared with the well made, well kept apparahoes of the mule-train. One outfit consisted of a small pack-saddle, shaped something like a diminutive saw-horse, partly covered with patches of leather and blanket, and girt with a broad belt of shaganappi. The second horse carried two large bags, made of moose-hide, that hung like panniers, one on either side. Another was equipped with what appeared to be either the rudiments of a riding-saddle brought into use before it had been finished, or the remains of a saddle in an advanced stage of decay;—and so with the rest. We were not, however, in a humour to criticize severely, but, thankful for such an unexpected conveyance, we were ready to adopt what is called the Hudson's Bay fashion,—that is, to use any thing you can get which will serve your turn, and let the next man forage for himself.

The trail leads up to a broad terrace which skirts the base of a hill known as the Buffalo's Head. The hill takes this name from a favourite camping ground close by, which has, for many years, been marked by the head of the last buffalo that was shot in this part of the Peace District. From its summit a wide sweeping view may be had of the valley of the river westward to the giant peaks that girt the Pass, and eastward towards Dunvegan where it flows through fertile plains. We had hoped to ascend this summit while delayed near the head of the Cañon, but a dense haze like that of a day in the Indian summer, only heavier, hung over the mountains, obscuring the view. The trail passes over rolling country, partly open pasture land, partly wooded with aspen, poplar, spruce, black pine and tamarac. On the north side rises the Buffalo's Head, a bare and rugged bluff, its sides covered with grass,—and facing it to the south of the trail, some five or six miles from top to top, stands the Portage Mountain, called formerly the Mountain of Rocks, raising its huge shoulder above all around, and flanked by a cluster of smaller hills that seem to lean against its sides, converging towards the summit. These may be regarded as spurs or foot-hills of the Rocky Mountains, although fifty miles east of the main range.

It was late in the afternoon when we left the head of the Cañon, and a thunder storm, which had been threatening us for some hours, broke over us while on the trail. As we trudged along however, Charlie, our old pilot, who knows the country from Red River to Victoria, whiled away the time with stories of the old mining days in Omenica; how he had been among the first to "strike" a paying bar on the Omenica, how Joe Evans, Bill Roberts, Twelve-foot Davies and he had gone in as the advanced guard of a rushing multitude; how flour sold at a dollar a pound, and other provisions in proportion; how Charlie himself turned his attention to the provision market, and made twenty-five dollars a day by catching and selling fish, while his klootchman, or Indian wife, made five dollars a day by washing; and how, when the Cassiar mines were opened, and Omenica was "played out," he turned back to Fort St. James, having no wish to wander as far as the banks of the Stickine. He recalled, with evident satisfaction, the fact that he had never known any case of assault among the miners except one, in which he was himself the victim, when, at an evening party, at which in his capacity of fiddler he refused to play some particular tune, he was attacked by an inebriated Irishman. He had never known a case of theft among the miners, and, although for a time he carried the express for Rufus Sylvester, Major Butler's old travelling companion, and was known to be often the solitary bearer of large sums of gold, yet none ever attempted in the least degree to rob, molest or annoy him. He attributed this excellent order in Omenica, as also elsewhere throughout our British Columbia Mines, to the efforts and reputation chiefly of Sir Matthew Begbie, for whom the miners have a profound esteem ever since his memorable caution to them at Kootenay:—" Boys! if there is any shooting at Kootenay, there will be hanging at Kootenay."

The rain was falling heavily, and the lightning playing about us, as we pitched camp at the lower end of the Portage, on a plateau about ninety feet above the river. On the opposite side, down near the water's edge, we saw a solitary light glimmering in the small log-house that is known as Hudson's Hope. We had passed the Mountains, and had entered on the vast Prairie Region.

CHAPTER VII.

HUDSON'S HOPE TO DUNVEGAN.

The Prairie Region.—H. B. Company and the North-West Company.—Hudson's Hope.—Moose.—The Climate.—Fertile Flats.—The Plateau.—On the Raft.—Appearance of Country.—Fort St. John.—Massacre at the Old Fort.—Bear Hunting.—Dunvegan.—Highlanders Abroad.—Peace River Indians.—Moostoos, and his fight with a Grizzly.—Missions to the Indians.

During the past century much has been done to explore the extreme north of what is now the Dominion of Canada; for, although the Hudson's Bay Company received their charter in 1670 few travellers ventured beyond the shores of Hudson's Bay until about 1770, when Stearne discovered Great Slave Lake and traced the Coppermine River to its mouth. Subsequent explorers, some of whom were inspired by the hope of discovering a north-west passage by sea from the Atlantic to the Pacific, acquired much information regarding that lonely north-land, and mapped out the country that borders the Arctic Ocean. But, while the labours of Franklin, Back, Dease, Simpson, Rae, Richardson, McClintock and others were making the world familiar with the shores of the Northern Sea, a vast territory was lying between that remote north-land and the western United States which was almost entirely unknown to any except the Hudson's Bay Company officials and Indians until 1857, when Captain Palliser made an expedition from Lake Superior to the Rocky Mountains. The lonely regions of the north may long continue to be, as they have been for ages, the home of the musk-ox, the summer resort of the elk, the hunting ground of the Indian, and the preserve of the fur-trader, unless indeed their minerals should prove of sufficient value to attract capital and population; but this more southern and more central territory, about which the outer world was long kept in ignorance while those who held it on lease retained it for buffalo and beaver and other fur-bearing animals, is one of the most fertile parts of our empire, and may soon become one of the chief granaries of the world.

This district which is sometimes called the Prairie Region of Canada, and which includes the best portion of the North-West Territories, may be roughly described as a great triangle, one side stretching for nearly one thousand miles along the international boundary line—the 49th parallel; another extending from the boundary northward, in part along the foot of the Rocky Mountains, for about eight or nine hundred miles; while the base of the triangle is formed in a broken and irregular way by the chain of lakes that stretch from the Lake of the Woods, a little east of Manitoba, north-westward to Great Slave Lake.

The estimated area of this prairie region is not less than three hundred millions of acres, that is, about ten times the size of England. Manitoba, covering nine millions of acres in the south-east corner of this vast triangle, is as compared with the whole territory little more than one square on the chess-board. It is unwatered by a great system of rivers that flow into the chain of lakes which bound it along the north-east, and these lakes, in turn, are emptied by another river-system that flows through the remoter north land into the Arctic Ocean and Hudson's Bay. The Peace and the Athabasca cut across the northern portion of this territory; the Saskatchewan cleaves its way for a thousand miles through the rich central districts; while through the south-eastern portions flow the Assiniboine and the Red River, which unite their waters at Winnipeg, the capital of Manitoba and present gateway of the North-West.

This immense territory, as well as that lying to the north, was, for two centuries, held by the Hudson's Bay Company. For a time their exclusive right to it was disputed by a rival fur-trading corporation, the North-West Company, which was formed in 1783, consisting chiefly of French and Scottish residents in the old Province of Lower Canada. This Company following the track of

Verandaye, who had travelled from the **St. Lawrence to the Saskatchewan**, pushed the fur-trade with great vigour, extending their operations even to the Pacific. They soon came into collision with the older corporation, and not content with the peaceful **rivalry** of commerce, the servants of the two companies had many a bloody conflict, until the antagonism that was proving fatal alike to the lives of the traders, the profits of the traffic, and the peace of the natives was ended by **the amalgamation of** the two companies in 1821, under the **title of the older corporation**.

Thus reinforced, **the Hudson's Bay Company** secured increased privileges **and extended their sway over all** except our older Provinces from ocean to ocean, and from the mouth of the McKenzie to the borders of California, for there was no doubt nor dispute at that time about the rightful ownership of Oregon. Subsequently their territory was diminished, first by the sacrifice of Oregon to the demands of the United States, and **later, when Vancouver Island and British Columbia** were erected into Crown Colonies, but it was not until 1870, on the transfer of the North-West Territories to Canada, that the Hudson's Bay Company, the last of the great monopolies that have figured so largely in the colonial and commercial annals of England, gave up their exclusive right to the vast country that they had so long possessed.

During their tenure of the land, it had been the policy

of the Company to retain it as a great fur-preserve, and therefore, they kept the outer world as far as possible in ignorance of its resources and its capabilities, of its illimitable fertile prairies and its inexhaustible stores of coal, of its capacity to support a population perhaps twenty times as large as the present population of Canada. But **the time had come** when the gates must be unbarred, **when, through the** efforts of successive travellers the **character of the country was** becoming known, while competent men declared that the greater portion of the **wheat-lands of the continent were** contained within this territory that had so long been sacred to the fur-trade. **The settlement of the** country could be delayed no longer, and the Company, recognizing the necessity that **had been thrust upon them, and unable** to secure the continuance of all their chartered privileges, transferred to Canada their right and title to the whole territory; and, **although** on the Prairie Region the diminished yield of **furs, the increase** of competition, and the progress of settlement must reduce their traffic, yet, in the remoter north-land competition **will be** powerless for many years to come, and both soil and climate will protect them from the inroads of colonisation.

The Company, consisting originally of Prince Rupert and seventeen others, acquired their right and title as "the Governor and Company of adventurers trading with Hudson's Bay," under charter from Charles the Second on the easy terms that two **elks and two** black beavers should **be** paid to the king whenever he might come into the country. They received in extinction of their claim the payment of one and a half millions of dollars, the grant of fifty thousand acres selected in the vicinity of their forts or trading-posts, and the reserve of one-twentieth of the so-called "fertile belt," that is, of the portion of the prairie region lying south of the north branch of the Saskatchewan.

When we reached Hudson's Hope we had completely passed the Mountains, even such outlying spurs as the Portage Mountain and the Buffalo's Head; **and here,** still following the Peace, **we entered on the great Prairie** Region, for the river carves its way through the upper portion of this vast fertile triangle in its course to **the** Northern Sea.

The Hope is an outpost of the Hudson's Bay Company station **at** Fort St. John, forty-three miles further down the river, and is the most western post of the Dunvegan district. The agent, Charlette Dumas, an active, sinewy, kind and trustworthy half-breed, with a guest of his, Bob Armstrong, gave us a cordial welcome when **we** visited them soon **after our arrival.** Bob is a specimen of character more frequently met in British Columbia than elsewhere **in** Canada, **an** educated, intelligent rambler, gold-hunter and trapper by turn, captivated **by** the wandering life for which this country affords abundant scope, and now grown so accustomed to it that a city would seem to him like a prison. He had just returned from Moberley's Lake where he had been "fishing for the dogs,' as he expressed it, that is, catching fish to feed the dogs, for dogs must be fed summer and winter, in order to be ready for their winter's work. While feeding the dogs, Bob had also been doing something towards the provision supply of the post, but this responsibility rests mainly upon the Indian hunters, while Dumas himself attends to fur-trading. As the hunters usually devote themselves to one kind of game at a time, the people at the Hope, as at the other smaller trading-posts, have not much variety of food; when they have moose they have little else than moose, and when they have fish or bear it is, as Armstrong said, "fish or bear straight."

Throughout the Peace River country the moose is to the Indian almost everything that the buffalo is to the hunter of the plains, for this is the best moose country in Canada. The flesh is his chief article of food; the skin, when tanned, is the great material for dress, at least for winter costume, while untanned it is used for countless purposes, among others, as the covering for his tent or tepee; and cut into strips, in which form it is known as "shaganappi," it serves in almost every manufacture, and for all kinds of repairs. When moose are plentiful traders and Indians live well, for moose mouffle and tongue is a dish for kings to dine upon. Sometimes, however, when the hunters are unsuccessful for several weeks, the people at some of the posts may be reduced to the verge of starvation. Two years ago Dumas was compelled to kill one of his horses for food, and last spring he and his family had to eat some of the parchments which had served as window panes, and only regretted that they had not enough of them.

Yet, while dependent for food on the precarious supply of the chase, they might at this trading-post, as at every other throughout the Dunvegan district, raise abundance of stock and excellent crops with very little difficulty. The soil of the broad river flat on which the house is situated is of the richest loam, and in the little garden attached to it wheat and vegetables grow to perfection. On the elevated plateaux, far above the river level, the grass is so abundant that horses and cattle can feed in large numbers. The horses can winter out, and sufficient wild hay could, with no great labour, be cut for winter-feeding a large number of cattle. Dumas informed us that sometimes frost occurs late in the spring, although potatoes are usually planted by the first week in May. It had occurred, for instance, on the 15th May preceding our visit, but they rarely have any frost from that time until September, the river being usually open until the beginning of December.

Indeed, we had already observed the marked change

that there is between the climate on the east, and that on the west side of the Rocky Mountains, that on the east being drier and much warmer. This is probably due in part at least, to the fact that the prevailing westerly winds blowing from the Pacific have, by the time they come so far inland, been relieved of much of their moisture,—first by the Cascade Range, and then by the Rocky Mountains,—and becoming drier they become warmer, while at the same time the general level of the country here is lower than that of northern British Columbia. But the temperate climate is, no doubt, caused also in part by the warm current of air, the Gulf Stream of the atmosphere, that flows from the south along the central part of the continent. From the Gulf of Mexico, a great plain occupies nearly all the central portion of North America as far as the Arctic Sea. Along this region of plain and prairie the heated air of the tropics must move northwards, and probably to this, as much as to the winds from the Pacific, we owe the moderate climate of our North-West. One naturally forms an impression of the climate of this country from the latitude, an impression that in the minds of many has been confirmed by reading Butler's *Wild North Land*, a record of a winter trip when the lakes and rivers were ice-bound and the country was covered with snow. But one might as correctly form his impressions of the climate of Ontario by the wintry photographs that English visitors in

Canada so frequently send to their friends at home. Here, at Hudson's Hope, for instance, the climate is as conducive to life and comfort as it is in Ontario, ten degrees further south, while, throughout the North-West Territory, with its dry air, its bright sunshine, and its cool summer nights, fevers and bronchial affections are almost unknown, and the conditions for health and labour are peculiarly favourable.

At Hudson's Hope the fertile part of the Peace River district may be said to commence, for above the Cañon the land suitable for farming is very limited. As yet, indeed, the only places occupied by the white man, throughout this vast northern country, are the Hudson's Bay Company posts, a few mission stations, and two or three "free-traders'" establishments, and these are uniformly found on the fertile flats near the river's edge. On these flats the soil is usually of the richest character; the garden at the Hope, for instance, though but poorly cultivated, yields as good vegetables as are found in any of our eastern markets, with excellent wheat and barley, though these are grown in quantities so small as simply to serve as samples of what the district might produce. On a similar flat at Fort St. John, wheat, barley, and a great variety of vegetables, are successfully cultivated, while a still greater variety, including cucumbers, are grown at Dunvegan, ninety-seven miles below Fort St. John. It is the same at all the Hudson's Bay Company posts along the valley of the Peace. Wheat is grown as far north as Fort Simpson in lat: 62°; while wheat and barley grown at the Chipewyan Mission, on Lake Athabaska, in lat: 58° 42″, fully 600 miles north of Winnipeg, took a medal at the Centennial exhibition in Philadelphia in 1876.

By the Peace River district, however, we do not mean merely the fertile flats that skirt the river, but the vast plateau that, with few interruptions, extends in unbroken level for many miles on either side, at an altitude, in this western part, of about nine hundred feet above the river level, an altitude that gradually diminishes to about fifty feet below Vermilion, five hundred miles further down the river. This plateau, through which the Peace winds with a gentle current and almost as uniformly as a canal, is narrow near Hudson's Hope, but widens as it stretches eastward. Along the north bank, for a width varying from twenty-five to seventy miles, the land is known to be very fertile, partly well timbered, partly covered with light poplar, partly prairie, with rich herbage, luxuriant wild hay and pea-vine, at least as far as the Salt Springs on Slave River; while on the south side it embraces one of the most fertile and promising tracts of the North-West, known as *La Grande Prairie*, and, pursuing a south-easterly direction across the Athabasca to Edmonton, the greater portion of the land is fit for cultivation.

For our journey down the river below the Cañon we could not procure a boat, nor could we even obtain canoes; we were therefore compelled to make a raft, on which we drifted slowly down to Dunvegan, one hundred and forty miles, the current of the river being here somewhat slacker than it is nearer the mountains. Sometimes the river is not more than eight hundred feet in width, but frequently it broadens to half a mile, encircling islands in its flow. These islands are very beautiful, some being thickly wooded, and gracefully arched, rising like domes from the water's level—others, such as Les Isles des Pierres, about five miles below Hudson's Hope, being rocky, with flat lightly-wooded tops and precipitous sides, along which the sandstone strata are clearly marked, looking at a little distance as regular as masonry. The benches or terraces, continue, but not in so marked a manner, nor in so great a number as above the Cañon. Occasionally we ascended the plateau and found the soil uniformly fertile,—in some parts heavily timbered, in others lightly wooded with poplar copse,—with occasional stretches of open prairie that increased in number and extent as we moved eastward.

Drifting down a large and gentle river on a raft is not very exciting; it had, however, in our case at least, the one advantage of allowing us leisure to observe the scenery, which, though here not wild nor mountainous, is by no means monotonous. The river flows in long, sweeping curves, with easy equable current. Borne onward by its flow one fails to recognise the even level of the upper plateau, as the lofty banks are so varied by valley and ravine, by slope and terrace. Sometimes they are steep, almost precipitous, walls of shale, sandstone or indurated clay,—sometimes they are fringed by wooded flat or shelving beach, with here a land-slide exposing a bank of clay, there a deep gorge, its sides peeled to the bare sand-stone or clothed with foliage. Now the valley broadens, so that the expanded waters flow more gently, again it narrows as if to impede the river, which is thus forced into a stronger current. Each afternoon, for it was now the last week of July, a heavy haze, deepening as the day wore on, hung over the river, and, looking behind us, it seemed to take a warm golden tinge from the light of the westering sun. It was not fog nor smoke; it reminded us of pictures of tropical scenery in which form and colour alike grow indistinct as river and bank and island are shrouded in dimness caused by the vapour and the heat.

In a wide bend on the northern bank of the river where the valley broadens to nearly a mile, backed by grassy and lightly wooded slopes, nestles the little post of Fort St. John. An older building than the present one stood, some years ago, on the opposite bank, where the garden of the Fort is now; and a still older Fort St. John once stood about fifteen miles below this, at the mouth of the North Pine River The present Fort is of the usual pattern of the smaller Hudson's Bay posts,—a very plain building of squared logs, with store and outhouses attached; while nearer the beach stands the log cabin recently occupied by the notorious Nigger Dan.

We ascended the plateau and walked back about a mile. The soil is surprisingly rich and the vegetation very luxuriant. Mr. Selwyn, who rode about seven miles from the river over the table-land or plateau, describes it as "a fine level or slightly undulating country, covered with the richest herbage of astonishing luxuriance," and he adds. "I have seen nothing in the Saskatchewan region that at all equals it; both the soil and the climate here are better."* Nigger Dan, however, who is an experienced gardener, and to whom we are indebted for some of the most recent records of climate at Fort St. John, where he lived for several years, differs from Mr. Selwyn in this comparison of the valleys of the Saskatchewan and the Peace. Having spent, unwillingly, the summer of 1879 at Fort Saskatchewan, he says that he considers the Edmonton District superior to the Peace River country both in regard to soil and climate.

The day being very clear and cool with a strong wind from the west, we could see the Rocky Mountains, some seventy miles away there being apparently nothing but prairie between us and them. To the south of the Peace

---

*Report of Progress, Geol. Survey of Canada, 1875-76, p. 51.

the country seemed to be about the same level as that on which we stood, that is, about nine hundred feet above the river, at least as far back as the valley of the Pine River, which joins the Peace about five miles below Fort St. John. Beyond the Pine River we could see low rolling hills, but between the two valleys, away up as far as Hudson's Hope, there was unbroken plateau.

It was now indeed, for the first time, that we began to realize the character of the country on which we had entered. Thus far we had only seen the western end of this fertile plateau, where it narrows towards the mountains. To the east it stretches for many leagues, in almost unbroken level, as far as Lesser Slave Lake;—to the north we know not accurately how far, as exploration has hitherto been confined to the vicinity of the river valley. To the south-east, after you have passed the foot-hills of the Rocky Mountains, the plateau extends, with few interruptions, to the valley of the Saskatchewan.

Some parts of this plateau are indented with valleys, or broken by low ranges of hills, some are wooded densely or lightly, and others are covered with the richest grass. Turn up the soil and almost everywhere you find it rich with promise of the most bountiful returns for any that will till it. Follow the course of the broad Peace River as it winds in long sweeping curves through this vast fertile country, and though you find its sides, now grooved by land-slips or carved and rolled into terraces, now covered with trees or grassy as a lawn, yet, above and beyond all the windings of the river and the varied contour of its banks, stretches the prairie in miles of superior soil, vast, rich and silent, traversed only by the few Indians that disturb the solitude. Records of the climate kept at Fort St. John shew that the first snow-fall usually occurs towards the end of October; the average date for the first appearance of ice on the river is about the 7th November, and for the opening of the river about the 20th April, while planting begins early in May, and potato digging about the third week in September. The average depth of snow does not exceed two and a half to three feet; and here, as throughout the district, the horses winter out, finding abundant grass on the neighbouring slopes and plateaux. Major Butler states that when he passed here he encountered the first mosquito of the year on the 20th April, an incident that to many in Ontario may be expressive of the early opening of the season.

We left Fort St. John at noon on the 30th July. Five miles below the Fort we passed the mouth of Pine River which flows in from the south, a river that has become well-known to many, at least by name, in connection with one of the proposed routes of the Canadian Pacific Railway, as the valley of the Pine River offers perhaps the easiest and most practicable Pass through the Rocky

Mountains. Were it desirable to select a Pacific terminus for our trans-continental road as far north as Port Simpson, there would be no serious engineering difficulties in constructing a line from the prairie region, by way of Pine River Pass and the neighbourhood of Babine, down the valley of the Skeena to the coast. Below the mouth of the Pine the Peace is dotted with numerous islands, which have apparently been produced by land slides or by alluvial deposits washed down by the current, as they show evidence of good soil similar to that on the flats along the river banks.

Later in the afternoon we passed the mouth of North Pine River, which joins the Peace about ten miles below the mouth of the stream of the same name that flows in from the south. Here stood the old Fort St. John which was in 1823 the scene of a horrible massacre. Hughes, the only white man then at the fort, had in some way aroused the anger of an Indian, who, entering the store soon after with some companions, threatened to take his life, and before any defence was possible shot him dead. At the time a party of H. B. Company voyageurs were coming down the river from Hudson's Hope, and were approaching the Fort immediately after the murder, when an old woman shouted to them to keep away, as the Indians had already killed the agent. Either not understanding or not believing her they landed, but as they did so the whole crew, four in number, were shot.

Shortly after another crew coming down the river towards the Fort, were hailed and warned by the old Indian woman. The interpreter, Charlette Lafleur, who was in the canoe, believing the woman's story, told the rest of the crew, and they at once took the other side of the river and passed down to Dunvegan. A few days later a solitary Indian, who is still living at Fort Vermilion, was coming down the river with letters from Hudson's Hope. Landing at Fort St. John, he found the place utterly abandoned, except by dogs that held carnival over the unburied remains of the dead. As soon as word was brought to Dunvegan Mr. McLeod, the agent then in charge, sent men in pursuit of the murderers, but the whole band, who were not Beaver Indians but Sicanies, had vanished, some crossing the Rocky Mountains, others fleeing in the direction of the Lower Mackenzie, all escaping beyond capture. Even the Beaver Indians fled for a time from the country, so that the whole district was abandoned. Dunvegan had to be deserted, as there were no longer any to trade with. Subsequently the Beavers returned to their old hunting grounds, and asked the Company to re-open their post at Dunvegan, which they did in 1828; but forty years passed before a station was re-opened in the neighbourhood of old Fort St. John, and then it was not at the scene of the massacre, but at a spot above it on the opposite side of the river, from which it was afterwards removed to the present site.

Our life on the raft was varied by the excitement of looking for bears along the grassy slopes of the north bank, as there is here a great profusion of saskatum, or service-berry bushes, and the bears, being exceedingly fond of these berries, come out upon the high sloping banks to enjoy them. Sometimes we saw ten or twelve in a day, although in almost every instance they were beyond range of our rifles, and we could not spare time for hunting. The day after we left Fort St. John, however, we saw one so near that McLeod, Major and I were induced to go ashore for a chase. Snubbing the raft to a tree, up we went through the thicket and along the flat, and then over the low grassy hills, one of the young Indians leading at a rapid pace. We had tried to arrange a plan of action so that the rifles would be stationed to the best advantage before we closed in upon our game, but Peter the Indian was so eager that he simply gave chase like a sleuth-hound, while we three followed to the best of our ability, hurrying to such points as we thought the bear might probably pass if escaping the nearest rifle. We soon heard the crack of the Indian's gun, and saw a huge black bear rolling heels over head down the hill in a direct line for Major, who fired at him, and then stepped quickly and gracefully aside to give him the road, thinking that he must be already in the throes of death. None of us, except the Indian who could not speak English, knew that a bear, in hurrying down hill, frequently prefers to roll heels over head, as he makes more speed in this way than by running, his fore legs being so much shorter than his hind legs. What was Major's surprise to find that the bear, after rolling to the foot of the hill, instead of resting in eternal stillness hurried off into the bushes. We gave chase, tracking him, as best we could, by the blood which stained the grass and bushes, but we frequently got off the scent for a time and so made slow progress. We had a dog, the property of our foreman, McNeill, but whistle and call alike failed to wile him from the provision stores on the raft, so, after following the blood-stained trail for about a mile, we gave up the chase, and returned to the raft, finding the remaining members of the party in a state of eager expectation, which was soon changed into bitter disappointment as our failure dispelled the vision of bear-steak that had risen before their minds. In the afternoon of the same day we had another bear hunt; this time it was a grizzly. We thought we had him as an easy prey, for he was swimming across the river, and though at some distance above us seemed to be carried towards us by the current; but the same current was hurrying us on also, and a raft is rather unwieldy in a strong stream. Bang! bang! went rifle and shot gun, but, though a shower of lead fell around him, he seemed to have a charmed life, or something was seriously wrong with our rifles,—we shall not say with our riflemen. In the evening around the camp-fire there was a general feeling of self-condemnation that we had to make our supper off the old stand-by of bacon and beans, instead of having a toothsome slice of fresh bear.

Several times in our course down the river, when we ascended the plateau, we were unable, on account of the clumps of wood, to obtain any very extensive view. The trail by which Messrs. Macoun and Horetzky travelled, in 1872, runs below Fort St. John, on the south side of the Peace. Of the country along the southern bank, at a little distance from the rough and thickly wooded part that borders the river between Dunvegan and Fort St. John, Mr. Horetzky writes:—" The whole country passed over
" during these few days was varied in appearance, the trail
" passing through wood and prairie, principally the
" former, and for the last two days through a rough coun-
" try covered with dense forest. A good many large
" creeks were crossed, and they invariably flowed through
" deep depressions cut out by themselves, to a depth of
" three and four hundred feet where we passed over them.
" Some very beautiful prairie land was also seen, but we
" always kept to the north of La Grande Prairie, which
" unfortunately we had not time to visit. Still the
" favourable appearance of the country we had passed
" through argued greatly in favour of the more southern
" section about which we had heard so much."*

---

* Canada on the Pacific: p 47.

Gently but steadily we were swept onward towards Dunvegan, the central H. B. Company's post of the Peace River district, reaching it on the 1st August. Since leaving Fort St. James, at Stewart's Lake (the central depôt of New Caledonia), this was the point towards which our thoughts were turned, for here we would rendezvous for a short time, here would begin for some of us the homeward journey, and here, though still more than twelve hundred miles from Winnipeg, we would at least seem to be nearing home.

The name Dunvegan recalled a scene very different from any to be met with on the banks of the Peace. Far away on the north coast of Skye, on a rocky steep washed by the wild Atlantic, stands Dunvegan the Castle of McLeod. To the west can be seen the lonely Island of Lewis, but for the rest that western view is one of sea and sky,—the ocean in calm and in storm,—the sky in dull grey or deep blue, its clouds torn and broken in the tempest or resting motionless in purple and gold near the setting sun. To the south rise the grim hills of Coolin; to the east the mountains of the main land. From that country of beauty and romance, of wild scenery, weird legend and thrilling memories, came one of the McLeods, many years ago, with fond recollections of his northern home, and, as he planted this fur-trading post in the distant west, he named it after the chief castle of his clan.

How fondly and frequently the thoughts of the Scottish Highlander turn to the home of his childhood. He recalls the outline of each hill as if it were some dear familiar face; he sees the well-known loch, now mirroring the sky, and now whipped into foam by a squall from some neighbouring glen; he treads again, as in boyhood, the winding path to the church, joins in the service with lowly and simple worshippers, and lingers in the kirk-yard where the dust of his fathers is laid. He may pass from that early home through the impulse, it may be, of an honourable ambition, or perhaps forced through the selfishness of the lords of the soil. Let him revisit the land of his fathers, he may find many of the glens now silent save for the bleating of the sheep, the old church perhaps closed for very lack of worshippers, monuments in the kirk-yard to the memory of those who have now no living representative in the land that once knew them, while in some little church-yard in Glengarry or Pictou, or other parts of Canada that were settled by Scottish Highlanders, may be found tombstones bearing the same names, and, close by, the living heirs of the men that once peopled those Highland glens. Yet meet him where you may you will find that, so long at least as he is true to the habits and the memories of his early years, the Highlander is strong in courage and fidelity, strong in self-reliance and in simplicity of life, and, as a tender tribute to the memory of the old land, he transfers at least the names of her lochs and hills and castles to the land of his adoption.

Very unlike the original Dunvegan is this H. B. Company's post that bears that Highland name. It stands on a broad low flat in a large bend, on the northern bank of the river, some thirty feet above the water level. Behind it rises an abrupt ridge, broken by grassy slopes and knolls, and leading to the rich pasture land of the plateau that spreads its vast expanse eight hundred feet above the fort. A new residence has recently been built, and a new store is in course of completion, but with these exceptions the buildings have a neglected, outworn look, as if in the prospect of the new the old had not been protected against decay.

At the time of our visit the Indians from the surrounding country had gathered near Dunvegan, to collect service-berries for spicing their moose pemmican, and to procure supplies for their autumn hunt. As they came in on the Sabbath morning to the Roman Catholic mission in the neighbourhood of the Fort, they inspected us and our tents with the liveliest curiosity, many of them lingering around the fire where the cook was at work in evident anticipation of some show of hospitality on our part. They presented every variety of Indian dress and fashion, except the war paint; some wore the old Hudson s Bay capôte of navy-blue cloth with brass buttons; some wore skin coats richly tasselated; others were gorgeous in embroidered leggings, or in hats trimmed with feathers and gay ribbons; while the women were dressed simply in tartans, bright patterns being evidently preferred, as if Scottish taste prevailed in the selection of imported goods as well as in the naming of the forts. And Scottish influence does largely prevail,—for almost every H. B. Company's agent from Dunvegan to the mouth of the Mackenzie is a Scotchman by birth or by descent, and it is a common saying there, as in other parts of the North-West, that the success of the Hudson's Bay Company is due to Scotchmen and shaganappi.

One of these Indians, Moostoos by name, was worth seeing, for he had passed through the rare experience of fighting a grizzly bear and living to tell it. The black bear is a common enough foe for these men to face, but few men survive a hand-to-hand encounter with a grizzly. Moostoos had come unexpectedly upon one that he found gorging himself on the remains of a black bear, and the grizzly at once turned on him. The Indian kept his ground, and as the bear rose on his hind legs to attack him he aimed at his breast, drew the trigger, but the old flint-lock missed fire. Immediately the grizzly sprang forward, and as he did so the Indian drew his knife, but with one blow the bear struck it from him and then felled him to the ground utterly defenceless. His only possible chance now was to feign death, for many a wild animal, if not hungry, will leave a man as soon as he seems to be dead. With tooth and claw the bear tore his flesh, at one stroke taking away his scalp, carrying the right ear with it, at another stripping a large piece from his shoulder, at another rending a piece from his side. Through all this torture poor Moostoos remained conscious, but was motionless as a corpse till the grizzly, apparently thinking that he was dead, moved off, and then the lacerated man dragged himself to the camp. He has never wholly recovered, though it is four years since this happened, but he still hunts with much energy and success. It is hardly possible for him, however, to go nearer to the jaws of death without finding them close on him for ever than he did in his fight with the grizzly.

There is a Roman Catholic Mission near Dunvegan conducted by Pére Tessier, one of the Oblate Fathers, who was sufficiently liberal in spirit to join with us in our service on the evening of the Sunday that we spent here.* The Pére told us that he had observed some improvement among the Indians of later years, which he ascribes to the influence of the Mission, especially in their increasing regard for the marriage tie, and their

---

* The form of service used by us, on this as on almost every other Sunday was one of those which, prepared by three clergymen of the Anglican, Roman Catholic and Presbyterian Churches, have been published under the title of *Short Sunday Services for Travellers*, by Dawson Brothers, Montreal.

carefulness in observing the Sabbath—things not only good in themselves, but probable indications of improvement in other respects. It used to be common enough for husband and wife to desert each other according to the attractions offered by some third party, as well as for the husband to take to his wigwam more than one wife, his practice of polygamy depending chiefly upon the amount of his worldly property and on his ability to keep his lodge supplied with game. Gradually however they are improving in this respect, as they are also in keeping the Sabbath. As yet their chief way of observing it is by abstaining from travelling or hunting, though sometimes, like their better educated white brethren, they try to bring conscience and desire into harmony by starting on a journey on Saturday and pleading the necessity of continuing it on Sunday. Yet some of them regard this, as one of themselves expressed it, as "trying to dodge the devil around the stump."

Mission work, however, must make very slow progress among them, if for no other reason, on account of their wandering life, as they are hunting during a great portion of the year, and while hunting they are generally separated, or banded perhaps in groups of not more than two or three families. There is thus little or no opportunity of educating their children, or of acquainting either old or young with more than the outward forms and requirements of Christianity. Several missions are maintained in this remote part of the North-West by the Oblate Fathers, the only Protestant missions throughout the district being those of the Church of England under the direction of Bishop Bompus, the Bishop of Athabasca, whose head-quarters are at Fort Chipewyan. In addition to the bishop there are four clergymen scattered throughout this vast diocese, one at Vermilion, two on the Mackenzie, and one on the Yucon. They labour unweariedly among their widely scattered flocks, the bishop himself, as well as the others, very frequently visiting the Indians on their hunting expeditions. They have to face many discouragements, not only from the difficulties of travel but from the slow and small results that they can witness from their labours, as the wandering life of the people precludes anything like the success that has attended some of the missions to the Indians of British Columbia, notably that established by Mr. Duncan at Metlahkatlah. Efforts are being made to secure the education of the children, and if possible to induce some of the Indians to cultivate the soil, but where game is so abundant it cannot be expected that the Indians will take to farming for many years to come.

CHAPTER VIII.

PEACE RIVER COUNTRY.

Province of Unchagah.—Outfits of exploring parties.—Old journals at Dunvegan.—Records of climate.—Beaver Indians.—Cree music.—Expedition to Battle River.—Character of country.—Bear-hunting.—Size and character of Peace River Country.—The climate.—Danger of summer frosts.—Increased sunlight.—Temperature.—Coal-beds.—Facilities of communication.

The Peace River country, which is destined to become an important province,—the Province of Unchagah, let us call it,—may be said, so far as agricultural resources are concerned, to begin near Hudson's Hope. West of that the areas of fertile land are confined to the river flats and to some restricted benches, and even for some distance eastward till you approach Fort St. John the arable land is very limited. From Fort St. John it stretches southward and south-eastward along the foothills of the Rocky Mountains to the banks of the Athabasca, eastward to Lesser Slave Lake and the hilly country that lies between it and the Athabasca River, north-eastward as far as Lake Athabasca. The great river that unwaters it and that gives it its name, entering this fertile tract at the Cañon, flows for nearly two hundred and fifty miles in an easterly course, till fifty miles below Dunvegan, after receiving from the south-west its chief tributary, the Smoky River, it turns suddenly northward. Then, after flowing in many curves and with gentle current for about three hundred miles it bends again, near Fort Vermilion, to continue its winding course eastward for two hundred miles more till it meets the waters that empty Lake Athabasca. Here it drops the name that it has borne from its entrance into the Rocky Mountains, to be known as the Slave, and lower down as the Mackenzie, as it rolls towards the Northern Sea.

We spent the month of August in this district of the great Unchagah, traversing the lower portion of it in different directions, our explorations extending northward seventy miles from Dunvegan, eastward as far as Lesser Slave Lake, and, including some subsequent examinations made by Messrs. Dawson and McLeod, southward to the banks of the Athabasca.

Dunvegan was our head-quarters, and though we deeply regretted the absence of the factor, Mr. Macdougall, we were greatly assisted by his clerk, Mr. Kennedy, in making all necessary arrangements. Of course we were dependent on " the Company " for the supply of horses, as the mule-train from Pine River could not reach Dunvegan before the middle of August; and we were also dependent upon their agent to secure some Indian guides. The horses, however, were running wild upon the plateau, and the "horse-guards" moved slowly in search of them, so that we could only procure enough to carry tents, provisions, etc., for two small exploring parties. Even after the horses had been secured, pack saddles required repairs, large supplies of shaganappi had to be provided, and a number of *etceteras* collected, as varied as the outfit of a small family on a holiday trip to the seaside. When other arrangements had been completed there would invariably be some delay in concluding terms with the Indian guides. The Indian is never in a hurry, except when running down game. In the ordinary concerns of life he endorses the saying that "hours were made for slaves;" as for himself, being a freeman, he can take time in large allowance and deal with it liberally. Try to secure him as your guide, and up to the last moment he will hesitate, like a gun that hangs fire. However attractive your offer may be, and however much he may really desire to go with you, an Indian will seldom show any anxiety to accept your offer, especially if he thinks that you are at all eager to engage him. He may be wooed; but he will not be deprived of his rights of courtship. Even after he begins to yield, having determined from the first to go, he will picture all sorts of difficulties, either by way of testing your courage and determination or by way of showing his own extraordinary self-denial. And after all is arranged, and you have stipulated how many skins' worth of goods he will get for his services, he will loiter around the camp, and until he sees you active and in earnest he will not bridle a horse; but when he is fairly started, though often lazy he is always trustworthy.

Messrs. Cambie and McLeod having secured the necessary conveyance and outfit, started on exploring trips in different directions through the southern country. I was anxious to go north as far as Battle River, but could not for lack of horses. During this enforced delay, I had the opportunity of examining the old journals of Dunvegan, and of growing somewhat familiar with life at an H. B. Company's Fort. The oldest of these records is of date 11th May, 1828, when the post was re-opened after it had been abandoned for five years on account of the massacre at Fort St. John. The entries of that date tell that the buildings were found in a very dilapidated condition,—that numerous tracks of buffalo, moose, etc., were noticed all around the Fort,—and add, " the men " commenced to get a plough and harrow ready to sow " and plant wheat, barley and potatoes, having brought " up a quarter keg wheat, one keg barley and ten kegs " potatoes." A little later, there is the following reference to the visit of Sir George Simpson, who passed Dunvegan on his tour to the Pacific :—" *Wednesday*, 27*th* " *August*, 1828. In the afternoon was agreeably surprised " by the arrival of two canoes, being Governor Simpson,

" and suite, consisting of the following members—
" namely—A. Macdonald, (Chief Factor), Dr. Hamelyn,
" William McGillivray, clerk, and nineteen men, two
" women and one child. They are on their way, around
" by New Caledonia, to Columbia. *Thursday 28th August.*
" Busy making up pemmican, etc., for the strangers. The
" Governor had some conversation with the Indians, and
" his speech to them was much to the purpose. The
" sounding of the bugle, the piper dressed in Highland
" dress playing the bag-pipes, and every appearance,
" made the Indians stare and wonder."

Judging by these old records, life at Dunvegan has not been very exciting for the past fifty years. There are horses to be sent in one direction or another, hunters to be fitted out for a fresh start, repairs and improvements to be made about the establishment, occasional fresh arrivals of Indians requiring attention, the crops or the garden in need of care, inventories to be made of goods received or despatched, parcels to be forwarded when occasion offers, trips to be made in different directions, on foot, on horseback, in canoe, or with dog-train, according to the country to be traversed and the season of the year. Matters of this kind seem trivial enough to the readers of newspapers, but they are the subjects around which, for the most part, the thoughts and actions of the white man in this northern land have centred ever since white men were seen here.

Sometimes the entries in these old journals indicate the extreme loneliness of the situation. The entry for December 15th, 1874, is: "What a glorious country for "a convict settlement; the last news from the civilized "world was in the beginning of June"; while that of April 11th, 1878, is: "Cry of starvation all over the country." Indeed, the want of food seems to prevail among the Indians more or less every spring, as at that season the hunters have often very little success. On the fly-leaf of one or more of the journals, as in those of many other H. B. C. posts, may be found the familiar verse, attributed to Alexander Selkirk, calling in question the charms of solitude.

Sometimes these records convey important information about the climate. They show, for instance, that, for the past six years, the average date for the departure of ice from the river opposite Dunvegan has been the 18th April; a fact worthy of note in regard to the Peace River, in any comparison of this district with Ontario, since April 30th was, from 1832 to 1870, the average date for the opening of the Ottawa River at Ottawa. While ice usually begins to form at Fort St. John about the 7th November, the river does not close opposite Dunvegan until the first week in December. Potatoes are usually planted here about the 4th May, and are gathered about the 23rd September, the yield being sometimes in the proportion of forty to one, twenty-five kegs having yielded one thousand kegs in a field adjoining Dunvegan.

The Beaver Indians are lords of the soil throughout the district from Hudson's Hope to Vermilion, where the territory of the Chipewyans begins; but they have intermarried of late years with some Crees who came here from the Saskatchewan to escape the ravages of small-pox in 1870, and with some Iroquois who formerly lived near Jasper House, where a number of them had settled in the old days of the North-West Company. They are not a strong tribe, probably not more than five hundred in all, including the hundred and fifty Crees and Iroquois that are now united with them. With the exception of a small Cree settlement at Sturgeon Lake, none of them engage in farming; their only occupation is hunting, and, while indolent at every thing else, they hunt with the energy and determination of weasels.

The Beavers appear to be mentally inferior to the Crees, and many of them become the ready dupes of the Cree medicine-men. One of them, for instance, named Alec, who lives near Dunvegan, has been for some years unwell. His sickness was originally caused by a fall, but he persists in attributing it to an Indian at Lesser Slave Lake who has, he imagines, cast a charm over him, and who sends invisible pieces of bone, wood and iron through the air, that enter his body and produce racking pains. Though Alec is nominally a member of Père

Tessier's flock, yet he puts himself into the hands of the Cree medicine-men. They go through certain incantations and then profess to extract from his arm, chest, or shoulders some pieces of wood, bone, or iron, and the enraptured Alec, seeing his own views confirmed, and imagining himself greatly improved, becomes more completely than ever the victim of the medicine-man's imposture.

As yet no treaty has been made with the Indians of this district as has been done with the tribes on our southern prairies, so that the Government are not in a position to offer for settlement any of the country north of the Athabasca, that being the present boundary, in this direction, of the territory embraced by the Indian treaties. The natives, however, would offer no opposition to any settlers, as they are of a harmless and very friendly disposition; but they may possibly ere long be impressed with a sense of their own importance by being called to conclude a treaty with the Government. Yet even if reserves were set apart for them and provision made for their instruction in farming, it can hardly be expected that as large a proportion of them as of the Crees, Blackfeet, Saulteaux, and others will cultivate the soil, or adopt the habits of the whites, as their country is still plentifully supplied with large game. It is the gradual extinction of the buffalo that is forcing the Indians of the southern prairies to take to farming.

One evening while delayed at Dunvegan I had a specimen of Indian music from Chantrè, the chief Cree singer and drummer of the district. His song, if such it could be called, was a wild dirge-like chant, with no rhythm nor any perceptible air. His performance on the drum, which he kept beating with a small stick, seemed to have no connection whatever with the song except to add to the volume of sound, the drum being a rude form of tambourine. The effect was as confusing as that produced upon the uninitiated in listening to selections from Wagner's *Lohengrin*. In lack of melody, if in no other respect, the Indian music of the past agrees with the German music of the future.

On the afternoon of the 16th August, the party from Pine River under the direction of Dr. G. M. Dawson, accompanied by the mule train, arrived opposite the Fort. We had left them on the banks of the Parsnip, at the mouth of the Misinchinca, on the 19th July, and they had been travelling as steadily as possible since that date, coming up the valley of the Misinchinca and down the valley of Pine River until they reached the prairie country, across which they travelled to Dunvegan. By the arrival of the mule train with saddle-horses and pack-mules we were enabled to make our projected trip northwards. On the following Monday, Mr. McConnell, (Dr. Dawson's assistant) and I started for Battle River, accompanied by Chamois, the packer, Nato, an Indian guide, and Tom, a half-breed cook and interpreter, while Dr. Dawson started on an exploring expedition across La Grande Prairie, to return by way of Elk and Smoky Rivers. We took the trail leading almost due north from Dunvegan, over the plateau that stretches its broad expanse about 800 feet above the level of the river. For about forty miles we traversed open prairie that was dotted by occasional clumps of aspen, and that was covered with luxuriant grass and with a great abundance and variety of wild flowers. The soil is uniformly a dark loam of the richest character, and the abundant pasture is cropped only by the horses, belonging to the Company, the priest and the Indians, that roam unfettered over it summer and winter. There are no badger-holes here, as there are on the prairies of the Saskatchewan, making small pit-falls for the horse; we could ride at full gallop, without fear of a cropper, in any direction that the willow and poplar groves would allow, sometimes over several miles of unbroken open prairie.

Occasionally we passed lakelets that abound with duck, but these are left almost entirely undisturbed, for such small game is unworthy of an Indian's regard. The large mallards, however, with the prairie chicken which are very numerous through this part of the country, formed a welcome variation from the orthodox bacon and beans.

Forty miles north of Dunvegan we crossed a ridge

that rises about 550 feet above the plateau, closely wooded with poplar and spruce. This ridge, or low range of hills, runs westward as far as Hudson's Hope, where it comes within about twenty miles of the Peace, and in some parts it rises to a height of 1200 feet. Beyond this, after traversing about a mile of mossy swamp, we came upon a country as rich and fertile as that which lay south of the ridge. In some parts it is closely timbered with poplar, cottonwood, and occasional black pine, but the soil is almost uniformly excellent even as far as Battle River, one part of it known as White Mud Prairie being particularly attractive. Between this ridge and Battle River we had fourteen degrees of frost on the night of the 20th August: we found afterwards that there had been a very widespread frost that night throughout the Peace River Country, but it was more severe in this northern portion than on the prairies to the south of Dunvegan.

Nato, our guide, was a fair specimen of the Beaver Indian,—lazy and indolent except when engaged in eating or in hunting, the two occupations that called forth his energy. Every day gave us opportunities of witnessing his vigour at table, or rather at meal-time, for it is needless to say that there was no table; and one afternoon we had a special opportunity of seeing his enthusiasm in hunting. We were about to pitch camp when we saw three bears at some little distance. As a considerable stream lay between us and them we hesitated about giving chase, whereupon Nato flung himself on the ground in passionate disgust, as if life had been robbed of every attraction. I offered him my rifle; with a sudden outburst of energy he sprang up, snatched it eagerly, and started in pursuit like a blood-hound, running for a few minutes at a speed which his former laziness would have led us to think was utterly impossible for him. He was soon close to his game, and within half an hour he returned to camp, having succeeded in killing two of the three. That night he revelled over a supper of bear's meat, and having gorged himself apparently to the limits of safety, he roasted two of the paws as a special tit-bit; then he stretched himself before the camp-fire thoroughly sated, and next day he relapsed into his natural laziness.

Among the various theories that have been proposed to account for the original settlement of Indians in this country, it is a wonder that none have argued for their origin from some son of Nimrod, or other mighty hunter, who may be supposed to have followed game across Asia, and around by an easterly course to our North-West. Hunting is the one work in which, apparently, the white man cannot excel them. With a keenness of the senses, in a great degree inherited and largely sharpened by necessity, they lay their grasp on all kinds of game, so that the strength or the cunning, the speed, vision, or hearing of moose, bear, or beaver fail as a defence against them. Sometimes they may have days or weeks of hunger, and their life, as a whole, is far more toilsome than what would be required of a farmer in this fertile country. But their wild, wandering habits, their intense love of the chase, their sense of power and of conquest in bringing down their game, their manner of life developed and confirmed through long generations, render it extremely difficult for the hunting tribes of Indians to take up the occupations of civilised communities. In this remoter land, where such game as moose, bear, and beaver are still very abundant, many years may elapse before necessity compels them to adopt more settled habits; yet in course of time the herds of moose must meet the same fate of gradual extinction as has already overtaken the herds of buffalo on our southern prairies; and it would be well for the Indians of the Peace if, ere that day comes upon them, they could be induced to take to farming as some of the Indians of other tribes are already doing.

On our way north we passed a number of Indians who had started from Dunvegan a short time before us with a band of horses that they were driving to Vermilion for the H. B. Company. Their families accompanied them, and, as they required to hunt for their living, and as most of them journeyed on foot, their progress was slow. The men hunted and looked after the horses, the women did all the work of pitching camp, gathering wood, cooking, etc., each child that was old enough to walk being required to help about the camp, while even the hungry, cadaverous dogs were compelled to render unwilling assistance in the way of carrying packs. They took little provision with them except tea, and their baggage consisted chiefly of the skins that formed their tepees, the forest always furnishing them with lodge-poles. Sometimes the hunters ride, but the women and children are compelled to walk, for wife, horse and dog share much the same treatment at the hands of the red man.

Battle River, which is about seventy miles north of Dunvegan, is a beautiful stream, twenty yards in width, with an average depth of about two feet, the water being very clear, of a slightly brown or amber hue, very different in appearance from the turbid streams that flow from the Rocky Mountains, and probably fed from the low range of hills that lie between it and Dunvegan. The scenery along the river is very pleasing; the banks for the most part slope gently, though sometimes there is a precipitous side, exposing a rich loamy soil on a bed of sand or clay. We rode for some distance along the trail that skirts the northern bank of the river, and found the soil and foliage very much the same as that on the southern side; and although in the river-bed there are many pieces of limestone, yet we saw no rock along either bank. Indeed from Dunvegan to Battle River we scarcely saw a solitary stone, and, so far as we could judge, the same is the case with the country lying immediately to the north of this, a country that, from all we could learn, has not yet been traversed by white men. The whole tract over which we travelled is well-watered, and has abundance of good pasture, so that we had no difficulty in finding good camping ground each evening. Whatever may be its value for the growth of cereals, it is already evident that it possesses very great advantages for stock-raising.

We returned to Dunvegan on Thursday, 28th August. Between that date and Monday, 1st September, the other members of our party had completed their exploratory trips east, west and south; we therefore met to compare notes and to form some estimate of the country that we had been traversing.* This southern portion of the Peace River District, to which our attention had been confined, embraced from north to south between Battle River and the Athabasca, covers an area of not less than 30,000 square miles, a territory about the size of Scotland. With few exceptions the country is one of extraordinary fertility, a large part being open prairie covered with luxuriant grass, while other portions are wooded more or less densely. It is well-watered, some of the streams, such as Smoky River and its chief affluents, being rivers

---

*In this description of the country I take the liberty of drawing freely upon the reports presented by my fellow-travellers, which are published in the Report of the Engineer-in-Chief of the Canadian Pacific Railway for 1880.

of considerable size. All its waters flow into the Peace, except a few small tributaries of the Athabasca that drain the southern portion of the district. These rivers are, at their upper waters, near the prairie level, but their channels constantly increase in depth till they reach the level of the main river. Their valleys are frequently wooded, sometimes with patches of the original forest, but usually with second-growth timber such as is commonly found on the prairie. Although much of the prairie is now open, it must all at one time have been densely forest-clad. Some of our southern prairies appear to have been always treeless, if we may judge by the absence of all remains of forest or of drift-wood in their alluvial soil; but it has evidently been otherwise with the prairies of the Peace River Country; these must all have been wooded at one time, and they have, no doubt, been cleared by fire. Although at present the woodlands may be less attractive to the farmer than the open prairie, yet, where the soil is fertile they must ultimately be as valuable as those parts that are now ready for the plough.

Along the southern borders of the district near the Athabasca, is found the largest tract of poor land which it contains. Here the country, which is for the most part closely wooded, is elevated considerably above the adjoining prairie, and is ridgy and sandy, with occasional patches of swamp. Along part of the eastern borders, also, there are mossy swamps that render much of the land unfit for agriculture, while, between Smoky River and Lesser Slave Lake much of the country is at present covered by swamps and beaver-dams, though parts of it might ultimately be converted into good farm-land.

Making ample allowance, however, for the inferior and useless land we may with confidence estimate three-fourths of this southern portion of the Peace River Country, or about 23,000 square miles, to be well suited to agriculture, while many sections of it possess exceptional fertility.

But there are also large tracts of fertile land to the north of that which we traversed, areas that, being unwatered by the **Peace, may be properly** included in our so-called Province of **Unchagah.** Those familiar with that northern portion assured us that from the confluence of the **Peace** and Smoky Rivers, as far as Lake Athabasca, there is a belt of fertile soil bordering the **river for a** width varying from fifteen to fifty miles. East of the Peace, however, though drained by its tributaries, and lying between **Lesser Slave Lake** and Lake Athabasca there is an area of about 25,000 square miles that is broken by hills, lakes, streams, and marshes, which render it unfit for farming. This is the best hunting-ground for beaver known to the H. B. Company, 8000 beaver-skins having been received in one year from this district at the single post of **Lesser Slave Lake.**

In 1875 Professor Macoun passed down the river from Dunvegan to Fort Chipewyan, the "capital of the north," on Lake Athabasca. On that occasion he had opportunities of seeing some of the northern portions of the country, and wherever he examined the soil he found it excellent, and in some places astonishingly rich. Of the country near Vermilion he says: "The whole country around this post is a plain not elevated at its highest point more than one hundred feet above the river, but the greater portion of it is less than fifty feet. From the highest point I reached, the view across the river extended to the Cariboo Mountains, distant about forty miles. The intervening country seemed to be perfectly level or else to slope gradually upwards towards the mountains. The soil examined is of the very best description."* When somewhat more than half-way between Vermilion and Chipewyan he spent a day at the H. B. Company's post at Red River, regarding which he writes: "The vegetation indicated that Red River was even warmer than Vermilion, and all garden vegetables are much more advanced."† Of this northern portion of the district we may safely estimate an area of from 20,000 to 25,000 square miles to be fertile, possibly a much larger area; so that within the District of Un-

---

* Report of Progress of Geological Survey of Canada for 1875-76, pp. 159, 160.

† Report Geol. Survey 1875-76, p. 161.

chagah,—exclusive of its great beaver-ground,—we may confidently expect to find fertile territory almost equal in extent to the united area of England and Wales.

But what about the climate, for fertile soil is of little use without favourable climate? Will it admit of the cultivation of wheat throughout this large district, for this is the crucial test now applied to climate in our North-West Territories? Let us gather up some of the facts that may enable us to answer this question, at least to give such a partial answer as our limited data will allow.

So far as actual experiment is concerned wheat has not been cultivated on the prairie level,—that is, on the general level of the country exclusive of the river valleys,—except at Lesser Slave Lake, where it thrives admirably. All other attempts at wheat culture throughout the district have been on the flats that fringe the river, which at Dunvegan is about 800 feet lower than the plateau; but this difference of level between prairie and river decreases further down the stream till at Vermilion it is not more than from fifty to a hundred feet. Should this difference of altitude lead us to expect a less favourable climate on the prairie than has been found on the river-flats? Probably not. Professor Macoun, speaking of the vicinity of Fort St. John, says: " Notwithstanding the difference of altitude the berries " on the plateau ripened only a week later than those

" near the river, and Nigger Dan stated that there was
" about the same difference in the time the snow disap-
" peared in the spring on the plateau and in the valley."*
In October, 1872, Mr. Horetzky when traversing the
prairie south of Dunvegan, found that, " curiously
" enough, the vegetation upon these uplands did not
" appear to have suffered so much from the effects of
" frost, this being probably due to the fact of the air in
" these upper regions being constantly in motion, while
" in the deep and capacious valley of the river the winds
" have often no effect."† Dr. Dawson, writes‡ " In my
" diary, under date September 5th, I find the following
" entry:—Aspens and berry bushes about the Peace
" River Valley now looking quite autumnal. On the
" plateau 800 or 900 feet higher, not nearly so much so.
" Slight tinge of yellow only on some aspen groves."
And again, " We found some rude attempt at cultivation
" also at the ' Cree Settlement,' which consists of a few
" loghouses built by Indians on the border of Sturgeon
" Lake, about seventy miles south-west of the west end
" of Lesser Slave Lake, and is at the average level of the
" country, with an elevation of about 2,100 feet. Here,
" on September 14th, the potato plants were slightly
" affected by frost, but not more so than observed with

---

* Report of Geol. Survey, 1875-76, p : 155.
† *Canada on the Pacific*, p. 44.
‡ Report of Engineer-in-chief of C. P. Railway, 1880, pp. : 116, 117.

"those at Dunvegan two weeks before." At Dunvegan I was informed that although the growth in early summer is usually more advanced in the valley than on the plateau, yet, as the moisture lingers longer on the upper level, the growth there seems to make more steady progress when it has once begun, while very little difference has been observed between the upper and lower levels, in regard to the time of the ripening, fading, and falling of the leaves. We may, therefore, regard the climate of the prairies as probably not less favourable than that of the river-flats.

Now the ordinary experience at such places as Hudson's Hope, Fort St. John and Dunvegan is that wheat thrives well. The season is long enough and warm enough, the only danger being from summer frosts. When Messrs. Selwyn and Macoun visited Peace River in 1875, they had no frost until September, and were assured that frost rarely occurs in July or August. At Vermilion on the 12th August, Mr. Macoun found barley standing in shocks in the field, which had been sown on the 8th May, and reaped on the 6th August, having been in the ground just ninety days, while he found some ears of wheat fully ripe at the date of his visit, and was assured that often a whole season passes without any frost occurring from early in May until late in October. In less than a day he observed 151 species of plants which seemed to him to show conclusively that the climate at Vermilion was much warmer than at Dunvegan. Between Hudson's Hope and Fort Chipewyan he collected 591 species of flowering plants and ferns of which 434 are found on the western plains, 411 in Ontario and 402 in Quebec, from which he concludes that the temperature of the growing season throughout this district is much like that of the southern prairies and of central Ontario.*

Our own experience, however, was not quite so favourable. Each of our small parties had frost on several occasions in August, at places widely separated, and although on some of these it may have been local, on others, especially on the 20th the frost was widespread. There was sufficient frost at Dunvegan on the 20th and 25th to injure beans and cucumbers, and although some of the wheat had ripened before the 20th August, the frost of that night affected the rest to such an extent that on our return on the 28th it did not appear to be any farther advanced than it had been a fortnight previously. It was similar with the wheat at the Mission, adjoining Dunvegan, and with a small patch at Hudson's Hope: in both instances it was hopelessly injured by the frost. This injury, however, had been sustained after some of the wheat at Dunvegan had fully ripened; and it is not improbable that if more attention had been paid to the selection of seed and to the time of sowing, all injury

---

* Report Geol. Survey 1875-76, pp.: 159, 167.

and loss by frost might have been avoided. Besides, it may be remembered that the summer of 1879 was a somewhat exceptional one, the weather of the early months being cold and wet throughout much of the North-West.

Returning home by way of Edmonton I found that there had been no frost there during August, that the wheat had ripened to perfection and that a large crop had been harvested. So far, then, as present information extends, it seems that the one danger to wheat crops in the Peace River Country is from early frost, that the seasons when such frosts occur must be regarded as exceptional, that care in the selection of seed and in early sowing may obviate even this exceptional danger, and that the Peace River prairies are more liable to this than the prairies of the Saskatchewan.

Every wheat-growing country, however, seems to be exposed to some influence by which occasional crops may be more or less injured. There are seasons when much of the grain of Britain remains unharvested on account of the excessive rainfall. Parts of the Western States and Territories will probably be always subject to periodical invasions of locusts, such as have devastated large areas as recently as 1874. Neither of these injurious influences threatens wheat-culture in the Edmonton district or in the Peace River Country, for the rain-fall though adequate seems never to be excessive, and the northward course of the locust seems, according to Dr. Dawson, to be " limited by the line of the coniferous forest which approximately follows the North Saskatchewan River."*

It must be noted, too, that the increased proportion of sunlight in these northern districts must very largely promote the rapid and vigorous growth of plants. At Dunvegan, for instance, the duration of sunlight on the 21st June is one hour and a quarter greater than it is at Winnipeg, while it is nearly two hours and a quarter greater than it is at Toronto, a difference which of course decreases to zero at the 21st March and 21st September, while it is reversed during the winter months. The average daily duration of sunlight from the 15th May to the 15th August,—the wheat-growing period,—is at least an hour and a half greater at Dunvegan than at Toronto. This must largely enhance the value of the northern prairies for agricultural purposes, and it may in some measure account for what climatologists have often observed, that the quality of wheat improves the more closely you approach the northern limit of wheat-growing lands. While the wheat-crop of the Peace River district may possibly suffer occasional injury from early frosts, barley, rye, and all the ordinary varieties of roots may be regarded as a sure crop, and these with the abundant and luxuriant pasture

---

* Geology of the 49th Parallel, p. 305.

would render this country peculiarly well adapted for stock-raising. The winter is severe but apparently not more so than that of the Edmonton district. The snow-fall, which averages from one-and-a-half to two feet, is not sufficient to prevent horses wintering out, while, at Dunvegan, cattle are usually home-fed only from the latter part of November till about the middle of March. Here, as throughout all our Canadian North-West, the cold of winter is much less severely felt than those living near the sea-board would, from the indications of the thermometer, be led to suppose, as the climate is dry and steady, and the temperature seldom so extreme as to prevent travelling, although travelling any distance involves camping out at night.

The average summer temperature is as high as that usually enjoyed ten degrees further south in Ontario and Quebec, without the discomfort of oppressively warm nights. Indeed, there is a very great difference between the temperature of the day and that of the night. During the first fortnight of August, 1879, the average midday temperature at Fort Dunvegan was 77° above zero in the shade, while the average minimum at night was 42°, a fair example of the difference ordinarily observed as between the day and night temperature of summer, although sometimes the variation is much greater. This depression of temperature, to whatever cause it is to be ascribed, produces a very heavy dew-fall, which probably assists very greatly in promoting vegetation, and the change after a warm day is almost as refreshing as a breeze from the sea.

In addition to its great agricultural resources the Peace River district possesses not only extensive timber lands, large portions of which are within easy access of the Peace or its tributaries, but it is also rich in coal. Although no seams of great thickness have yet been discovered, the area throughout which coal or lignite has been found is so large that there can be little doubt that valuable seams will yet be developed. These coal-beds that underlie the Peace River district extend, it seems, in increasing thickness to the south-eastward. Dr. Dawson says that " one of " these reported to be eight feet thick, occurs near the " projected railway-crossing of the North Pembina " River, while between Fort Edmonton and the mouth of " the Brazeau River, on the Saskatchewan, a seam of " coal fifteen to twenty feet in thickness was discovered " by Mr. Selwyn in 1873;" and he adds:—" While " neither of these can be classed as true bituminous " coals, they are fuels of great value, and compare closely " with those brown coals used extensively on the line of " the Union Pacific Railway in the Rocky Mountain " region."* It has been estimated that " the total area " of the western part of the prairie region between the

---

* Report of Engineer-in-Chief Can. Pacific Railway, 1880, p. 130.

" forty-ninth and fifty-fourth parallels, now known by
" more or less connected lines of observation to be under-
" laid by the lignite and coal-bearing formations, does
" not fall short of 80,000 square miles; and should future
" investigation result in affixing some of the fuels to the
" Lower Cretaceous, it must be very much greater."*
It has been established by the explorations of 1879 that
coal does exist well down in the Cretaceous formation.
The localities, says Dr. Dawson† in which coal is known
to occur in the lower or certainly Cretaceous zone are:
Table Mountain, which is on the south bank of Pine
River, Coal Brook a tributary of the south branch of
Pine River, Portage Mountain at the Cañon of Peace
River, and on the lower part of Smoky River. This is a
fact of considerable importance, for not only has the
coal-bearing area been thus proved to extend northward
to the fifty-sixth parallel, and thereby increased from
80,000 to probably 100,000 square miles, but it seems to
confirm the supposition that the former estimate is much
too small for the coal-fields between the Athabasca and
the international boundary line. The value of these
coal-fields in a country which, like our North-West, is in
some large areas very destitute of wood, can scarcely be
exaggerated.

In any development of the resources, whether of the
farm-lands, the forests or the mines of Peace River Dis-

---

* Dawson; Geology of 49th parallel, p. 180.
† Report of Engineer-in-Chief Can. Pacific Railway, 1880, p. 128.

trict, the great extent of navigable water presented by the Peace and by several of its tributaries will furnish facilities for communication throughout a large portion of the country. Although our Canadian Pacific line will not pass through it, and although it may not for many years be found necessary to embrace it in our system of railways, yet it is known that a branch line would be perfectly feasible and for the most part easy of construction, extending from the vicinity of Edmonton to Pine River or to Dunvegan. The district must naturally be peopled by immigrants coming from the east, and therefore not until large portions of the country between Manitoba and Edmonton have been cultivated need we look for many settlers on the banks of the Peace; but none who traverse it can doubt that the Province of Unchagah must in due time prove to be a most valuable portion of what is, as yet, the undeveloped interior of our Dominion.

CHAPTER IX.

DUNVEGAN TO EDMONTON.

Leave Dunvegan. — Farewell view of Peace River.—Cooking.—Lesser Slave Lake.—Another Stage.—Postal Arrangements.—Indian Hospitality.—Athabasca River and Landing.—Gambling. — Road to Fort Edmonton. — Telegraph Office. — Cree Camp. — Our Indian Policy. — Farm Instructors.—Treaties. — Sioux.—Edmonton District.—Canadian Pacific Railway.

Our party separated at Dunvegan, some to return by way of Pine River Pass to Vancouver Island, others to examine the country bordering the Athabasca and the facilities for railway connection between the Peace River District and the Saskatchewan, while I came by way of Lesser Slave Lake towards Edmonton.

On Tuesday, the 2nd September, I left Dunvegan on a small raft, my only companion being the half-breed Tom, who had accompanied me to Battle River; and, borne along by the gentle current of the Peace, we reached next afternoon the Hudson's Bay post near the mouth of Smoky River. The Peace had fallen greatly since our arrival at Dunvegan on the 1st August, and the water, which was then turbid, had become clear, though still possessing that greyish tinge which seems to be an ordinary characteristic of the streams from the Rocky Mountains. The country through which the river winds is similar to that above Dunvegan, but here the banks slope more gently from the water, and the plateau seems to be somewhat lower. Gravel beaches frequently fringe the banks on either side, and a number of well-wooded islands dot the river.

At Smoky River depôt Nigger Dan, the notorious, when on his way to be tried at Edmonton, had left a protest in the form of an inscription on the door of the storehouse: "Daniel Williams, prisner of Her Majesty under fals pretenses." Public opinion in the Peace River country had centred more on him than on any other subject during the summer of 1879. We had heard of him beyond the mountains. We found him to be the one unfailing topic of conversation at each of the H. B. Company's posts that we had passed. At Lesser Slave Lake and at Edmonton he continued to attract a lively interest, and even at Battleford one of the first points in regard to our explorations in the Peace River country, about which the civil and military authorities of the North-West made enquiries, was the accurate longitude of Fort St. John, so that they might know whether it was in the N. W. Territories or in British Columbia, and thus decide whether Nigger Dan should be tried at Edmonton or at Victoria.

At Smoky River depôt I was again thrown upon the

help of the Company's agents, through whose kindness I was supplied with a prairie-cart, two horses and an Indian guide, while an Indian boy accompanied us on horse-back. Indeed the traveller in the North-West, at least in the remoter districts, is almost entirely dependent on the H. B. Company for conveyance. On the more frequented prairie trails you may meet, during the summer, long bands of carts belonging to independent freighters, or you may at some points find that the "free traders" can forward you more quickly and more comfortably than the Company; yet the assistance of the Company's officials, who are almost invariably energetic, hospitable and courteous, is of essential importance in traversing the remoter north, while even on the more familiar prairies they are the chief forwarders as well as fur-traders. At nearly every post the Company keep a large number of horses, for this costs nothing except the hire of a few men to herd them, as the horses find abundant pasture, both summer and winter; and if the agent at any post has no horses under his charge he can usually make arrangements with Indians, half-breeds, or, in some cases, with white settlers to provide them; and thus the traveller is forwarded by stages from the Rocky Mountains to Winnipeg.

The road from Smoky River depôt to Lesser Slave Lake, about sixty-three miles in length, is a tolerably good waggon-road, although grooved occasionally into deep ruts by the heavy traffic upon it, for **the supplies of the Peace River district** are forwarded from Edmonton to Lesser **Slave Lake, and by** this route to Dunvegan. Leaving the depôt the road passes at once to the plateau about six hundred feet above the river, and **as** it nears the upper **level** the view, looking back upon **the Peace,** as seen on a fair September evening, **is one of the** loveliest in the North-West. The plateau stretches away on either hand an **almost** unbroken level of fertile, virgin soil; the slopes leading from it **to the rivers, which here** blend their strength, are broken **into** all varieties **of** terrace and knoll, now grass-covered, now rich **with groves** that were already **tinted** with **the mottled glory of** autumn; the well-wooded islands break the smooth and steady current into ripples; the mighty **river** winds its slow northward course; and over all, from an unclouded sky, stream the rays of the setting sun. From such a scene one turns unwillingly **away.** More than a month's acquaintance had made us familiar with the great Unchagah. We had followed it from away beyond the junction of the Parsnip **and the** Finlay, where it first assumes the name of the Peace River. **We had been** borne by it through the range of the Rocky Mountains along many a league, where it winds in graceful curves between banks of **ever changing loveliness. We had** dreamed dreams of the **time when this broad belt of the** silent north-land which it unwaters would smile with happy homesteads, when the music of the reaper and of the mill-wheel would be heard here, and when it would bear upon its breast some portion of the commerce of a thriving people. But henceforward its scenes of grandeur and of beauty were to be enjoyed by us only in memory, as we left it on our eastward journey.

After leaving the river the road passes for the most part through a beautiful tract of country, rolling prairie alternating with woodland, the soil being excellent, while the vegetation becomes richer and the pasture more luxuriant on approaching Lesser Slave Lake. This part of the journey afforded some new experience. Throughout the various changes of conveyance and of attendance, since leaving the Pacific, we had always enjoyed the services of a cook, and one of the recommendations of the Indian guide, whom I took from Smoky River depôt, was that he could do any such plain cooking as I might require. I soon found, however, that his knowledge of "plain cooking" was confined to the boiling of a kettle, and dropping into it anything he had, whether bacon, fresh meat, or pemmican; and, to make matters worse, I was unable to converse with him. I had been told that the boy who accompanied us could speak French, and I thought that he might act as interpreter, but after a few futile efforts to make myself intelligible to him, I concluded that we had learned French from different masters, and so, during the two days of our journey, all our communication was by silent gesture, a simple but not always very definite method of intercourse. Attempting to improve upon the cooking of my guide, I became for the first time initiated into the mysteries of frying bacon, of boiling rice, of making oatmeal porridge, and of preparing the few other stores that I had brought with me from Dunvegan. For some time the result of these efforts was a very dismal kind of success; but hunger is a good sauce, and necessity soon developes ability. Considerable anxiety and effort, too, were expended upon one of the cart-wheels. The cart was of the ordinary prairie-cart pattern, with the addition of iron tires. One of these tires had become loose. I afterwards found that I might have left it behind, as a prairie cart will run as well without one; but, in my ignorance, I bound and re-bound it with rope and shaganappi, until, from its numerous bandages, the wheel looked as if it had been fractured at every joint. The road is so free from stone that the rope and shaganappi were scarcely at all worn, and in no case cut through, by the time I reached Lesser Slave Lake.

Approaching the lake the road leads over a broad marsh, which yields abundance of excellent hay. With such an ample supply of fodder the H. B. Company's agent at this post raises a goodly number of cattle; and the hay-stacks piled upon the marsh, with the cattle feeding on the rich pasture or standing knee-deep in the shallow water by the margin of the lake, gave to the vicinity of the Fort a more cultivated, pastoral appearance than that of any place we had seen since leaving Victoria.

The Fort at Lesser Slave Lake consists of shop, storehouses and dwellings of the Company's servants, ranged in a quadrangle, and surrounded by a palisade, while at a few yards distance is the agent's residence, recently erected. A hundred yards off is the dwelling of the Roman Catholic priest, and a little further the establishment of the free-traders, where Stobart, Eden & Co., have a branch, while, in another direction, there are a few small log-houses and Indian lodges. A number of Indians, —" free-men," that is, men not in the regular service of the Company,—live in the neighbourhood, being employed by the Company as occasion may require, and able to support their families with very little labour by fishing and shooting. The lake abounds with delicious white-fish, rivalling those of the lakes of Ontario, and in autumn with countless ducks, wavies and wild geese.

The Indians make no attempt at agriculture beyond the cultivation of some small potato-patches. They scarcely regard flour, potatoes or other vegetable diet as any substitute for animal food. They want their rations of meat, particularly of buffalo pemmican, which has until recently been the staple provision from Peace River to Winnipeg. While such large game as moose, bear and beaver continue, and while the lakes abound in fish, they cannot see any use in farming, unless perhaps it might be in stock-raising, since the richest crops would not lessen their demand for animal food. Some vegetarian missionaries might be of service among them. There is not much land in the vicinity of the lake fit for cultivation, for, although wheat is grown here with marked success, yet the flats near the water's edge are valuable chiefly for their marsh-hay and for the facilities they afford in this respect for cattle-feeding. Beyond these flats the country is broken by hills and ridges varying in height from 150 to 800 feet above the level of the lake, while to the north of the Fort a large extent of territory is covered by muskeg, swamp, lakelet and stream.

The lake, which is about seventy miles in length, is emptied by Lesser Slave River into the Athabasca, which, near Fort Chipewyan, meets the Peace in its northward flow. The Athabasca, after receiving the waters of Lesser Slave River, flows for about fifty miles in a southerly direction; then turning sharply it resumes its former course. At this bend or elbow there is a freighting station of the H. B. Company, known as the Athabasca Landing, for the Company have taken advantage of this part of the river for the transport of their stores, furs etc., as the route by Lesser Slave Lake and River and by this part of the Athabasca is a very direct one, and, in connection with the waggon-road by which we came from Smoky River depôt and a waggon road from the Landing to Edmonton, forms the most favourable route from the Peace to the Saskatchewan.

I had proposed going by canoe to the Landing, about 165 miles, and, in lack of easier conveyance, walking from there to Edmonton, if I could secure Indians to carry my tent, baggage and provisions; but the agent, Mr. Young, assured me that the Company's boat would be going to the Landing in a few days, and would there be met by carts that would at once return to Edmonton. A heavy storm, which continued for three days, made it impossible to proceed by canoe; so I waited for the speedier and more comfortable York boat. The delay was irksome, for the season was getting well advanced, but it was relieved by the hospitality of the Fort and by the pleasure of meeting Mr. and Mrs. Macdougall, of Dunvegan, homeward-bound from Edmonton. Mr. Macdougall spent several years on the Yucon, and regards his present post as in the very centre of civilisation, when compared with the remoter north-land that borders Behring's Straits.

We left the Fort with a fair breeze which soon freshened almost to a gale: the shallow waters of the lake were whipped into foam, and, in the absence of projecting promontory or sheltering island to form a harbour, we ran under close-reefed lug-sail almost from end to end without halting, covering the distance in about nine hours. When we had once entered the river we were largely dependent on our oars, for the stream winds by many a curve and with very gentle flow. It maintains throughout most of its course of forty-five miles a width of about twenty yards, being regular and monotonous as a canal, until nearing the Athabasca it passes over a series of small rapids where it broadens to a span of about fifty yards. Its banks are low, fringed for the most part with willows, while on either side there is a fertile plateau covered with luxuriant vegetation and abounding in wild-cherry trees, whose ripe fruit frequently detained the Indian crew that accompanied me.

The Athabasca where it receives the Lesser Slave River is nearly two hundred yards wide. For a short distance after their waters meet the two streams may be recognized by their colour, that of the Slave River being brown, while the Athabasca has the gray colour characteristic of the streams that flow from the Rocky Mountains. Very soon, however, they are blended beyond all recognition.

At the junction of the two rivers I set up a post office and left a mail bag. The office consisted of a tree well blazed; the bag, a fragment of a flour sack which was tied to the tree, enclosed a letter for Dr. G. M. Dawson, "to be left till called for." It was his intention to come down the Athabasca from a point some distance west of this, and my letter was to inform him that he would find certain provisions cached for him in a small house at Athabasca Landing. Any stores thus left for a traveller in these regions though placed, as in this case, in an unlocked hut, or even though fastened to the branches of a tree, are as safe from all disturbance by the hand of man as though they were guarded by a regiment. The wolverine may sometimes help himself to them, and it requires thoughtful arrangement to secure them against his cunning, but every Indian, or other traveller, holds it a matter of sacred faith to leave them untouched, and passes them as if they were not. The letter and provisions were both in due time found in perfect safety by Dr. Dawson.

After I had completed these postal arrangements my boatmen were attracted by the sight of an Indian lodge near the river, and, recognizing some friends, they went ashore. After they had been gone for some time I found them comfortably engaged at tea in the lodge, and on my appearance the Indian woman at once asked me to join them. As the tepee was hung round with dried moose and beaver-tails, I ventured, with the assistance of one of the men who acted as interpreter, to express admiration of this abundant store of provisions. The Indian at once took down some moose-meat and some beaver-tails, and presented them to me. It is customary among the Indians that if one expresses fervent admiration of some article belonging to another, the possessor at once gives up the coveted article to the admirer of it, although he probably takes an early opportunity of repaying himself by admiring some of his friend's possessions. It is told of a surveyor, Gore by name, who was engaged in laying off the H. B. Company's lands near Lesser Slave Lake, that, when seated with his men one evening around the camp-fire, he expressed frequent and fervent admiration of a new pipe which one of the Indians was smoking. The owner handed it to him bidding him take it. The others assured the surveyor that it would give great offence if he refused, so he reluctantly accepted it. Next evening the Indian was loud in praise of a very fine otter-skin cap which Gore was wearing. All turned towards him; he knew what was expected; and taking off the cap he passed it most unwillingly to the Indian, who thanked him and immediately threw him his own old well-worn one in return. The surveyor restrained all further expression of admiration for the property of the Indians.

Accepting the proffered gift of our Indian acquaintance, we reciprocated his hospitality by a gift of flour and tobacco, and continued our journey down stream. The current of the Athabasca, though swift nearer the mountains, is here probably not more than two miles an hour. Its banks, which are generally bordered by a beach of sand or clay, slope rapidly up from the water's edge to a height of from one to two hundred feet. Where broken they expose a light, loamy soil on a bed of sand and clay; but they are, for the most part, closely wooded, chiefly with poplar and spruce. Nearer the Landing, however, the banks become more varied, sometimes abrupt, with here and there a land-slide, sometimes low and flat, although at a short distance from the water's edge the land seems to maintain a pretty uniform level. The weather was beautifully fine, the woods were rich with many-tinted foliage, the shores gravelly, grass-grown, and sandy by turns. No sign of life was visible except an occasional beaver on the beach. The Indians, knowing that they would be in ample time to meet the carts from Edmonton, simply allowed the boat to be borne onward by the current, while, coiling themselves in their blankets, they passed hour after hour in sleep, for they have an unlimited capacity for doing nothing when they are not spurred into action by necessity.

Between the Landing and Lake Athabasca the river passes over two falls, where somewhat heavy portages would be required, and on that account freight for Fort Chippewyan and the northern districts, instead of passing along this portion of the river, goes from Fort Carlton along the old route by way of Lacrosse, Portage La Loche, and the Clearwater, one of the best known and most frequently travelled routes of the north. On both sides of the Athabasca, as it flows northward from the

Landing, the general altitude of the country decreases, as it does along the course of the Peace River. Indeed, this northward dip commences near the boundary line, for the 49th parallel, though arbitrarily chosen as the international boundary, marks approximately the watershed of this portion of the continent, where the southern tributaries of the Saskatchewan rise near the northern tributaries of the Missouri. From that, northward, the general level falls towards the Arctic Sea.

We reached the Landing on the evening of Wednesday, the 17th September. The conveyances from Edmonton which we expected to meet there, did not arrive until Friday morning. During this delay, and fearing that there might be some unforeseen detention, I proposed to the Indian boatmen that they should pack for me to Edmonton. As only one of the four could talk English, and as my proposals to the others were necessarily made through him, he being himself disinclined to accept, probably modified my offers. At any rate the Indians would not agree to go. Fortunately, however, the arrival of the conveyances on Friday removed all further difficulty. When the freight train from Edmonton had come, the Indians from the lake and those in charge of the carts spent the evening in the red man's favourite recreation, gambling. The stakes were small, usually a fig of tobacco, but the excitement was as lively as it used to be at Baden-Baden. They play in much the same way as boys play "odds or evens," holding something in one hand, folding their arms akimbo, jerking the body, and droning a so-called song, that they may give as little indication as possible to the rival players as to which hand contains the treasure. While play continues a drum, or some appropriate substitute such as a tin pan, is beaten, noise of some kind being apparently a necessary accompaniment.

On Saturday morning the boats were loaded, and the carts started on their return trip, while I had the advantage of a buck-board which had been sent out with Mrs. Young, whom we met on her way to Slave Lake. The road from the Landing to Edmonton, which is an excellent waggon-road, ninety-six miles in length, was made by the Company to avoid the necessity of freighting goods for the north by the old and difficult trail which passed by way of Fort Assineboine to Lesser Slave Lake. After leaving the river it leads very quickly to the plateau which is here about 350 feet above the level of the Athabasca. The country for several miles south of the Landing is broken into ridges, the soil being at first rather poor, but it gradually becomes undulating prairie. Sometimes the road passes over sandy soil through groves of pine, while here and there the landscape is dotted with clumps of spruce; but twenty miles from the Athabasca the country becomes more beautiful, rich with luxuriant grass and pea-vine, watered by frequent

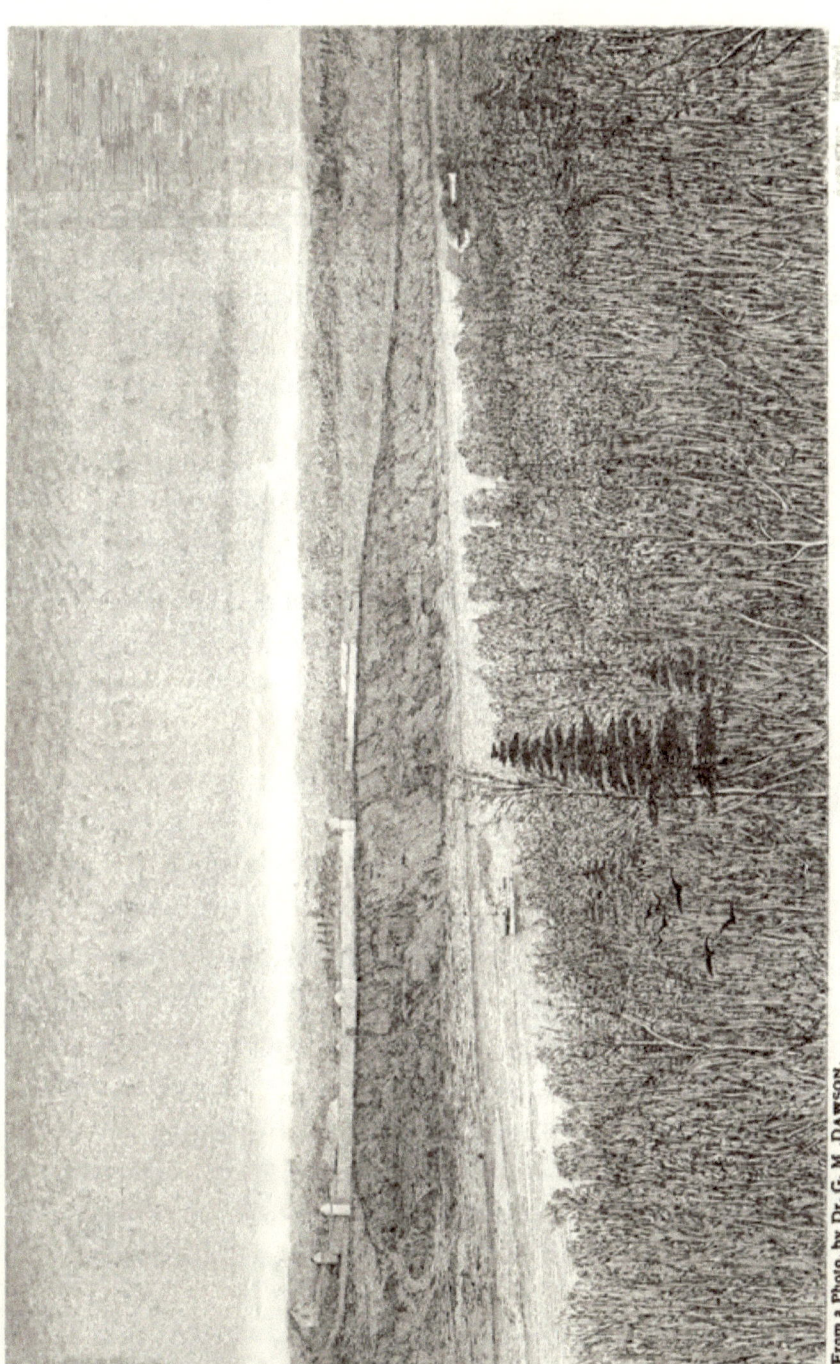

From a Photo. by Dr. G. M. Dawson.

FORT EDMONTON.

streams and lakelets, with loamy soil, occasionally dotted with aspen copse. Nearing Sturgeon River, which the road crosses about twenty-five miles north of **Edmonton, the country** becomes peculiarly attractive, there being **already upon** this river, about **two miles above our crossing,** a thriving settlement with grist-mill and other appliances of an agricultural community. Between Sturgeon **River and Edmonton** the country is of the richest undulating prairie character ; **the soil is excellent, and** the road **leads for** miles **by** luxuriant hay meadows and through gently rolling land of great fertility. Much of the hay had recently **been cut and stacked, and** the large stacks gave a **cultivated appearance to** the country. **As** we approached Edmonton **we** passed many **wheat**-fields where the grain, already cut, was being garnered, the hearts of the settlers having **being** gladdened by an abundant harvest. **We** came unexpectedly **on a** little clump of houses on the plateau overlooking the river, and then **a** little further, and somewhat **lower down,** on a slope leading to the **river, we entered Fort Edmonton,** the most important **H. B. Company's Post in the North West Territories.** The shops, store-houses, offices, servants' dwellings, etc., **are** enclosed by a palisade, while at a short distance, and a little higher up the bank, outside of the palisade, stands the factor's house, where, after this stage of the journey eastward, the large-hearted hospitality of Mr. and Mrs. Hardisty was peculiarly welcome.

The telegraph line has been recently extended to Fort Edmonton, but, in the summer of 1879, the nearest telegraph station was at Hay Lakes, a point on the located line of the C. P. Railway, about thirty-five miles distant from the Fort. Being anxious to send messages eastward, I hurried, by an excellent road, to Hay Lakes. The country traversed by this road that runs southward from Edmonton, is even superior to that lying north of the Saskatchewan. It is rich in the extreme, consisting chiefly of gently rolling prairie, dotted with groves of aspen, poplar, etc., and covered with luxuriant herbage. The telegraph office was a very rude shanty, but to one who had for months been cut off from tidings of friends and of the world it seemed like a temple of science, as it enshrined a battery and instrument that made it possible to communicate with any point along the world's four million miles of wire. Messages were soon sent to Battleford, Winnipeg and Ottawa, and the hours passed slowly until the click announced the coming reply. The day was fine, and the ducks on the neighbouring lakes temptingly abundant, but we did not care to leave the house lest we might lose the earliest opportunity of continuing our correspondence.

A large number of Crees had pitched camp in the neighbourhood, waiting for some reliable report regarding the approach of the buffalo across the border, and meanwhile living on ducks and prairie chicken, of which they daily killed several **hundreds**. Even the fattest and largest mallard ducks were regarded by them as **inferior food**. Until recently they would not have wasted powder upon them, but the gradual extinction of the buffalo is enhancing the **value** of small game. As far back as memory or tradition can reach, the Indian of the prairies has relied upon the buffalo **for** supplying **food**, clothing, tent,—almost everything requisite for his **maintenance**. The herds that **annually visited the northern plains and prairies** seemed practically **unlimited; year after year** thousands fell before **the rifle of the Indian and of the half-breed**, while the fur-trade furnished **continual inducement** to procure an **increasing annual supply of robes;** but the work of destruction, **carried on upon both sides of the boundary,** has gradually thinned off the herds to **such a** degree, that already on **our Canadian prairies the** buffalo has become almost extinct.

This change has **of** necessity forced the Indians into new lines of life, while at the same time **it has** laid upon our Government increased responsibility **in its** treatment of the prairie Indians. Food **must be furnished** for many, who, from long habits of dependence upon the buffalo, would starve if no aid were given **them**. Some **of** the Indians indeed, especially **among the Blackfeet,** take their stand **upon** the argument: "We had plenty of food until the white man came; **now if, as you tell us,** the great mother sends her white children here, then,

17

since the buffalo are failing, the great mother must supply us with food." Their creed has at least the merit of simplicity, and, as they have been trained only to hunt, and are as yet incapable of maintaining themselves by farming, it is absolutely necessary that the Government should assist in feeding them until they are educated into more settled ways of life. Looked at even as a matter of policy, it is cheaper to feed than to fight them, and the latter alternative might be forced upon us if the former were not accepted, while, at the same time, this humaner policy would be only in accord with the considerate treatment that has always been shewn by the British and Canadian Governments towards the old possessors of the soil. Much relief however would annually be required, if the Indians were not trained into self-help, and therefore, to reduce this burden, as well as to educate the Indians, as far as possible, into diligent and useful citizens, the Government has appointed farm instructors to teach them practical farming on the reserves that had previously been allotted to them.

Thirteen such farm-instructors have been appointed, stationed on different Indian reserves between Manitoba and the base of the Rocky Mountains.* It is as yet too early to pronounce upon the results of this system,

---

* The locations at which the various instructors in farming have been stationed are : Qu'Appelle, Touchwood Hills, Fort Pelly, Prince Albert, Duck Lake near Carlton, Battleford, Fort Pitt, Saddle Lake near Victoria, Edmonton, Blackfoot Crossing, Fort Calgarry, Fort McLeod and Fort Walsh.

but there is every likelihood of its ultimate success. Already a number of Indians, following the example of their chiefs, are taking to farming, and in this they seem to be much more influenced by the example of the half-breeds than by that of the whites, as the half-breeds are hunters like themselves, and were for many years almost as dependent upon the buffalo. Yet, even if this attempt to make the Indians self-supporting should prove a failure, the establishment of government farms on which large quantities of root crops can be raised will greatly reduce the expense of feeding them.

There is no reasonable ground for any apprehension of danger from the Indians, nor any likelihood of trouble arising between them and the settlers. From the first the Government have carefully respected their claims; they have extinguished, by treaty, the Indian title to the land, before offering an acre for settlement; and the Indians know that the Government will keep faith with them. This is the open secret of Canada's success in dealing with her Indians. In all, seven treaties have been made with the tribes of the North-West, covering the entire territory from the boundary line northwards to the Athabasca, the Beaver and the Nelson Rivers, and from the Rocky Mountains eastward to Ontario.

These treaties guarantee, on the part of the Indians, the entire surrender of the territory, with the exception of certain reserves, it being understood that they continue at liberty to hunt and fish without restriction over all unoccupied lands; and, on the part of the Canadian Government, the payment of a certain annuity to each family of the tribe, the yearly distribution of a fixed amount of ammunition, the establishment and maintenance of schools, the gift of cattle, agricultural implements, etc., with some other less important provisions.

The only Indians in the southern portion of the Territories, not yet under treaty arrangement with the Government, are the Sioux, who crossed from the United States under Sitting Bull in 1876, and who are camped near Wood Mountains. Reserves had been allotted them by the U. S. Government in the Black Hill country, not far from the boundary. It was afterwards found that the reserves contained rich mining-lands, and the Sioux were therefore asked to move to other reserves without any compensation for the sacrifices demanded of them. They declined; and the Government resorted to the powder argument, which was too strong for the natives, who then sought refuge on Canadian soil, where they have since remained on sufferance. Their chief contends that his men are British subjects, that they never legally became wards of the U. S. Government, that the territory in which they dwelt belonged by right to Britain, and should never have been ceded to the United States, that therefore he and his men were improperly transferred to a foreign government,—an opinion in which Sitting Bull shows a pretty clear knowledge of the history of our boundary negotiations. Another band of Sioux, however, who crossed into Canada immediately after the Minnesota massacre, in 1862, are settled near Prince Albert and on Bird Tail Creek, where they have had reserves allotted them by the Government, but receive no further relief.

The Sioux under Sitting Bull have, in some degree, cut off the supply of buffalo that would otherwise have helped to sustain our own Crees and Blackfeet, but that is the only injury inflicted by them. It is most improbable that they will show any hostility to the Government or people of Canada; indeed they are clear-sighted enough to see that, since the gradual extinction of the buffalo, their chief prospect of sustenance lies in the friendship of the Canadian Government, and that they would forfeit this by any injury inflicted upon the settlers. At the same time the Crees, Blackfeet and Sioux have too much dislike, distrust and jealousy towards each other to form any union for aggressive purposes against the whites. In travelling from Edmonton to Winnipeg we occasionally met sensational rumours regarding alleged acts of violence on the part of the Indians, but further inquiry always proved these rumours to be baseless. Even when sorely pressed by hunger, and when pained by the sight of friends suffering from starvation they displayed the utmost patience and endurance, and made no attempt to procure relief by violence. Throughout the whole country the white settlers are undisturbed by any anxiety about them; and the natural course of events must tend to make the whites every year more and more secure against any likelihood of trouble from this quarter.

The district around Edmonton is one of exceptional fertility and promise, the most promising indeed of all the North-West Territories. Nowhere do settlers reap larger crops "off the sod," that is, the first season that the soil is ploughed. In some parts of the North-West the land yields little or nothing the first summer, so that the settler can only plough it up that the grass roots may rot and that the soil may be ready for seed the following spring. In most parts of the Saskatchewan valley, however, good crops may be raised on newly broken land. Not only do the horses winter out, but frequently the cattle also, for, even when the snow averages three feet in depth, as it sometimes does, it is so light, and the meadow hay and pea-vine are so tall, that cattle have little difficulty in foraging for themselves, at least in the neighbourhood of Hay Lakes.

This Edmonton district, as I saw it for thirty miles south of the Fort, for more than twice that distance to the north, and for any distance less than 200 miles eastward, to which the name can be properly applied,—and, as reported by other travellers, for a considerable distance westward,—possesses not only the richest soil, but is for the most part well-wooded, being indeed heavily timbered along the upper waters of the Saskatchewan. It is well supplied with coal, which is now used for domestic purposes at Fort Edmonton. Gold-washing on the sand-bars of the Saskatchewan yields from $1 to $6 a day. The country is well watered; it is connected by a line of steamers with Winnipeg; its climate is enjoyable in the extreme; its fitness for wheat culture equal to that of any part of the country west of the Red River valley. Out of such a district a prosperous Province must ere long be formed.

It is natural that the Government should regard Edmonton as an essential point to be traversed by the Canadian Pacific Railway. Not only is it destined to be the centre of an important district, it is also most favourably situated as a distributing point for the country to the north and south. To the north and north-west lies the fertile Peace River district. To the south-west lies the rich Bow River country, which is already recognized as perhaps the best grazing district in Canada, including a territory of about 20,000 square miles, running, that is, from the boundary line about 200 miles northward, and from the base of the Rocky Mountains about 100 miles eastward. Owing to the "Chenook" winds, as they are called, which apparently come from the Pacific across the country once held by the Chenook Indians, near the Columbia River, this district enjoys an exceptionally mild climate that renders it comparatively free from snow even in mid-winter, so that cattle are enabled throughout the whole year to graze upon its rich well-watered plains. If our trans-continental railway were to pass by the northern route through the Peace River country to the Pacific, the traffic of this great grazing district to the south of Edmonton would necessarily be thrown into the United States railways, whereas it can easily be drawn towards our own line, if that line should pass not further north than Edmonton. At the same time the Peace River country, as soon as circumstances may require, can without much difficulty be connected with the trunk line by a branch from the neighbourhood of Edmonton.

How soon will the railway reach Edmonton? If the North-West is to be rapidly peopled,—and on its settlement must depend much of Canada's future prosperity—facilities of communication must be provided, and the railway, as a great colonisation road, must precede or at least accompany settlement. And while the peopling of the North-West requires the construction of the railway to the foot of the Rocky Mountains, other reasons, such as the interests of British Columbia, the closer union of the Provinces by lines of traffic, and the development of commerce with Asia, demand railway extension to the western seaboard.

The line from **Lake Superior to the Pacific** consists of the following sections:—

		MILES.
1.	Fort William to Selkirk....................	406
2.	Selkirk *viâ* Edmonton to Jasper Valley.....	1000
3.	Jasper Valley to Kamloops	335
4.	Kamloops to Yale........................	125
5.	Yale to Burrard Inlet.....................	90

Total **from** Lake Superior to the Pacific...... 1,956

On section 1, the rails are laid **136 miles west of Fort William** and 90 miles east of Selkirk, and the remaining 180 miles will be completed by **July 1882.** On section 2, 200 miles are already under contract from Selkirk westwards. Section **4** is under contract. On sections 3 and 5 nothing has yet been done beyond the location of the **route.** There are thus, (exclusive of the Pembina Branch, 85 miles in length, from Emerson to Selkirk,) 226 miles in running order and 505 miles under contract.

With the strong tide of immigration that may at once be expected to pour into the North-West, and the facilities for railway construction from **Selkirk to Jasper Valley,** ten years are surely an outside estimate of the time required to extend the line across the prairies to the Rocky Mountains. According to the terms of the contract, it is contemplated that the section from Kamloops to Yale will be completed in five years. Is it extravagant to expect that with the work of construction proceeding on both sides of the Mountains, we shall, by the close of the present decade, have our through line complete? The claims of the prairie section for speedy completion are more urgent than those of the British Columbia line; and the sale of lands and the increasing traffic to be secured by it, as well as the cheaper cost of construction, must make it the best paying portion of the whole line. At the same time the completion of the line to the western coast may be regarded as a political necessity, and, as it will develope the resources of British Columbia, as it will give a seaport on the Pacific by which the produce of our plains can be distributed westwards, and as it will afford a route from Europe to China for through traffic about 700 miles shorter than any other, it is of manifest importance that the part west of the Mountains be constructed as speedily as the finances of the country will allow.

But will the finances of the country allow its construction at all? Regarding the line from Lake Superior to the Rocky Mountains leading statesmen, on both sides of politics, and other competent authorities seem to be of one mind. On the smallest reasonable allowance for the increase of population in the North-West this portion of the line will not only prove directly a good commercial enterprise, but indirectly a source of large increase to the revenues of the country. For the remainder, the same cannot with as great confidence be expected. The cost of the line from Jasper Valley to Burrard Inlet is estimated at from thirty to thirty-five millions of dollars. If none of this were defrayed by the sale of lands in the North-West, it would entail an annual expenditure of nearly a million and a half of dollars of interest on cost of construction, on the part of the Dominion, and it might be questioned, whether, for a country with so limited a revenue as Canada, this outlay would be compensated for by the advantages that it would secure. But even the least sanguine can hardly suppose that the completion of the line would lay this burden upon the revenues of the country, for there can be little doubt that the sale of lands in the North-West will pay for the entire construction of the railway. At the same time, the country cannot afford to peril too much on mere expectations, however well grounded, and therefore, until a large immigration and extensive sales of public lands be secured in the North-West, it would be well to "make haste slowly" with the British Columbia section of the line.

But our Pacific railway may well be regarded as a work of Imperial as well as of Canadian importance. It concerns the welfare of the empire both as a colonisation road and as part of a trans-continental highway. The settlement of our North-West must very soon and very seriously affect the wheat supply of the mother country. At present that supply is drawn largely from the United

States and from Russia, and as these countries, being foreign, might become unfriendly, the receipt of breadstuffs from these sources might any season be imperilled; whereas, if our own vast prairies were developed the policy of foreign countries could not seriously disturb the wheat market of Britain. Besides, the welfare of the empire is concerned in the extension of this line of railway to the western seaboard, as it would not only provide speedy communication through British territory with British possessions on the Pacific, but would supply the great missing link in a rapid route from England to Eastern Asia that would be safe against foreign interference.

CHAPTER X.

EDMONTON TO BATTLEFORD.

Steamers on Saskatchewan.—Prepare to cross the prairie.—Trails —Prairie travel.—Pemmican.—Victoria.—Half-breed farmers Christian Missions in North-West.—Victoria to Fort Pitt.— Royal mail.—Dog-driving.—Fort Pitt.—The trail again.— Treeless prairies.—Tree Culture.—Battleford.—Government of North-West.—Climate.—Character of country.—Great Plain —Homestead and pre-emption law.—Prospect of settlement.

I left Fort Edmonton for Battleford on Friday, 26th September. Earlier in the season I might have gone down the Saskatchewan by steamer, for during the summer, a line of steamers belonging to the H. B. Company plies between Edmonton and Red River. The "Lily," a boat of light draught runs from Edmonton to Fort Carlton, a distance of about five hundred miles; and, as the river becomes deeper below Carlton, a larger boat, the "Northcote" runs from that point to the head of the Grand Rapids at the mouth of the Saskatchewan, a distance of about four hundred miles. These rapids, forming a complete barrier to navigation, necessitate a portage of three miles, which is traversed by a tramway, connecting the steamers on the river with those on Lake

Winnipeg. Another steamer, much more strongly built than the river boats to stand the rough waters of the lake, runs from the mouth of the Saskatchewan, two hundred and eighty miles to the mouth of Red River, and when the water is high, thirty miles up the latter river to the Stone Fort, within twenty miles of Winnipeg. The navigation of the Saskatchewan is much impeded at some places during low water by rocks and sand-bars, but these could be removed and the river rendered navigable throughout all the open season at an estimated outlay of $50,000. Were these increased facilities for navigation supplied, the cost of living in many parts of the North-West would be greatly reduced. At present the average rate of freight by cart across the prairies is $1.00 per cwt. for every hundred miles from Winnipeg, that is, $5.00 per cwt. to Prince Albert, $8.00 per cwt. to Battleford, $10.00 per cwt. to Fort Edmonton, rates that seriously affect the prices of imported goods. Besides, it requires from fifty to seventy days, according to the weather and to the state of the roads, to carry freight from Winnipeg to Edmonton, and nearly as long to make the return trip, whereas, if the necessary improvements were made on the Saskatchewan, the round trip, from Winnipeg to Edmonton and back, could be made in about twenty-five days.

Unable, however, to proceed by steamer down the Saskatchewan, and unwilling to go by canoe, I made pre-

From a Photo. by Dr. G. M. Dawson.

PRAIRIE CARTS EN ROUTE.

parations for crossing the prairies. Through the kindness of Mr. Hardisty I secured the services of an English half-breed, Fred. Rowland, who, though sometimes a little lazy in the morning, was faithful, cleanly, and intelligent. Our waggon, which was single-seated, but with space enough to hold provisions, baggage, tent, etc., piled up in the rear, was drawn by two horses, while two others ran loose, to take their turn in harness or under the saddle with which I occasionally relieved the tedium of the drive. The only care that these horses require is that at least one of them, the bell-mare, be hobbled at night, so that they may readily be found in the morning; they can easily find food and water, and they can travel thirty-five or forty miles a day without difficulty. A prairie journey is now little more of a novelty than a trip across the Atlantic; yet, like an ocean voyage, it is full of interest to one who makes it for the first time. The primitive prairie cart is the conveyance most frequently employed, but it is well, if possible, to have saddle-horses for the sake of comfort, and to leave the carts for tents, camp outfit, baggage, etc. In many instances, however, the cart has been abandoned for more pretentious vehicles. The light waggon, covered with a cotton awning that gives it the name of "prairie-schooner," from its fancied resemblance to a sail-boat, the two-horse spring-waggon similar to the ordinary "democrat" waggon of Ontario, and the double buck-board are the greatest favourites. Of these the buck-board is the best, because least liable to injury, an important advantage, for, when you are on the prairie there is no blacksmith's shop round the corner at which to repair a spring or to replace a bolt.

The chief trails across the prairies are so distinctly grooved and worn that there is no danger of losing the way, unless at some fork or cross-road where a finger-post has not yet been erected. Sometimes the trail winds over gently rolling country, or by aspen copse, so that the track can be seen only a short distance ahead; at others it stretches over a dead level plain, like an invitation into boundless space, the numerous parallel grooves that have been cut and worn by carts year after year being regular as railway lines, while near any centre, such as a farming settlement or a trading-post, the converging trails remind one of the lines near a railway depôt. Occasionally one meets immigrants or freighters, with their bands of prairie carts, at first almost as rarely as a ship on mid-ocean but more frequently on moving eastwards, like the increasing number of vessels that are seen when nearing port.

Each day you pass places that have evidently been the camping-ground of others. The square of sod, dug out by the careful freighter to form a fire-place that shall not endanger the prairie grass, the lodge-poles left lying on the ground, the ashes of recent camp-fires, the little enclosure, some ten feet square, fenced in to contain the extensive "smudge" of grass and leafy boughs, around which the horses gather on summer evenings to secure in the smoke a respite from the mosquitoes,—these mementos of previous travellers are frequently seen and are unfailing objects of interest.

One need have little difficulty in keeping the pot well supplied with game, especially if accompanied by a retriever, for abundance of ducks can be found in the numerous lakelets that border the trail, and prairie chickens are plentiful in all except the more settled districts. As day after day passes one becomes more and more in love with the climate as well as with the country, and can understand how it should be noted for its peculiar healthfulness, and especially for its freedom from fevers and from diseases of the throat and lungs. Though one day so closely resembles another in its ordinary routine, yet there is a continual freshness and interest in the journey, and if one has pleasant travelling companions, and is favoured with fine weather, a trip across the prairies, particularly after the mosquito season is over, may be like a prolonged pic-nic.

On leaving Edmonton the larder contained some fresh meat and fresh butter,—luxuries unknown for months, as well as the ordinary substantials of bacon, pemmican, etc. Buffalo pemmican will soon be a matter only of tradition and memory upon the prairies. It is not the

18

most enjoyable **variety of food** ; indeed, the first day that a man has to live on pemmican he finds that he is not very hungry; and yet white men as well as half-breeds and Indians find it a peculiarly nourishing diet, while it has the advantage of comprising a great deal of food in very small bulk, and of keeping fresh for an indefinite period. The appetite of both whites and Indians around Fort Edmonton for buffalo meat must have been keen in the days when buffalo were abundant. Capt. Palliser gives the daily ration of fresh meat served out at the Fort in 1858, as 406 pounds to ninety-four persons. How the Indians must long for the " good old times," when they mourn over the extinction of the buffalo.

We took the trail along the north bank of the Saskatchewan, it being in some respects preferable to that which passes by Fort Saskatchewan along the southern bank of the river. Already the autumn was upon us ; the trees were rapidly losing their leaves ; the cart-ruts and the small streams were filled with fallen foliage; the numerous plants scattered among the grass began to wear a withered look, although still presenting almost as much variety of colour as the foliage-plants in our gardens in mid-summer. The days were warm and clear, the nights cool, sometimes frosty. It was impossible for us to keep long hours of travelling, as day-light is necessary both for pitching and for moving camp, at least if it is to be done in any comfort, and so our average daily drive was from thirty-five to forty miles.

Two days brought us to Victoria, seventy-three miles from Edmonton, the trail throughout this distance leading through a country of almost unvarying excellence. There is a post of the H. B. Company at Victoria, connected with that at Edmonton, and about a mile from it there is a settlement composed almost exclusively of English half-breeds, who came here some fifteen years ago, or, as they themselves usually express it, five years before " the transfer," dating this and other incidents from the transfer of the Hudson's Bay Territory to the Canadian government, in 1870.

Unlike the French half-breeds the Scotch and English half-breeds take readily to farming. When the French voyageurs, who came from Lower Canada in the old days of the North-West Company, intermarried with the natives, the children seemed more Indian than French; but, when the Scotch servants of the H. B. Company married Indian women, the children showed few Indian characteristics. If the Scotchman did not raise his wife to his own level, he at least succeeded as a general rule in uplifting his children, whereas the Frenchman seemed almost at once to be drawn down to the level of the Indian. The half-breeds, however, even at best are inferior farmers, for, having sown their seed they spend much of the summer in hunting or in freighting for the

H. B. Company. At Victoria their farming is conducted on a very small scale, but, as their land is a beautiful black loam, which has yielded excellent returns of wheat year after year without any manure since they have settled upon it, they might evidently farm to great advantage, or at least their lands might be cultivated to great advantage if they were in the hands of capable farmers. There is a grist-mill about a mile from the settlement, and good prices can be secured for flour and grain as the Government, the Company and the new settlers must all be large purchasers. The Government will, for several years, require considerable quantities of flour for Indian supplies. The Company purchase largely to supply their own men, as they give scarcely any attention to farming. Even at those posts, such as Edmonton, where farming was attempted, it was often in an expensive way with hired labour and by men who were not practical farmers, while the conduct of the Indians, who sometimes used the fence-rails for camp-fires and let loose their horses in a field of young grain, was adverse to the success of such experiments. And new settlers coming, as they must ere long do in large numbers, to the Edmonton district will require both food and seed, so that the half-breeds of Victoria will find ready market for their produce. Better farmers than the half-breeds, however, are required to disclose and to develop the wheat-growing capabilities of the North-West.

There was a large Cree camp at Victoria not long ago, and an important Mission, in connection with the Methodist Church, was established here by the late Rev. G. Macdougall about the time that the half-breed settlement was formed. At present there is no resident missionary among them, but they receive an occasional visit from the Anglican and Methodist clergymen at Edmonton. On the Sunday that we spent in this neighbourhood we had the pleasure of uniting with them in Divine Service.

Until recently the Christian Missions of the North-West were necessarily confined to the native tribes, the servants of the Company, and the French and English half-breeds, for as yet " the settler " was unknown. The first Christian Missions were those of the Roman Catholic Church. The early French explorers, such as M. de la Verandaye, were usually accompanied by a priest, and as trading-posts were planted Missions were established, the first being in 1818 at St. Boniface where it has ever since been vigorously maintained, and where now stands an imposing range of ecclesiastical buildings familiar to every visitor to Winnipeg. From that centre the work was extended westwards, so that not only the early French traders and the numerous French half-breeds, or Metis, but also many of the Indian tribes adhered to the communion of the Romish Church, and now the diocese, presided over by Archbishop Taché, includes Missions in the ecclesiastical provinces of **St. Boniface, St. Albert** (on the Saskatchewan), Athabasca, Mackenzie and British Columbia.

The first Protestant Mission was that of the Church of England, which from a small beginning on the banks of the Red River in 1820 has, under the fostering care of the Church Missionary Society aided by private benefactions, extended to Hudson's Bay, to the Mackenzie, and to the far distant Yucon. In connection with this Mission the North-West has been divided into four dioceses:— Rupert's Land, with head-quarters at Winnipeg, Moosinee, with head-quarters at York Factory on Hudson's Bay, Saskatchewan, with its bishop's residence at Prince Albert, and Athabasca, where the bishop travels far and wide among the Indians but makes his home at Fort Chipewyan. The Methodists have also been very active in mission-work among the Indians, their pioneer, the late Mr. Macdougall, one of the most earnest and useful missionaries ever known in the North-West, being distinguished for his influence among the Indians from Winnipeg to the Rocky Mountains. They report six missionaries at present labouring among the Indians, and twelve among the white settlers. The Presbyterian Church, although later in commencing mission-work among the Indians, has now thirty missionaries in the North-West, three of whom are specially designated to missions among the natives.

Of recent years, however, Christian Missions in the North-West have presented new features and have assumed new proportions. A new element of population has entered, one which will ere long overshadow all previous tenants of the soil, the white settlers, who came not to serve the fur-traders but to unfold the vast resources of the land. It will tax the energies of the Canadian Churches, even with such aid as they may receive from the mother-country, to meet the demands laid on them by this increase of their home-mission fields.

Having spent a Sunday at Victoria we left next morning, and on the following Wednesday evening, 1st October, we reached Fort Pitt, two hundred and five miles from Edmonton. We were occasionally delayed at some of the creeks or gullies, which, being too narrow and too deep for fording, had been bridged, but the bridges had fallen into decay. Apparently the process of decay goes on until some freighters or other travellers find the bridge impassable and so repair it for their own and the public good. All these creeks have Indian names, and many of the names might as well be left untranslated by our mapmakers. Nameepee, for instance, is a more musical name for a stream than "Sucker," and Ahtimsegun is decidedly better than its English equivalent " Dog's-rump." The trail is good, the soil almost uniformly excellent, the land well-watered by numerous streams and generally well-wooded, chiefly with willow and poplar, though occasionally with small groves of pine. Only in the neighbourhood of Saddle Lake and again in the immediate neighbourhood of Fort Pitt did there seem to be any scarcity of wood. Near Saddle Lake, where we camped on the first evening after leaving Victoria, we had to continue driving after sunset on account of the difficulty of finding a combination of wood, water and grass, the three requisites for a good camping-ground. We spent Tuesday night near Moose Creek, about forty miles from Saddle Lake, at one of the best and most frequented camping-grounds on the trail, where the numerous lodge-poles and the ashes of old camp-fires gave evidence of previous travellers. Next day the trail led by numerous lakelets, some, such as Stone Lake and Simpson Lake, being of large size and very beautiful, and all abounding with duck. These, with the extent of timber and the number of the streams in the vicinity, combined with the general excellence of the soil, must in due time render this district as attractive to the settler as it is pleasing to the eye of the traveller.

The afternoon being wet and cold with threatenings of a stormy night, we pushed on towards Fort Pitt. About sun-set we met the mail, the driver having already camped for the night. He drove a very humble, unpretending conveyance, a common prairie cart, very unlike the dashing mail-gig, or the imposing stage-coach, which association connects with the words "royal mail." However, it is a stride forwards, as well as an indication of general progress, to find the mail running every three weeks between Winnipeg and Edmonton, and kept up with remarkable regularity summer and winter.

At first the winter mail was carried by dog-trains, but now, in winter as in summer, it is run with horses. For winter travel dogs have hitherto been largely used, as with light loads they are much swifter than horses. To drive a team of dogs it is said that one must be able to swear in English, French, or Cree, while to be a first-rate dog-driver requires a fluent command of profanity in the three languages; yet there are some excellent dog-drivers in the North-West. Some years ago a well-known Winnipeg ecclesiastic was making an extended winter trip; the dogs, though frequently whipped, made little progress, so the bishop remonstrated with the driver. That functionary replied that he could not make them go unless he swore at them. Absolution was given him for the trip, and the dogs, hearing the familiar expletives, trotted along gaily. Dog-driving, however, is passing out of use in the North-West, as it is becoming much more expensive to keep dogs than to keep horses. While buffalo were abundant, and every post and wigwam could have unlimited pemmican, it was easy for any man to keep a kennel, but as the buffalo are rapidly disappearing, and as the horses can forage for themselves at all seasons, whereas dogs must be fed throughout the whole year in order to be on hand for their winter work, horses are being used almost entirely on the prairies except in the more northern districts, where game and fish are still very abundant.

We reached Fort Pitt late in the evening, and the storm which had already overtaken us made the comforts of this hospitable house all the more enjoyable. Next morning, having inspected some wonderful wheat and potatoes grown at the Fort, and having experienced the proverbial difficulty in making an early start from a post of the H. B. Company, we crossed the Saskatchewan and took the trail for Battleford. The Fort is a comfortable two-story dwelling, with the usual accompaniments of store and outbuildings, partially surrounded by a low palisade. It stands about twenty feet above the river, and has, like many others, a number of Indian lodges, or tepees, in the neighbourhood, at which, even when most of the men with their families are off hunting, the lame and the sick remain, expecting to be kept in life and in some measure of comfort by the officers of the Company.

We left the south bank soon after mid-day, and, after rising about fifty feet from the water's edge, we crossed a plain of several miles, where the soil is light, but the pasture excellent, and then passed over rolling prairie, of good soil and rich grass, with clumps of willow, already brown and well-nigh leafless. We found plenty of wood and water, and no scarcity of good camping-grounds, but on account of our late start we did not make more than sixteen miles. Next day the solitude of our journey was relieved by our meeting a clergyman, who was on his way to Fort Pitt, expecting to reside there as missionary among the Indians of this district.

The country traversed was rolling prairie and grassy plain, partly good for the growth of grain, and partly for pasturage, the soil being sometimes light, sometimes rich loam, but generally lighter than that along the north bank of the Saskatchewan. Hour after hour wore on, and mile after mile was traversed, without our seeing any living creature except the ducks that still lingered on the lakelets, an occasional gopher or prairie squirrel, or a badger, popping up his grey head to watch us as we passed the little mound which he had scooped out of the earth, when making a hole for himself and a small pitfall for the horses. At night the last sound heard in the stillness was the call of the wild geese winging their way southward, the harsher cry of the land crane, or the rustle of the aspen leaves, now dry and ready to drop.

On Saturday we passed over rolling prairie country generally of light soil, scantily wooded, and soon after midday we reached Battleford, ninety-three miles from Fort Pitt. We had accomplished the first stage of the journey from Edmonton to Winnipeg; we had traversed a country of almost uniformly good soil, sometimes of surpassing richness, and were assured that we would have found it similar had we followed either of the main trails south of the Saskatchewan. In a few places there is a great scarcity of wood, a want that is felt in the vicinity of Battleford, though not as severely as in some other parts of the prairies. Before reaching Winnipeg, however, the traveller from the west becomes sufficiently familiar with treeless tracts. Probably on some of the plains no trees have grown for many centuries, as no roots nor any trace of decayed trees can be detected in the soil. For the most part, however, they have manifestly been denuded by fire, sometimes the result of accident but frequently set by the Indians as their mode of signalling each other. To quote Capt. Palliser: "The most trivial signal of one Indian to another has often lost hundreds of acres of forest trees which might have brought wealth and comfort to the future settler, while it has brought starvation and misery to the Indian tribes themselves, by spoiling their hunting-grounds. The Indians, however, never taught by experience, still use 'signal-fires' to the same extent as in former years." But, in justice to the Indian, he adds, when nearer the mountains: "Here I observed a very satisfactory proof that lightning in the mountains must very frequently be the cause of fires, and that all forests are not destroyed by the hand of man."* One

---

* Explorations of Brit. North America, p.p. 89, 93.

result of this destruction of trees, one which is quickly and keenly felt, is the scarcity of firewood, for in crossing the prairies one suffers more frequently from the want of wood than from the want of water; and fresh water can usually be found by digging for it. This scarcity of wood can, of course, be remedied by increased tree culture; and the growth of trees would also secure partial if not complete defence against the ravages of the locust, from which for several years Manitoba and the North-West suffered severely, and by a recurrence of which they might again be seriously injured. No barrier is so effectual against them as belts and groves of trees.

But a result even more serious than the lack of fuel or occasional ravages of grasshoppers, that may be attributed to this widespread treelessness, is the gradual reduction of the rainfall. It is known, from long-continued observations, that the moisture of the climate has on the treeless portions of the prairies been diminished, as is manifest, for instance, from the fact that many of the lakelets are slowly drying up; so that, if nothing were done to counteract this process, there might, in a few generations, be seen on our prairies results similar to those already seen in Palestine and in parts of Northern Africa, where from the destruction of the woods and the consequent reduction of the rainfall, lands that were once fertile have become utterly unproductive. And conversely where groves and forests are multiplied the moisture is increased, for not only do the trees, by the shade which they afford prevent rapid evaporation and so preserve the streams and rivulets, but probably the foliage reduces the temperature near the earth and so contributes to the formation of clouds. Already in portions of the Western States the cultivation of trees has had a marked effect upon the climate. "When the Mormons first settled in Utah, they found the district barren. Water had to be brought almost incredible distances, in wooden pipes. Trees were carefully planted, and nourished with the water so brought, and now the district may be termed the garden of the world, and is not dependent on water brought from a distance, but enjoys a steady rainfall."* Even in 1867 it was noticed that "the settlement of the country and the increase of the timber have already changed for the better the climate of that portion of Nebraska lying along the Missouri, so that within the last twelve or fourteen years, the rain has gradually increased in quantity, and is much more equally distributed throughout the year."† And the work of tree-culture is neither slow nor difficult; not difficult, for the chief requisite is to break up the land, and to sow seeds or to plant cuttings;

---

* Quoted by Dr. Dawson, Geol. of 49th Parallel, p. 318.
† U. S. Geol. Surv. Territ. quoted by Dr. Dawson, *op. cit.*, p. 318.

and not slow, for soft maple will attain a height of fifteen feet with diameter of seven inches in seven years, increasing in three years more to ten inches, so that in ten or fifteen years a plantation may be raised even from the seed, and much more speedily from cuttings. As long as the supply of our woodland is adequate to the requirements of the country, and until the well-timbered tracts of fertile soil are occupied, the need of tree-culture may not be severely felt; but even for such general reasons as providing barriers against the grasshoppers and for improvement of the climate, as well as for the increase of fuel and of building material, the cultivation of trees should be liberally encouraged by the Government. Not long ago an excellent act was passed, entitling settlers to "tree-claims" not exceeding 160 acres, for which patents would be issued at the end of eight years, provided that a certain area had been planted in trees, tree-seeds or cuttings, and that there were a certain number of living and thrifty trees to each acre. One fatal restriction, however, has been laid on this law. It does not apply to the railway belt, the belt of one hundred and ten miles on each side of the located line of the Canadian Pacific Railway; and, as the southern margin of that belt approaches the international boundary, while on the north it includes large tracts of timber-land, the law, in its present form, is useless.

Battleford has for three years been the capital of the

North-West Territories. It is situated on the south bank of the Battle River, near its confluence with the Saskatchewan, and in addition to a number of good dwellings, the chief of which is Government House, it boasts a printing office, where the *Saskatchewan Herald* is published, an H. B. C. Post, a few shops, etc., while at a short distance, on the opposite side of Battle River, are the quarters of the North-West Mounted Police, as a detachment of the force is always stationed here.

The present arrangements for the government of the North-West are simple but seemingly effective, for law and order are admirably maintained. For the administration of justice the Territories are divided into three Judicial Districts, each large enough for an empire. The Saskatchewan District is bounded on the south by Red Deer River, the south branch of the Saskatchewan, and the Saskatchewan River, on the west by British Columbia, on the east by Keewatin, on the north by the Arctic Sea. The remaining portion between the Saskatchewan district and the U. S. Boundary line on the north and south, and the Rocky Mountains and Manitoba on the west and east is divided into two districts by the 108th meridian of west longitude, the western one being named the Bow River District, the other the Qu'appelle District. In each of these three districts justice is administered by a Stipendiary Magistrate, who seems to possess the power and to perform the functions of the combined courts of any of the older Provinces.

For the general affairs of government there is a Council, of which the Stipendiary Magistrates are *ex officio* members, presided over by the Lieutenant-Governor. Every district, not exceeding 1,000 square miles, that contains a population of not less than 1,000 adult inhabitants, exclusive of aliens or unenfranchised Indians, may elect one member of Council. When the number of members increases to twenty-one, the Council shall cease, and a Legislative Assembly be formed, but, meanwhile, the Council possesses powers similar to those of the Legislative Assemblies of the other Provinces. They have no direct control over Indian affairs, these being administered through the Department of the Interior and the Indian Commissioner, but the interests of the Indians are often of necessity matters of consideration for the Council, just as the administration of justice to the Indians as well as to the whites is a duty of the Stipendiary Magistrates.*

The Government are enabled, through the North-West Mounted Police, to enforce their laws promptly and

---

* The North-West Council at present consists of Lieut.-Governor Laird; Lieut.-Col. Richardson, Stipendary Magistrate of the Saskatchewan District; M. Ryan, Esq., Stipendiary Magistrate of the Qu'Appelle District; Lieut.-Col. Macleod, C.M.G., Commissioner of N. W. M. Police, and Stipendiary Magistrate of the Bow River District; and Pascal Breland, Esq.

efficiently, the services of the police being specially required in carrying out the prohibition of the liquor traffic, in conveyance of certain criminals to Winnipeg, as no penitentiary has yet been provided for the Territories, and in similar offices where the argument of physical force is necessary.

The wisdom of selecting Battleford as the capital of the North-West Territories has been as much questioned as the propriety of making Ottawa the capital of the Dominion. Its opponents say that there is no abundance of good soil in the neighbourhood, that there is a great scarcity of wood, that settlers are not being attracted there, and that Prince Albert, near the junction of the North and South Saskatchewan, would be much more suitable; while its advocates maintain that its situation is central, that to move it eastward would be a mistake and an injustice to the western districts, all the more so as the western limit of Manitoba may, if Manitobans get what they want, be moved some distance westward. The arguments on both sides are good and true; meanwhile, Battleford has possession of Government House, and the argument of possession is a very strong one.

The season here, as throughout a large portion of the North-West Territories, is earlier than in the Eastern Provinces. From records that have been kept at Battleford, for instance, since its selection as the seat of Government, it is found that in 1878 ploughing commenced on the 19th March, the soil being dry almost as soon as the snow had disappeared. On account of frost in April, however, wheat was not sown that year until the 4th of May. In 1879 wheat was sown on the 12th April, ploughing having been begun on the 10th April; potatoes were planted on the 12th April and used on the 1st July, while wheat was cut on the 11th August, the crops being excellent. The end of May and the month of June are usually wet, but the remainder of the summer is almost invariably dry and warm, with only sufficient rain to secure good harvests and with invariably cool nights.

The Saskatchewan, at Battleford, opens about the 10th April, and, although winter commences at the beginning of November, nearly a month earlier than in Ontario, yet spring opens about a month earlier. The average temperature at Battleford, from April to August,—that is during the wheat-growing months,—is higher than it is at Toronto, so that even although the average for the year is, on account of the colder winter, lower than in Western Ontario, yet the temperature is more favourable to the growth of grain. And the climate is much the same all along the Valley of the Saskatchewan. From numerous observations, Dr. Dawson says: "Enough is known to prove the remarkably uniform progress of the spring along the so-called 'fertile belt,' which, passing north-westward from the Red River Valley, nearly follows the Saskatchewan to the Rocky Mountains, and will be the first region occupied by the settler. From the data now at command, I believe that the difference in advance of the spring between any of the above stations (that is, Dufferin in Red River Valley, Cumberland House, Fort Carlton and Fort Edmonton) is not so great as that obtaining at the same season between the vicinity of Montreal and that of Quebec."*

And while the climate is thus favourable, these southern prairies even in the least attractive districts are much more suitable for settlement than has till recently been supposed. For years the wonderful fertility and excellence of such districts as Edmonton, Prince Albert, Touchwood Hills, Little Saskatchewan and others have been familiar to many, but the country to the south of Battleford from the Hand Hills to the valley of the Qu'Appelle has hitherto been known as the Great Plain, and has been regarded as sterile, barren and useless. Last year, however, Professor Macoun traversed those plains from east to west, and although he found some parts unfit for settlement he found in many others rich loamy soil and abundance of grass. In a region adjoining Red Deer Lake, where Palliser twenty-two years ago, found numerous species of large animals and the grass eaten so low that he could not get food for his horses,

* Geology of 49th Parallel, p. 283.

Mr. Macoun found the grass knee-high, the wild animals all gone and the poor Indians perishing from famine.* The close cropping of the grass by herds of buffalo, accompanied by the general treelessness caused by fire, may in some measure account for the unfavourable report hitherto given of those more southern prairies. Summing up his experience of this district, Mr. Macoun says: "After seeing the 'Great Plain,' I can state distinctly that the rainfall throughout the whole region is sufficient for the growth of cereals, coming as it does, in June and July, when the crops actually need it, and ceasing when ripening commences. Wherever the soil was suitable for the growth of grasses, there they were." And, after referring to the arid clays and uncultivable parts, he adds: "A more minute examination of the country will locate these apparently unproductive soils, and show that they are a very small percentage of the whole. After seeing the country at its worst, when it was suffering from intense heat and dry winds, I wrote: 'Wherever there was drift without these clays there was good grass, but wherever this soil prevailed, aridity showed itself at once.' Many of the hilltops were dry and burnt up, but, had they been ploughed in the spring, would have yielded a good crop, as the summer rains, which undoubtedly fall over the whole country, would have passed into the soil, instead of run-

---

* Report of Engineer-in-chief of Can. Pac. Railway for 1880. p. 197.

ning off or passing in a few hours into the air, as they do under the present condition of things." * We may reasonably suppose that a similarly favourable opinion may yet be justified regarding much of the southern plains that have hitherto been considered as unfit for settlement.

It may as yet be premature to attempt to estimate, even approximately, the extent of cultivable land in the North-West; but, in the light of the most recent information, and making large allowance for arid and useless land, it has been set down at one hundred and fifty millions of acres. Mr. Taylor, the U. S. Consul at Winnipeg, "Saskatchewan Taylor," as he was called years ago from his familiarity with the country, contends that "four-fifths of the wheat producing belt of North America will be found north of the international boundary." These estimates may be excessive, and yet each year, with its ampler examination of the country by surveyors and its increasing testimony from settlers, tends rather to confirm than to refute these figures. This vast area, the largest unoccupied tract of farm-lands in the world, has been opened for settlement on the most liberal terms. The land is laid off into townships of six miles square, each of the thirty-six square miles being called a section. Within a belt of one hundred and ten

---

* Report Engineer-in-chief, C.P.R. 1880, p. 200.

miles on each side of **the proposed line of the** Canadian Pacific Railway **every** alternate section is reserved **for** railway lands and is offered for sale at prices varying from one dollar to five dollars per acre, according to the proximity of the land to the railway. The remaining lands in this belt are open for homestead and pre-emption. Any person who is the **head of a** family, or who has attained the age of eighteen years, is entitled to be entered on these unappropriated **lands for a** homestead of a quarter-section, **that is** one hundred and sixty **acres,** and, on his compliance with certain requirements in the way of settlement and cultivation of the soil, he receives, at the end of three years, a Crown patent confirming him in absolute proprietorship. In addition to this **free** homestead the settler may acquire another block of one hundred and sixty acres by pre-emption; that is, he **has** the right of purchasing the quarter-section adjoining his homestead, so that he may thus become proprietor of a farm of three hundred and twenty acres, the price of the pre-empted land varying from one dollar to two dollars and a half per acre, according to its proximity to the line of railway. The value of this vast tract of unoccupied land where a free homestead is offered to **the settler,** come whence he may, is greatly enhanced **by the ad-**mission, on the part of competent authorities in **the** United States, that nearly all the free agricultural **lands** in that country have been taken up, those that are not held by settlers or speculators being to a great extent in the hands of railway companies.

Already the current of immigration seems to have set in towards those fertile prairies. Last year, 1879, the Government lands sold in the North-West were considerably more than those of 1877 and 1878 combined, amounting to 1,154,072 acres; and the receipts (one-tenth of the total value, since the price of these lands is paid in ten equal annual instalments,) were $218,409, exclusive of $42,910 received for homestead and pre-emption fees; and this notwithstanding the unfavourable land regulations then in force which restricted the homestead claim to eighty acres. With the increased homestead and pre-emption claims, with the favourable reports of tenant-farmers and others who came last year to spy out the land and to see the size of the grapes in our Canadian Eshcol, with the recent unfavourable harvests in Britain that have led many to think of founding new homes in this part of the empire, and with the wider spread of information regarding the resources and the attractions of the country, a large and increasing influx of population to the North-West may soon be expected. The immigration already witnessed is only

> "The first low wash of waves, where soon
> Shall roll a human sea."

CHAPTER XI.

BATTLEFORD TO WINNIPEG.

Battleford to Carlton.—Duck Lake.— A blizzard.—Fellow-travellers.—South Saskatchewan.—Delayed by snow.—Humboldt.—Alkaline lakes.—Touchwood Hills.—Indian farming.—Breakdowns.— Prairie-fires.— Qu'Appelle.— Fort Ellice.—Township surveys.—Colonisation Companies.—Prohibitory Liquor Law. — Shoal Lake. — Salt Lake. — Little Saskatchewan. — Enter Manitoba. — Joe's temptations.—Heavy roads. — Portage La Prairie.—Winnipeg.—Prospects of immigrants.

After sharing, as an old acquaintance, the hospitality which Governor Laird is ready to extend to State officials, to familiar friends, to unknown travellers and to Indians, I left Battleford at noon on Monday, 6th October, and reached Fort Carlton, a hundred and eleven miles distant, on the Wednesday following, being passed along through the kindness of Major Walker of the N. W. Mounted Police, who was sending one of his men with a double buck-board to Duck Lake. The trail runs for the most part near the south bank of the Saskatchewan. The country is very level, the soil being generally light, but improving as you approach Carlton. With the exception of the river valley, it is almost destitute of wood, and, at the time when I saw it, looked peculiarly uninviting, having been desolated and blackened by recent prairie-fires. Our first night was spent about thirty miles from Battleford at a place which my driver assured me was an excellent camping-ground, but as darkness, accompanied by a storm of wind and rain, had overtaken us before we reached it, so that it was very difficult to pitch a tent and impossible to make a fire, I had to be satisfied with his assurance of its good character. Next night we camped at the Elbow, (for almost every river in the North-West has an "elbow,") a favourite and excellent halting-place with delicious water, supplied by springs in the river bank, and with abundance of wood and grass.

Knowing that Carlton is one of the most important of all the posts of the H. B. Company, I had hoped to procure horses there for my journey as far as Touchwood Hills, but was disappointed, as neither the Company nor the "freemen," living near the Fort, could forward me. I therefore drove on that same evening, fourteen miles further, to Duck Lake, where Stobart, Eden and Co., the chief rivals of the H. B. Company in the fur-trade of the North-West, have an extensive post; and through the kindness of their agent, Mr. Hughes, I was supplied with a light, strong prairie cart, two horses and a half-breed driver. Next morning, however, further progress was entirely stopped by a snow storm. I had been told to expect snow in the early part of October, and was most fortunate and thankful that the storm had not overtaken me on the open prairie. Though the weather was not cold, yet for a day the storm raged as wildly as any winter "blizzard," meeting the requirements of the stage-driver's description of a blizzard when he defined it as "one o' them 'ere mountain storms as gets up on its hind legs and howls."

A number of travellers were storm-stayed at Duck Lake; among others Colonel Osborne Smith and Mr. Acton Burrows, of Winnipeg, who were travelling eastward together, equipped with two spring waggons, and accompanied by a half-breed and an Indian. We joined forces; and as I had travelled for the most part alone from Dunvegan, save only as attended by half-breeds or Indians, it was most pleasant to have these gentlemen as fellow-travellers from Duck Lake to Winnipeg.

Colonel Smith had been organizing four companies of militia, for the purpose of allaying any alarm that the settlers of this and the neighbouring districts might feel on account of a recent influx of Sioux from the south. These Sioux had come from Sitting Bull's camp, perhaps in the hope of acquiring reserves, or else expecting to be better fed, either by the Government or by the settlers, than they could be if they remained with the rest of the tribe. They were almost invariably well-armed, and, when they entered the homes of the settlers asking for food, their excellent repeating rifles and their belts well filled with ball cartridge gave them such a persuasive appearance that their request was usually as effective as a royal command. Yet there was really little cause for anxiety, for the Indian is nothing in his own eyes if not armed; his rifle is to him a badge of manhood rather than a threat against the peace of the community, and, so far as intent is concerned, inoffensive as a walking-stick. The enrolment of 160 militiamen had, however, the beneficial effect of allaying all trace of alarm.

The snow-storm prevented our seeing this part of the country to advantage, but from Duck Lake to the junction of the north and south branches of the Saskatchewan, about fifty miles below this, the country is peculiarly rich and fertile. Prince Albert Settlement, which forms part of this district, is already well known as one of the most prosperous and promising in the North-West. With easy communication east and west by the river, and with advantages of churches, schools, mills, etc., its population is rapidly increasing; its free homesteads have all been taken up, and land is annually rising in value. A little further down the Saskatchewan, near the borders of the Carrot or Root River there is an excellent tract of country which, during last summer, was attracting a large number of settlers.

During the enforced pause at Duck Lake we were able to make the necessary arrangements for the next stage of our journey, a hundred and fifty miles to the H. B. Company's trading-post at Touchwood Hills. After a day's detention we started, but the recent snow-fall had made the roads so heavy that a day's travel brought us only to the South Saskatchewan, twelve miles from Duck Lake. We crossed the river at a point known as Gabriel's Crossing, so called because the ferry is kept by Gabriel Dumond. Another trail from Carlton to Touchwood, running a little north of the one we followed, crosses the river five miles lower down, at Batosche's Crossing.

Hitherto the South Branch of the Saskatchewan has been navigated only by canoe; yet the only part of it for several hundred miles unsuited to large craft seems to be a short reach near its junction with the North Branch. Mr Macoun who crossed it at the Elbow in July 1879, says: "Shoals and sandbars were numerous, with occasional islands, but nothing to indicate that the river at this point was unsuited for navigation;" and he adds:—"Why the South Branch should be thought unfit for navigation, I cannot understand. Mr. Hind, who passed down it in August, 1858, never speaks of its depth as being less than seven and a half feet, and the current as never more than three miles an hour, except when close to the North Branch. Palliser, who crossed the river about twenty miles above me, on 28th September, 1857, states that the water in the middle of the channel, where they lost their waggon, was twenty feet deep. While on the plains, I never heard of the river being fordable below the mouth of the Red Deer River. Palliser crossed it on a raft, 22nd July, 1859, about sixty miles above that point where the river was 250 yards wide, and from five to eight feet deep. When at the Blackfoot Crossing of the Bow River, a branch of the South Saskatchewan, 27th August, 1879, I found that it was with the utmost difficulty that horses could cross without swimming. No person ever mentions a rapid being anywhere in the river below this, so that I have come to the conclusion that there is nothing to prevent all the supplies wanted for the south-west being sent up the South Saskatchewan. Coal is abundant in the river banks at the Blackfoot Crossing, and farther eastward, so that there will be no difficulty as to fuel for steamers. Should an attempt be made to navigate the river, it will be found to have better water for a longer period of the year than the North Saskatchewan, as its head waters drain a greater extent of the mountains."*

We camped on the east bank, near Dumond's, a large number of freighters, some heavily-laden, others returning eastward with empty carts, being camped near us. Next morning, Saturday, we found the crust on the snow so strong that we could walk upon it, and although as the day grew warmer we tried to proceed, our horses

---

* Report of Engineer-in-Chief of C. P. Railway, for 1880, p. 196.

became so fagged after we had gone three miles that we were forced to halt. On Sunday we remained in camp all day, being unable to travel, had we desired to do so, our freighting neighbours being forced into similar inactivity. That night there came a thaw, and with the warmer weather the snow began to disappear, so that, although for some distance the road continued heavy, we were able to make from twenty to thirty miles a day.

We passed over undulating prairie, wooded with occasional aspen and willow copse, and well-watered. The numerous badger-holes gave us easy opportunity for examining the soil, which we found to be in some parts loamy and good, but generally light and sandy. This is the prevailing characteristic of the country, as seen from the trail, for the greater part of the distance from the Saskatchewan to the Touchwood Hills; but, though most of it is seemingly poor wheat-land, it may be well suited for grazing and stock-raising. Occasionally the trail skirted small lakes, some of which were alkaline. In the neighbourhood of the fresh water lakelets, and especially near the picturesque Morris Lake, which is thirty-five miles from the Saskatchewan, good camping-ground may be found; but a few miles east of Morris Lake there is a treeless plain, in crossing which, late in the day, as we did, it is well to carry wood lest it may be necessary to pitch camp ere the plain be passed.

On Wednesday morning we halted for a little at the

Humboldt Telegraph Station, some fifty-six miles from the Saskatchewan. We found that the telegraph line was down, that it had been down for a fortnight, and so here, as at Battleford, the only other station that we passed between Edmonton and Winnipeg, we were unable to send any messages eastward. Although a subsidy of $12,000 a year is given by Government to the contractors, communication is very frequently interrupted; and while there may be difficulty in keeping so long a line in repair through such a sparsely peopled and lightly wooded country, yet in view of the subsidy, and of the excessive rates charged by the contractors, better provision for the transmission of messages might be expected. Leaving telegrams to be forwarded as soon as the line would be in working order, we again took the road.

Thirty miles from Humboldt we entered on a salt plain, known as Quill Lake plain, named after the largest of the salt lakes in the vicinity. The plain is about twenty-three miles in width where crossed by the trail, and although the grass looks rich, yet it is hard and wiry, and so heavily impregnated with alkali that the horses do not care for it. The shores of these alkaline lakes, as well as the soil in their vicinity, when bare of herbage, are generally encrusted with a thin coating of salt. Sometimes quite near them there are fresh-water lakelets, but on the salt plain there is a great scarcity of fresh water, as as well as of wood, so that we were compelled to carry both for some miles for cooking purposes.

The formation of these alkaline lakes has been a frequent subject of speculation. It has been observed that they have no visible outlet, and it is supposed that alkali, left on the soil by the extensive prairie fires, is washed by the rain into these alkaline basins. Other lakelets may receive similar deposits, but, as they are emptied by running streams, the **supply of** alkali is carried off and the water in them **is thus** kept fresh. It seems probable that when, under careful administration, prairie fires become less frequent, **when tree-culture is practised** throughout a large portion of the North-West, and **when** the present rapid evaporation of the rainfall shall **thus** be reduced, the alkali will disappear from these lakes, and the soil in their neighbourhood, which in other respects is generally of good quality, will be thoroughly adapted for cultivation.

Very soon after crossing Quill Lake Plain we entered the Touchwood Hill district, **one of** the choice parts **of** the North-West Territories. **The country here is very** beautiful, more varied in scenery **than any other which** we had passed, with excellent soil and abundance of wood and water. This is the character of the country for about sixty miles east and west as crossed by the trail, and it is said to be similar for at least the same extent north and south. Indeed, a province could be formed out of this Touchwood Hill country, most of which would embrace land of special excellence for farming, while outside of the arable lands excellent grazing districts might be found.

For a time it was supposed that the whole of the so called "fertile belt," that is, of the part of the North-West Territories lying south of the North Branch of the Saskatchewan, was suitable for cultivation. Then came a reaction of sentiment, and it was supposed that very little was cultivable, whereas the fertile tract was thought to be further north. Fuller enquiry, however, is shewing that the good land is in districts rather than in one continuous belt, interspersed with tracts of less value. Only the advanced guard of immigration have as yet reached the Touchwood Hills, although many have settled further west at Prince Albert and Edmonton. The chief disadvantage of the district, as compared with those bordering the Saskatchewan, is that it is cut off from all communication by water east or west, and until the C. P. Railway passes, as it is expected to do, within easy access of it, it must be dependent for freight upon prairie-carts or other wheeled conveyance.

The name Touchwood Hills conveys an exaggerated idea of the character of the country. It is by no means mountainous; it can hardly be called hilly; it is simply rolling country, well wooded, with numerous gently swelling knolls, and dotted by many beautiful lakelets;

it is hilly only in comparison with the dead-level prairie. Soon after we had entered this fertile district, we crossed one of the Indian reserves, passing by the farm of Mr. Scott, the Indian farm-instructor. A number of the Indians were busily engaged in farm labour, while others, under Mr. Scott's directions, were building barns. As the chief, Day-Star by name, seems fully determined to adopt a settled life, and gives promise of becoming a tolerable farmer, his band will probably follow his example; and as the soil on their reserve is excellent they will have little difficulty in raising all necessary supplies.

On Friday, the 17th, we reached the H. B. Company's trading-post at Touchwood Hills, eighty-one miles from Humboldt, one hundred and sixty-three miles from Fort Carlton, having, through actual stoppage and short days' travelling, lost about four days by the storm. This post, which is one of several stations connected with Fort Ellice, is in the very heart of the Touchwood Hill country, and cannot fail to become ere long the centre of a rich farming district. They had only a little snow here on the day of our snow-storm at Duck Lake, and before noon next day it had entirely disappeared. In the immediate neighbourhood of the H. B. Company's post we found many strawberry blossoms, the wild vines having already yielded a large supply of berries, and now blossoming a second time.

Here we required to procure fresh horses, and I had to provide myself with a substitute for the cart that had come from Duck Lake, my fellow-travellers having brought their waggons from Winnipeg. The H. B. Company's agent furnished us with horses, and secured for me a spring cart from one of the settlers, and the services of an Indian driver. I was imprudent enough to advance the Indian a large part of his wages in the form of a blanket; and after he had been with me a day he feigned sickness so successfully that I was forced to allow him return. The spring-cart was as great a failure as the Indian. After driving twenty miles the axle broke beyond repair, and my only resource was to buy a prairie cart from a passing freighter, who fortunately was able to spare one. When the last and only cart breaks down the usual resource is to make a "travail." Two poles, longer than ordinary shafts, are fastened like shafts to the horse, while the ends trail on the ground a few feet behind him, kept apart by several cross-bars on which the load is bound. Those who are much accustomed to prairie life soon become experienced carriage-menders. A half-breed, Joe Bourrassa, who had accompanied Colonel Smith from Winnipeg, was invaluable in this as well as in many other respects. When a break-down occurred, whether from a lost bolt, a broken whipple-tree, or other cause, Joe would have the necessary repairs completed before an ordinary carriage-maker could have decided what should be done. He appeared to have an inexhaustible reserve of expedients; failing one, he would try another; and his ready resources were frequently of great service to us. By the time that our journey was over we thought, as no doubt many others do after similar experience, that we could have planned the best kind of conveyance for crossing the prairies, but our new and improved buckboard is still a thing of the future.

For about fifty-five miles from the H. B. Company's Post at Touchwood Hills the country is pleasingly varied with rich soil, luxuriant herbage, and abundance of water and of wood, the poplars here being sometimes eighteen inches in diameter. East of this, there is a treeless plain or "traverse," as such tracts are called, probably because when once entered they must be crossed ere good camping-ground can be reached. It is not always easy, however, to measure your distance and to time your day's journey so closely as to cross a traverse without camping, especially in such a case as this where it was thirty miles in width. Being forced to spend a night upon it we had to carry wood several miles for our camp-fire.

For three or four days the weather was very beautiful, realizing the promise held out by many regarding the Indian summer that would follow the first snow-fall. Even mosquitos appeared, although their hum had lost the business-like tone of July. Prairie fires were visible for several nights in succession; and a large expanse of country traversed by us had already been burnt over, while day after day the smoke hung heavily along the horizon. One favourable result produced by the surrounding fires was that a great abundance of game,—chiefly prairie-chicken,—was driven in upon the unburnt portion of the prairie over which we passed.

The distance from the trading-post at Touchwood Hills to Fort Ellice is one hundred and fifty-two miles, and although the soil in many parts after leaving the fertile district seemed light and poor, and had been rendered less attractive by the prevailing fires, yet some portions appeared rich and cultivable. We did not reach Ellice until mid-day on the 23rd. The Indian summer had passed; the nights had become cold, the thermometer one morning indicating seventeen degrees of frost; and the raw keen winds made us anxious to reach Winnipeg.

Early on the 23rd we crossed the sandy valley of the Qu'Appelle, the main tributary of the Assineboine. The river probably derives its name from the very distinct echo that is heard at several places along the valley. Voyageurs, finding that sounds came to them from the banks, might often have asked "Qu'appelle?" "Who calls?" and hence the name; although some, as might be expected, attribute it to a haunting spirit that occasionally disturbs the solitude and silence, leading the traveller to ask, in some anxiety, "Who calls?"

The valley of the Qu'Appelle is said to be **well suited** for sheep-farming, being better fitted for grazing than for grain-growing. It has evidently been at one time the bed of a much larger stream than that which now flows through it; and it has been generally supposed that the South Saskatchewan, instead of turning northward at **the** Elbow to join the North Branch near **Prince Albert**, formerly flowed eastward along the **valley of the** Qu'Appelle and of the Assineboine to join the Red River at Winnipeg. **Mr.** Macoun, however, has recently weakened the plausibility of this theory. **He says:** * " It having been supposed, and even stated as **a fact** during my stay in Winnipeg, that the waters of **the** South Saskatchewan could be easily **let into the** Qu'Appelle River, I considered it of so much importance to ascertain the correctness of this, that my assistant, an engineer, levelled back fifteen miles from the Elbow, and found that at that point the water surface of the Qu'Appelle was seventy-three feet higher than the Saskatchewan, on July 16th, 1879."

Soon after crossing the Qu'Appelle Valley we reached Fort Ellice, the central H. B. Company's depôt of **an** extensive district. The division of the country adopted by the **H. B.** Company in the formation of their districts suggests itself as a possible one **for** the formation of future provinces. Thus we might have the provinces of

---

* Report of Engineer-in-Chief, C. P. Railway, for 1880, p. 196.

Ellice, Carlton, Edmonton, Athabasca, Dunvegan (or Unchagah), Mackenzie, etc., each with territorial limits larger than some of our organised Provinces, while such a one as that which might be formed out of the Edmonton district, if it were settled according to its resources, would probably be not inferior to any province of the Dominion.

Fort Ellice stands near the confluence of Beaver Creek, the Qu'Appelle and the Assineboine, with a commanding view of the broad and fertile valley of the Assineboine, through which the river flows in serpentine windings at a level of about two hundred feet below the Fort. An older fort at one time stood some distance above Ellice on the banks of Beaver Creek, and the present one used to be surrounded by a palisade in the days when traffic with the Indians was conducted through port-holes, and when they had to give up their knives before receiving their rum. The soil around the Fort is too sandy and gravelly to be fit for cultivation, but the valley of the Assineboine is exceedingly rich and admirably suited for the growth of wheat, while it is large enough to afford farms for many thousands, and the neighbouring prairie to the north is an excellent grazing country. The river is navigable for steamers from Winnipeg to Ellice. We had to procure a fresh relay of horses at Ellice, as well as some fresh supplies, our next stage being from this to Portage La Prairie. As the corral was eighteen miles distant, there was a day's delay in fetching the horses. Having completed our preparations, we left on Friday the 24th, and after crossing the valley of the Assineboine we followed the trail eastward, reaching Shoal Lake that evening, a distance of thirty-three miles.

From Ellice to Winnipeg we saw every day the houses of new settlers, the country to this extent having already been surveyed into townships; but as yet the township surveys have not been completed west of this, except at some special localities. The township is six miles square, and each of the thirty-six square miles constitutes a section. Two sections in each township are reserved for the Hudson's Bay Company, and two others for the benefit of public schools. Of the remaining thirty-two, sixteen are reserved for railway lands, eight for free homesteads, and eight for pre-emption. The system is simple, its chief drawback being that the settlers are necessarily so widely separated from each other. Each settler, it may be supposed, will endeavour to secure at least half a section, 160 acres of free homestead, and 160 acres by pre-emption. Let an entire township be settled at this rate, and even if the railway lands be occupied, there will only be sixty-four families in the township of thirty-six square miles, while the number may be much smaller, and these so scattered as to be of little mutual service in the support of Churches, schools, etc. The Mennonites, who have received special permission from the Government to settle their townships according to their own plan, form a "dorf" or village in the centre, and, while thus living near each other for mutual benefit, they cultivate their separate farms in different parts of the township. Our Anglo-Saxon settlers, however, even were liberty given them by the Government, would probably decline to adopt the Mennonite system; yet until population becomes numerous, sections become sub-divided, and villages spring up in each township, they cannot take much concerted action in matters of religion, of education, or of other general interest.

Twelve miles from Ellice we crossed Bird-Tail Creek, on which, at some distance north of the trail, a tract of two townships has been secured by the Hamilton Colonisation Company, with a view to settlement. Colonisation Companies may serve for the North-West the same purpose, as immigration agents, that has been served by Railway Companies in the Western States. Such companies, spurred into activity by the prospect of profitable land sales, will probably be more zealous than Government immigration agents, and will naturally strive to secure the speedy settlement of at least a portion of their lands. At any rate they may be useful fellow-labourers with the Government in promoting immigration

At Shoal Lake there is a station of the N. W. Mounted Police, and as it is the first station west of Manitoba, and on the great highway of prairie traffic, all freighters and other travellers westward bound are examined here, and are compelled to give up all spirituous liquors, unless they carry them by special permit of the Lieut.-Governor, as the prohibitory liquor law of the Territories is rigidly enforced.

Ten miles from Shoal Lake we passed Salt Lake, so called from the character of the water, which is so impregnated with alkali that cattle will not drink it; indeed, for some distance in the neighbourhood of Salt Lake the soil appears to be largely affected by alkali. But, although it looked unfavourable for settlement, as seen from the trail, two days after we had passed it we overtook some Ontario farmers, who had been "land-hunting" and had selected homesteads a little north of Salt Lake. The land seen from the trail must frequently be poorer than that a little distance off, as ridges and gravelly soil, wherever such can be found, have naturally been selected for the trail, on the principle that good soil makes bad roads.

Nine miles from Salt Lake the trail forks into two, one of which crosses the Little Saskatchewan at Rapid City, the other, a little farther north, crossing it at Prairie City. Taking the latter, which passes by Badger Hill, we travelled for many miles through a beautiful country, well watered, with excellent soil, and crossed, near sunset, the fertile valley of the Little Saskatchewan, seventy-two miles from Fort Ellice. This valley, like many of those which we had crossed before, seems very large in proportion to the size of the stream that flows through it, but the absence of rock has allowed these creeks and rivers, as they coursed through the rich prairie soil, to carve out large channels for themselves. These valleys, or *coulées* as they are sometimes called, form the chief engineering difficulty in railway construction across the prairies.

Here, as at Shoal Lake and elsewhere, speculation was rife regarding the probable location of the C. P. Railway. All seemed glad that the line by the Narrows of Lake Manitoba had been abandoned for the more southern route, and settlers were anxious to ascertain where the Little Saskatchewan would be crossed and what route would be adopted further west.

This little Saskatchewan district is already well-known and justly esteemed both for its beauty and for its fertility; almost every part of it is fit for settlement, and the lands that are unsuited for wheat are admirably adapted for grazing. Encamped one evening near its banks we were visited by two Scotchmen, recent arrivals, one of whom had lived for some years in Ontario. After discussing the present and prospective merits of the country, I asked him how long it was since he had left Scotland. "Hoo did ye ken that I cam' frae Scotland?" he replied in the broadest Doric, imagining that he had lost his Scottish accent in Ontario; but the Scotchman is becoming ubiquitous in the North-West. Like other settlers with whom we conversed, these men gave us glowing reports of the soil, crops and prospects of the country. Much of the land in their neighbourhood had already been taken up, some of it in much larger blocks than the ordinary homestead. We were told, for instance, that Lord Elphinstone, has secured 12,000 acres of arable and grazing land, which he evidently intends to settle and cultivate.

Continuing our course eastward, we passed over similar country, rich and attractive, waiting to be tilled, and already in many parts taken up. Having crossed Snake Creek, about twenty-two miles from the Little Saskatchewan, we traversed the Beautiful Plain, as it is called, a stretch of the most luxuriant pasture-land we had ever seen, and, about forty miles east of Prairie City, we entered the Province of Manitoba. The country continued as fertile as any that we had come over, perhaps more so, but Manitoba is so very flat as compared with such districts as Little Saskatchewan, Touchwood Hills, or Edmonton, that it appeared somewhat monotonous. A level sameness of extremely rich farm land, however, affords rather a pleasing monotony. Only to the traveller in search of the picturesque does the country seem uninviting, many leagues being so level that a wheat-stack may be seen for miles, while a farm-steading is as distinct an object on the horizon as a hill is in Scotland.

Having entered Manitoba, and having crossed and re-crossed the White Mud River, first at Gladstone, a thriving border village, then at Woodside, and again at Westbourne, we camped near Westbourne. That first night in Manitoba was rather serious in its effects upon our half-breed driver, Joe Bourrassa, as he was once again within reach of liquor. For several weeks he had been practising enforced abstinence, but at last, like a sailor after a long voyage, he threw off the unwelcome restraint. Next morning poor Joe was rather unfit for his work. On each subsequent occasion on which we came within range of a public-house, it was necessary to watch him very closely, and as we approached Winnipeg, or "Garry," as all the half-breeds call it from the old Fort around which the city has clustered, his face beamed with delight at the vision of unrestricted whiskey. Within two hours after our arrival, Joe, dull of eye and incoherent of speech, came to ask for his wages, and on being told that he could only get them when he became sober, he begged for one dollar " to finish drunk."

Soon after leaving Westbourne we found the roads heavy through recent rain, and we were able in some measure to appreciate the difficulties of immigrants arriving in the wet season of early summer, and traversing Manitoba in May and early June. The roads through these extremely rich wheat-lands become almost impassable for some weeks after heavy rain, while walking is carried on under such conditions as to make every pedestrian appreciate the oft-repeated joke that "if you don't stick to the land, the land will stick to you." So far as travellers going west of Manitoba are concerned, this and kindred difficulties will be overcome on the completion, during the present year, of the first hundred miles of railway now in course of construction west of Winnipeg, but until that section is completed, we cannot expect a large influx of immigrants into the North-West. Although they may be told that our wheat-lands yield on an average from fifty to a hundred per cent more that the best wheat-lands of the United States, a larger yield per acre, of better quality, and of greater weight per bushel, although they may be familiar with reports of settlers, of British deputations, of immigration agents, and of Cabinet ministers, and although they may know that a free homestead can be had north of the international boundary line while farms worth having in Dakotah or Minnesota will cost at least from $2.50 to $6.00 per acre, yet the facilities of access and of traffic furnished by the railway system of the United States must induce many to remain south of the boundary till at least a portion of our Pacific road west of Winnipeg be completed.

At noon, on Tuesday the 28th, we reached Portage

La Prairie, more commonly called "the Portage," the largest prairie town west of Winnipeg. Situated on the banks of the Assineboine, with steam communication by river to Winnipeg, and with a tri-weekly stage, that will soon give place to several daily railway trains, in the centre of a magnificent farming district, this border town is rapidly becoming a place of considerable importance. The road to Winnipeg, about sixty-two miles, traverses a very level country of the richest soil, nearly all of which is under cultivation. As we passed, the farmers were threshing their wheat, and, being unable to use up their wheat straw, were in many instances burning it, simply to put it out of the way. Surely some means can be devised by which they may utilize their straw as fuel; if so, it would be a great saving to Manitoba farmers, for firewood generally is scarce and dear.

We met train after train of prairie carts, which would continue to move westward until the winter stopped the season's traffic. Already the roads were frozen hard, and, having been much cut up during the autumn, were now very rough. Following the main road we were frequently within sight of the Assineboine, which, unlike many of the rivers of the North West, is wooded on both sides, most of the streams being wooded chiefly upon the southern banks, the northern banks being more exposed to fires from the prairies, driven along by the prevailing north-westerly winds.

We reached Winnipeg on the 29th of October, just before the cold weather fell upon us, and found here, as at every village and shanty that we had passed since leaving Edmonton, a pulse of life and hope. Every one appeared to anticipate a bright future for the country, and an especially bright one for himself. The city, which was a small hamlet seven years ago, now boasts a population of about 10,000, and as it is the natural gateway of the North-West it must continue rapidly to increase.

We had crossed the prairies; we had seen the country in that uncultivated condition in which it is difficult for any but the experienced farmer to gauge its productive powers; we had traversed it, for the most part, after the flush and luxuriance of summer had passed, when the leafless woods and the withered grass made much of it appear uninviting, and when a still more desolate appearance had been given to large tracts by recent prairie-fires. We had seen it thus with but scant ability to estimate its resources, and under circumstances by no means the most favourable, but day after day the impression of its wonderful fertility and of its vast and varied attractions deepened upon us, while day after day the vision of its future became more glowing, as we seemed to hear the tread of advancing settlers and the blended sounds of coming industries.

We had reached Winnipeg from the west. How fares

it with the immigrant approaching it from the east? His passage from Liverpool, by way of Quebec, Sarnia, and Duluth, has taken about fifteen days, and has cost him from £9 to £28 sterling, according to the accommodation he has chosen by steamer and rail. From previous information he knows where to settle, and at once procures his "location" from the Dominion land agent; or, perhaps, he can afford a little time to look about him. If he has arrived early enough in the year, and has settled on land that yields a good return off the sod, he may be able to raise a crop his first season. If not, he must content himself with breaking up his land, to have it ready for the following spring, and with building his "shanty" and barn, providing himself with stock, and laying in winter supplies. He has availed himself of the liberal homestead law, and has pre-empted an adjoining quarter-section, so that he is now the possessor of a farm of 320 acres, having brought out his family, procured his land, and started with sufficient stock and implements for a new settler, at a total outlay of less than a single year's rental for a wheat-farm of a similar size in the mother-country. He will find an abundant market for all that he can raise, whether it be stock or cereals. New settlers will require food and seed; and the Hudson's Bay Company and the Government will probably be large purchasers, the former for their widely scattered posts, the latter on behalf of the

Indians. Indeed, there is every prospect that, for several years, the bulk of the grain raised in the North-West will be required for local consumption; and by the time that settlers are ready to export grain, the means of communication will be so much increased, and the cost of freight so much reduced, that they will be able to compete on most favourable terms for the supply of the British market. Competent authorities estimate that within two years, as soon as the railway is completed from Winnipeg to Thunder Bay, on Lake Superior, grain can be taken from Manitoba to Liverpool at a total outside cost of 45 cents per bushel. Wheat is grown in Manitoba at a cost that does not exceed, if it reaches, 40 cents per bushel; so that it will be grown in Manitoba and delivered in Liverpool at a cost to the producer, including all charges for transport, of 85 cents (equal to 3s. 6d. sterling) per bushel, or $6.80 (equal to £1. 8s. 4d.) per quarter. As the average price of wheat in England for the thirty years, from 1849 to 1878, was $12.72 per quarter—the lowest in that period being, in 1851, $9.50 per quarter—a sufficiently broad margin is left for the Canadian wheat-grower. *

And if such facilities for transport be not sufficient to secure for our North-West, where land yields from

---

* These figures are from a pamphlet entitled " Manitoba and the North-West," issued by C. J. Brydges Esq., Land Commissioner of the H. B. Company.

twenty to sixty bushels of wheat per acre, the chief supply of the British market, other and shorter lines of transport may yet be opened. Already a new route is projected, and a company is being formed to construct a railway, about three hundred miles in length, from the northern extremity of Lake Winnipeg down the valley of the Nelson River to Port Nelson on Hudson's Bay. This port is twenty-one miles nearer Liverpool than New York is. It appears that the valley of the Nelson offers a practicable route for a railway, although the river is too broken to be navigable, and the navigation of Hudson's Bay and Hudson's Straits can be relied on for at least three months in the year, probably for a longer period. This would allow the shipment of a very large amount of grain from the Canadian North-West, and also from the north-western portions of the United States by this route. Even if the year's crop could not be shipped during the same season that it was harvested, yet the difference in cost of transport would probably make it worth while to hold much of it over until the following summer rather than send it by the more expensive southern routes. But whether the grain of our North-West reaches the Atlantic by way of the St. Lawrence or by way of Hudson's Straits, it seems almost inevitable that it must in the course of time become a powerful, and perhaps a controlling, factor in regulating the wheat markets of the world.

While those rich prairies, that must yet be carved into a cluster of loyal provinces extending from Red River to the Rocky Mountains, offer homes to men of all nationalities, they offer special attractions to immigrants from the mother-country, for there the shield of the Empire will still be around them, and one scarcely knows how much he loves the old flag till he sees it float over some far-away trading-post in that lonely north-land. There was a time when those coming from Britain to Canada looked on the national life at home as something from which they had been severed, while their sorrow at that separation seemed almost beyond the solace of song. That time is gone; Canada is now something more than a Crown Colony; she must be regarded as an integral part of the Empire. No British statesman would now say to Canada "Take up your freedom," nor would any statesman of Canada counsel the Dominion to drift off into independence. One chief argument for independence has been based on the analogy of the family, and it has been urged that, as the children cannot always be gathered under the old roof-tree but should be so trained by their parents as in time to become self-supporting, independent heads of families, so colonies should be fostered into independent states. But the analogy does not hold; for, while there is a necessity for the extension, continuance and independence of families, since only in this way can the race survive the inroads of death, there is no similar necessity for a continuous succession of nations. It does not seem requisite for the world's welfare that the parts of a great empire should, as their strength increases, be lopped off, and be left to work out a separate life and destiny. We Canadians at least need recognise for ourselves no such necessity. We may regret the scant attention that colonial interests have commonly received at the hands of British statesmen; we may regard our present relations with the mother-country as capable of improvement; we may discuss theories of Imperial Federation that shall admit us to higher national duties and responsibilities as our powers increase; but we shall proudly and hopefully continue to share the life and destiny of the Empire.

www.ingramcontent.com/pod-product-compliance
Lightning Source LLC
Chambersburg PA
CBHW030001240426
43672CB00007B/780